GASPIPE

CONFESSIONS OF A MAFIA BOSS

PHILIP CARLO

WILLIAM MORROW

An Imprint of HarperCollins*Publishers*

For the author's continued safety, some names had to be changed.

HarperCollins books may be purchased for educational, business, or sales promotional use. For information please write: Special Markets Department, HarperCollins Publishers, 10 East 53rd Street, New York, NY 10022.

FIRST EDITION

Designed by Daniel Lagin

Library of Congress Cataloging-in-Publication Data

Carlo, Philip.
    Gaspipe : confessions of a Mafia boss / Philip Carlo.
        p.   cm.
    ISBN 978-0-06-142984-2
    1. Casso, Gaspipe, 1942– 2. Mafia—New York (State)—New York—
Case studies. 3. Gangsters—New York (State)—New York—Biography.
4. Criminals—New York (State)—New York—Biography. 5. Organized
crime—New York (State)—New York—Case studies. I. Title.

HV6452.N72C37 2008
364.1092—dc22
[B]   2008002683

08   09   10   11   12   OV/RRD   10   9   8   7   6   5   4   3   2   1

Dedicated to Laura Garofalo for all her help, support, and love.

And Lillian Delduca Casso.

In loving memory of Giovanni and Gaetana Carlo,

and Florenza and Alberto Mandato.

He who fights with monsters might take care lest he thereby become a monster. And if you gaze for long into an abyss, the abyss gazes also into you."

—Friedrich Nietzsche

Il lupo mangia con le sue zampe.
The wolf eats with its legs.

—Lucky Luciano

In Cosa Nostra, there is an obligation to tell the truth, but there is also a great reserve. And this reserve, the things that are not said, rule like an irrevocable curse over all men of honor. It makes all relationships profoundly false, absurd.

—Tommaso Buscetta (Sicilian Cosa Nostra boss)

CONTENTS

Preface   xiii
Introduction   xvii

BOOK I   **THE MAKING OF A BOSS**

Chapter 1   A Man of Respect   3
Chapter 2   Street Smart   8
Chapter 3   First Blood   13
Chapter 4   Last Standing   17
Chapter 5   Readin', Writin', 'Ritmatic   21
Chapter 6   A Very Close Shave Indeed   23
Chapter 7   Irrationally Violent   28
Chapter 8   When You Steal Without Hurting
               Anyone, It's a Lot of Fun   37
Chapter 9   Larceny-Hearted   39
Chapter 10   The Opposite Sex   42
Chapter 11   True Love   44
Chapter 12   Bensonhurst   47
Chapter 13   The Carlos   50
Chapter 14   Dreams   52

BOOK II   STONE COLD

Chapter 15	Making Bones	61
Chapter 16	The Burn Bar	67
Chapter 17	Casso's Crew	70
Chapter 18	A Blessed Event	73
Chapter 19	A Backstabbing Backstabber	78
Chapter 20	Straightened Out	83
Chapter 21	Rising Star	87
Chapter 22	Mia Figlia	92
Chapter 23	Anthony Junior	95
Chapter 24	Bad Apples	97
Chapter 25	Family Affair	101
Chapter 26	Crimes Pays	106
Chapter 27	The Forbidden Fruit	108

BOOK III   LA VENDETTA

Chapter 28	Inside Info	113
Chapter 29	Kennedy Airport	116
Chapter 30	Newfound Wealth	119
Chapter 31	The Seeds of the Windows Case	122
Chapter 32	The Secret Sweeper	125
Chapter 33	Double, Double, Toil and Trouble	131
Chapter 34	Great Usurper	134
Chapter 35	Sparks Steakhouse	138
Chapter 36	Justice, Mafia Style	141
Chapter 37	Toys "R" Us	144
Chapter 38	A Curse from the Grave	149
Chapter 39	Mean Streets	151
Chapter 40	Hssssssst	156
Chapter 41	The Golden Ox Incident: Gotti's Revenge?	158
Chapter 42	Honor Thy Father	163
Chapter 43	"You're Under Arrest"	167

Chapter 44   The Bull   171
Chapter 45   Housekeeping   176
Chapter 46   The Chin   181
Chapter 47   The Commission   187
Chapter 48   Sanitation   190
Chapter 49   Sausage Fingers   193
Chapter 50   Starter   196
Chapter 51   The Killing of Vinnie Albano   199
Chapter 52   Racketeering   202

BOOK IV   GONE WITH THE WIND

Chapter 53   Gaspipe's Crystal Ball   209
Chapter 54   Underground   213
Chapter 55   The FBI Comes Knocking   215
Chapter 56   Fat and Skinny   221
Chapter 57   Light on His Feet Pete   224
Chapter 58   Backfire   232
Chapter 59   Et Tu, Brute?   238
Chapter 60   Escape   243
Chapter 61   Tight-Lipped Vic   246
Chapter 62   King Gaspipe   249
Chapter 63   No, You Come Up   252
Chapter 64   Earthquake Rocks Mafiadom   257
Chapter 65   The 302s   269
Chapter 66   The Teflon Don   277
Chapter 67   Anathema   280
Chapter 68   A New Regime   283
Chapter 69   Contraband   286
Chapter 70   A New New Lease   289
Chapter 71   Gaspipe Meets the United
              States Senate   295
Chapter 72   No Comment   299

BOOK V   THE LIVING DEAD

Chapter 73   Hellhole   303
Chapter 74   Impartial Observation   304
Chapter 75   Chinese Torture   305
Chapter 76   Dumb Fuck   307
Chapter 77   Reconciliation   311
Chapter 78   No More Pain   317
Chapter 79   The World Suddenly Turned
              Upside Down   319
Chapter 80   Phoenix   321
Chapter 81   The Death of La Cosa Nostra   325

Postscript   329
Casso's Neighbors   333
Gaspipe Revelations   335
Appendix   "Government Witnesses: Getting
            More—or Less—Than They
            Bargained For?" by Joshua L. Dratel   339
Acknowledgments   345

PREFACE

Main Entry: ²revenge

Function: *noun*

Etymology: Middle French *revenge, revenche,* from *revengier, revenchier* to revenge

1 : an act or instance of retaliating in order to get even <plotted her *revenge*>

2 : an opportunity for getting satisfaction <sought *revenge* through a rematch>

Source: http://www.m-w.com/cgi-bin/dictionary

LA VENDETTA

Now, finally, Anthony "Gaspipe" Casso would have revenge. Twenty-two days ago, on September 14, 1986, there had been an attempt on his life. He had been shot six times, but luckily escaped. Even now, two slugs were still lodged in his body. He had become used to the dull, constant pain they emitted. Wearing a black leather jacket as soft as butter, and a diamond pinkie ring the size of a macadamia nut on his right hand, he sat in the Toys "R" Us parking lot just off Brooklyn's Belt Parkway, waiting for the man who was responsible for the attempt on his life. His dark eyes were cold, his lips a parched, unfeeling slit.

Seething, Anthony Casso was as still as stone, his mind playing over the world of pain he'd inflict on the man who'd tried to kill him. Colorful scenarios of torture slowly moved through Casso's head, like hungry sharks around a bleeding man. Until Casso had revenge, found out who was behind the hit, he would not be whole—he would not be complete. He would be a mere shell of the man he had been.

Casso looked left and saw the black Plymouth with blackwall tires cautiously approaching. There were two stoic men in the front seat. They were New York City detectives—crooked cops on Casso's payroll—ice-cold killers both. With few words exchanged, Casso took the car they were driving. Though he wanted to speed to the place of torture, fly there at 200 miles an hour, he drove slowly, the quintessential professional, making certain to abide by all traffic regulations, his muscles tense, his heart racing, adrenaline slowly seeping through his muscular body. He reached the safe house, pulled into the garage, and opened the trunk.

Trussed up like a Thanksgiving turkey was a big, blond-headed man. His wrists and ankles were cuffed tightly, his mouth taped shut. When he saw Casso, his eyes nearly popped out of his head, cartoonlike. Casso seemed possessed of superhuman strength. He grabbed the man by his handcuffed legs and wrists and effortlessly heaved him from the car.

The well-choreographed ballet of pain Casso had in his head was suddenly forgotten. Now a primordial, atavistic world of emotions overtook him. With an animal-like ferocity, he kicked and beat his enemy, his nemesis—this man who would have been his assassin.

Breathing heavily now, sweating, Casso dragged the man to the place where he would slowly die. To an uninformed observer, it looked like a carefully laid tarp in the corner of the room. In reality it was a grave, a popular place for mafiosi to murder. Casso took out a knife and proceeded to cut off all his victim's clothes. He was careful not to slice any arteries. He wanted this death to be long and drawn out; he was intent upon that.

Anthony Casso, like few others in La Cosa Nostra (LCN), had mastered the art of murder. Indeed, he had a doctorate degree in the killing of human beings. Casso—a boss in the Lucchese crime family—turned and walked the full length of the room. It was a finished basement with wood-paneled walls. There were no windows. No fresh air. It would soon be a tomb.

Casso, who had been an expert marksman since he was a young boy, now drew out a sleek blue-black 16-shot .22 automatic fitted with a silencer. The gun seemed a lethal, natural extension of his body. Casso's intention was not to kill the man but to make him suffer, make him talk. With a hand as steady as a diamond cutter's, Casso began the torture. The first bullet he put through the victim's left kneecap, the next through his right knee, and the third through the space midway between his ankle and knee.

Pow!

Pow!

Suddenly there were bullet holes in each of his victim's shins. He then took aim at the space where Christ had been crucified, the area just above the metatarsals, and fired. The man furiously twisted and turned to no avail.

The amazingly well-placed .22 slugs continued to drill holes in him—the left and right elbows, the wrists, and the shoulders were pierced.

Satisfied that he had hit most of the major bones of the man's body, Casso moved on to his large muscles. He shot holes in the biceps, the calves, the thick thigh muscles. He then scrupulously took sight of the folded mushroom that was his penis. He pulled the trigger. The man's shriveled up sex organ seemed to explode. It was suddenly no more.

Calmly, Casso reloaded the gun. He would leave the man alone for a while; he'd allow the wounds to swell and fester, the symphony of pain to begin . . . a Beethoven's Fifth of suffering.

Casso knew the wounds were now numb; the body's endorphins had been released into the man's bloodstream en masse. As the body's natural opiates diminished, the pain would begin in earnest. Each of the wounds would grow to the size of half a lemon; each of them would turn a dark purple color.

Silently, with the quiet stealth of a large cat, Casso turned and walked away, feeling whole and complete for the first time since he'd been shot.

When, several hours later, Casso returned, he began the questioning . . .

"Who," he demanded in little more than a growl, "hired you?"

INTRODUCTION

THE EYE OF THE STORM

Anthony Casso's story began in lower Park Slope, South Brooklyn. During the turn of the twentieth century, this area was a tough, violent Italian American enclave filled with coarse, Italian immigrant dockworkers and laborers. Bordered by Atlantic Avenue to the north and the sprawling hills of Greenwood Cemetery to the south, Prospect Park to the east and the docks of Red Hook to the west, South Brooklyn produced numerous Mafia luminaries. Al Capone came from this place. Both Carmine and Alphonse Persico also came from this neighborhood, as did Albert "Kid Blast" Gallo and "Crazy Joe" Gallo. Albert Anastasia, Harry Fontana, and Joe Profaci all hailed from this four-square-mile area.

Elia Kazan's immortal *On the Waterfront* was an in-depth study of the New York harbor docks, the stranglehold the Mafia had on the waterfront. The film garnered Oscars for Best Director and Best Film as well as an Oscar for Brando's brilliant performance. Who can ever forget his classic line in the film, "I coulda been someone, Charley—I coulda been a contender."

In a sense, to some Italians, becoming a member of the Mafia was all about "being someone," being "a contender" in life. The Mafia was an opportunity to become wealthy and treated with respect without a formal education, without having to walk the straight and narrow or follow the rules and regulations mandated by a hostile society.

To some degree, much of that had to do with the fact that society's rules and regulations were unfair, outright corrupt, specifically geared toward excluding Italian immigrants.

Italians, perhaps more than other immigrant groups before them, were marginalized and put upon. They were thought of as an uneducated gruff people who could not speak English, ate spaghetti, drank too much wine, and were oversexed. They were not, for instance, allowed in trade unions; they were outright shunned by American society.

For example, when the Central Park reservoir was being dug in 1904, an advertisement was posted in the *New York Times*, seeking men to dig the huge hole and lay the stone the reservoir required. The amount of pay was offered in three different ways—for "whites," for "blacks," and for "Italians." The Italians were paid the least.

However, these were a hardworking, industrious people with the blood of Dante, Caesar, Michelangelo, da Vinci, and Galileo running through their veins, and no amount of prejudice was about to keep them down, as has been made all too evident by the success of so many Italian Americans, from the ingenious inventor Gugliehmo Marconi to the baseball great Joe DiMaggio, tenor Enrico Caruso, jazz great Joe Venuti, filmmakers Martin Scorsese and Francis Coppola, the actors Robert De Niro and Al Pacino, Governor Mario Cuomo, Mayor Rudolph Giuliani, businessman Lee Iacocca, and entertainer Frank Sinatra.

New York's Tammany Hall, part of the most crooked administrations in government history, was a good example to the early Italian American immigrants of the blatant hypocrisy so rampant in both government and business; indeed, society at large.

With the millions of honest, hardworking Italians who emigrated from Italy to America between 1890 and 1921—some 4.5 million—also came a cunning criminal element known as La Cosa Nostra, which loosely translated means "our thing"; that is, the Mafia we have come to both loathe and be so fascinated by. Rather than supply a treatise here on the genesis of the Mafia, suffice it to say that the Sicilian Mafia began as a society of honored men in Sicily who banded together to fight the tyranny and brutalities of conquering nations. The Greeks, Turks, French, Spanish, and Normans had all invaded Sicily and subjected the Sicilian people to iniquitous treatment. The raping of Sicilian women and girls was the norm, not the exception. In the end, however, the Sicilians managed to outsmart, outwit, and outmurder their tormentors.

South Brooklyn was home to a large Italian community, and mafiosi inevitably set up shop and took deep roots here. Ultimately they decimated the competition for the lucrative underworld enterprises—vice, bootlegging and gambling, shylocking and hijacking, prostitution and racketeering. The Irish and Jewish gangsters, who fought the Italians tooth and nail, were eventually sent packing by the organized structure, efficiency (based upon the Roman legions), and deadly cunning of the Mafia. In the words of Owny Madden, a renowned Irish bootlegger and gangster of the 1920s, "Nobody kills better than the wops." (Wops referred to Italian immigrants who arrived at Ellis Island *without papers*.)

———

The road to the formation of the Lucchese family, beginning in Sicily and ending in Brooklyn, is a long bumpy one strewn with dead bodies. The family first formed at the turn of the twentieth century, when the business of the Mafia was secretive in the extreme, generations before the formation of the modern FBI. *Omerta*—the blood vow taken to become a "made man"—was considered a sacred oath, never broken or compromised in any shape, manner, or form.

The first known head of the Lucchese family was Tommaso Reina. He was murdered in 1930, during the so-called Castellammarese War between rival New York gangsters Joe Masseria and Salvatore Maranzano. Joe Masseria had Reina killed because he didn't want him joining forces with his mortal, sworn enemy, Sal Maranzano. The two men left in charge of the Reina family, Tommaso Lucchese and Tommaso Gagliano, hooked the families' fortunes to the Maranzano camp. This was a wise decision because Joe Masseria was soon murdered.

The Mafia, like a treacherous sea with strong undercurrents and swift moving tides, is constantly in flux, and several months later "the Two Tommys"—as they had become known—backed a carefully laid power play by Lucky Luciano, one of the most cunning foxes the Mafia ever produced. Lucchese helped set up Joe Maranzano, who was considered old-fashioned and backward thinking, in his New York office and was actually there when Maranzano was shot and stabbed to death.

A cautious administrator liked by his men, Tommy Gagliano successfully ran the family until 1952. That year, he died of brain cancer, a somewhat rare way of departing the earth for Mafia men in those days. Without strife or opposition, Tommy Lucchese took over the family in 1953, and he soon became a member in good standing on the Mafia board of directors, on "the Commission" as it has become known.

A wily, crafty individual with the dour countenance of a bulldog, Tommy Lucchese ran the family without difficulty until 1967, when he was diagnosed with brain cancer, which ultimately took his life. His successor was the powerful Lucchese capo Tony "Ducks" Corallo. Unfortunately for Tony Corallo, he was convicted of bribing the New York City water commissioner and sent upstate to Ossining State Prison—Sing Sing. By now Carlo Gambino was the *capo di tutti i capi* (the "boss of all bosses"), and with Gambino's blessing, Carmine Tramunti temporarily took over the family. Tramunti was soon convicted of selling heroin and wound up spending the rest of his life in prison.

When Tony Corallo was released from jail in 1970, he took over his former spot as head of the family. He was older, wiser, grayer, and more cautious, though apparently not cautious enough. Corallo's Jaguar was cleverly bugged by organized crime authorities, and the Lucchese family's involvement in labor racketeering, private sanitation, and major construction throughout the New York tristate area was exposed. Corallo wound up with a hundred-year sentence.

———

From a storytelling point of view, here is where this bloody, startling underworld drama takes a novel turn. When Anthony Casso married his childhood sweetheart, Lillian Delduca, and decided to leave South Brooklyn, they chose to live in Bensonhurst, Brooklyn.

In a very real sense, Bensonhurst was the other side of the proverbial tracks, thought of as a far better place to live—cleaner, safer, and also home to a large Italian American community. It, too, was where I lived with my parents, Dante and Nina Carlo, and my younger sister, Doreen. When the newlywed Cassos moved to Bensonhurst, they took up residence right next door to my family, a few feet away from the front steps of our home at 173 Bay Thirty-fifth Street. It didn't take long for my parents to meet and become friends with Anthony and Lillian Casso.

Casso took an immediate liking to my mom and dad. My father, like Casso, was born and raised in South Brooklyn, was a first-generation Italian American, and was a serious sports enthusiast. Unlike Casso, however, my father was not involved with the Mob; he had a nine-to-five straight job that he religiously went to every day. For this and other reasons, Casso was particularly comfortable around my family and in our home, and thus I got to know and see Anthony Casso in a unique, very intimate way that few journalists—if any—have had with the subjects of their books.

When the much-publicized relationship Casso had with two crooked NYPD detectives, Louis Eppolito and Stephen Caracappa, came to light, when they were put on trial in federal court, Casso was literally inundated with requests from writers and journalists who wanted to tell his story. However, he agreed to work with me, open his heart and mind and soul to me, because we "went back." Because he implicitly trusted me, a rare thing for Anthony Casso—trusting anyone—he opened himself up to me for this book, without asking for or expecting anything in return.

Eventually, the Cassos had a female child, a blessed event. My sister often babysat for them. Casso was excessively generous when he paid her. If Doreen was due $25, he'd give her $100. Several times over the years Casso even helped members of my extended family when they had problems; when a union tried to shake down my uncle Leo, Casso put a stop to it; when a connected individual tried to get money from my uncle Russi, who owned a grocery store in Brooklyn Heights, Casso again interceded. He asked for nothing in return.

Eventually, the Cassos bought a home in Mill Basin, Brooklyn, and moved away. My family stayed friendly with the Cassos, though they did slowly drift apart. Anthony had become the subject of intense police and FBI scrutiny and he didn't want to create any problems for my family.

Destiny, however, brought me back into contact with Anthony Casso after his arrest, and destiny's fickle turns, stops, and starts are, in a very real sense, responsible for this book.

BOOK I

THE MAKING OF A BOSS

CHAPTER 1

A MAN OF RESPECT

Anthony Casso was raised within the confines of a Mafia culture, mindset, belief system.

The youngest of three children, Anthony was born in Park Slope's Methodist Hospital on May 21, 1942. He had a brother, Michael, born in 1936, and a sister, Lucille, who was born in 1939. His parents, Michael Casso and Margaret Cucceullo, met in a bakery the Cucceullo family owned on Union and Bond streets in 1934, and it was love at first sight—*egli ebbe un colpo di fulmine,* struck by a lightning bolt, as Italians say.

This was the height of the Depression. Hard times were the norm. The world was starving. Men with hostile, gaunt faces filled with anger crowded soup lines and shamelessly begged. A mass exodus of able men left South Brooklyn and searched far and wide around the country for work, money, and a way to feed their families. Anthony's father, Michael Casso, however, managed to prosper during these hard times, for his best friend, Sally Callinbrano, Anthony's godfather, was a respected capo in the Genovese crime family, and he had substantial influence on the nearby Brooklyn docks. Michael Casso and Sally had grown up together and had been best friends since grade school. They played ball together. They stole together. They watched each other's backs. Sally made sure

Michael Casso worked every day, that he had access to the regular pilfering that went on at the docks, as a matter of course.

"It fell off da truck" was the phrase commonly used for their stealing. The shipping companies accepted the practice; they had no choice. They wrote it up as "da cost a doin' business," as a retired dockworker recently put it, an old-timer now eighty.

Each of Anthony's grandparents emigrated from Naples, Italy, one of the most corrupt, crime-ridden, and dangerous cities in the world, between the years 1896 and 1898. They were a part of the mass exodus of Italians from the Mazangoro. Hardworking, industrious people, Casso's grandparents prospered—the Cucceullos opened a bakery. Casso's paternal grandfather, Micali, opened a bowling alley on Union Street and Seventh Avenue. Both the Cassos and the Cucceullos prospered, and eventually attained the elusive American dream. The effects of the Depression were not that dire for them. Fewer people went bowling, but Michael Casso Sr. managed to make a living, and the Cucceullos' bakery was always busy. Most everything on the shelves was gone by midday. The bakery was ideally located near the Gowanus Canal where there were thousands of blue-collar workers, and Union Street was a main artery with a good deal of traffic. A busy trolley line traveled in both directions.

Michael Casso and Margaret Cucceullo's union proved to be a good one. They were ideally suited for each other, deeply in love, and they would stay together till death parted them.

Anthony Casso's childhood was a happy one. All his memories of his early years are good ones. He was showered with love from both his parents and grandparents, aunts and uncles. His father never hit him. Anthony wanted for nothing. One would think, considering how cold and mean Casso could be as an adult, that he'd been brutalized as a child, beaten and regularly put upon, but just the opposite was true. Even today, he says his best friend in life was indisputably his father.

Michael Casso was a bull of a man, as powerful as three average men. This was a genetic trait. He had the rock-hard body endemic to southern Italian males, and his regular working at the docks, stressing and straining his muscles, helped build his impressive physique. Anthony's father was a calm, easygoing man; he rarely, if ever, got angry and rarely raised his voice, but he was a fierce street fighter, one of the toughest men on the Brooklyn docks.

Michael Casso's nickname was "Gaspipe" because he always carried an eight-inch length of lead gaspipe that he used like an impromptu blackjack, or held in his huge, large knuckled fist when he threw a punch to add bad intentions to the blow. Anthony would, years later, inherit his father's nickname and become known through Mafiadom as Gaspipe, never Anthony, though he did not use a gaspipe as a weapon. It is no accident that most all street guys have nicknames. This was a simple though clever way to confuse law enforcement as to the true identity of any given made man.

———

Anthony Casso's first conscious recollections of the Mafia were Sunday outings with his father. He was seven years old. They'd get dressed up, get in his dad's car, a big, shiny Buick, and drive to his godfather Sally Callinbrano's club on the Flatbush Avenue extension and Bridge Street. They'd make their way straight down Flatbush Avenue toward the Manhattan Bridge. The young Casso very much enjoyed this time alone with his dad, just the two of them in the car cruising along. The year was 1949 and these are some of the warmest memories Anthony has of his childhood, him and his father slowly driving along Flatbush Avenue. Little was said during these private outings with his dad. Just the fact that his dad would take to him Callinbrano's club was, Anthony knew, an honor. Michael Casso was, in a very real sense, introducing his son to a secret society, a far different place from the straight world.

Sally Callinbrano was a prominent force, a highly respected capo in the Genovese crime family. He was a thin, distinguished, gray-haired individual. He was always in an impeccably cut suit, starched white shirt and silk tie, glistening leather shoes. He was perfectly barbered. A huge diamond pinkie ring adorned his right hand.

"He was a class act all the way," as Casso puts it. After the murder of Albert Anastasia in 1957, Callinbrano essentially took over his rule of the International Longshoremen's Association Union, ILA Local 1814, a powerful position that guaranteed prestige, honor, and money. Lots of it.

Anthony would watch through the innocent, though observant, eyes of a curious child all types of men—from all the five families—come to

Callinbrano's club, each showing him deference and respect. Callinbrano was always mild mannered. He was always a gentleman. This made an indelible impression on the young Casso. Even his father treated Callinbrano like "someone special, a man of respect," explained Casso. This, too, had a deep effect on the impressionable boy.

Casso also noted that Callinbrano never raised his voice, never bullied or browbeat anyone. Casso was not sure what Callinbrano was all about, but he wanted to be a part of what he saw. Without his knowing it, the young Casso was being weaned from his family, introduced and made a part of La Cosa Nostra, its unique culture, its beat, rhyme and rhythm.

By three o'clock every Sunday, all the men would dutifully return home to their respective families and have Sunday dinner, large three- and four-course meals, one of the many customs brought over from Europe by the Italian immigrants.

Family, *famiglia*, came first; it was the glue that held them together; it was the only way the Italian immigrants felt they would prosper in this country. With *famiglia* you were insulated and protected, your back covered no matter what; through thick and thin, your family was there.

Casso's mother, Margaret, was a particularly gifted cook. She was a thin, attractive woman with dark hair and dark eyes. She was fair-skinned and shy, though when she warmed to people she was outgoing and gregarious. Margaret made all their pastas by hand, and her tomato sauce was legendary throughout the neighborhood. She was also a gifted baker—she prepared all kinds of Italian cookies, pastries, and fresh bread. On holidays, especially Christmas and New Year's, all the extended family would eat huge meals together that literally went on day and night. It was as though they were making up for any lost meals they or their forebears might have suffered. A good meal, lovingly prepared and served, was like a religion, something holy to be revered. On holidays the men would play cards all night, fueled by Margie's pastries and espresso mixed with homemade anisette.

It was, interestingly, Casso's mother, Margie, who first let the young boy know that his doting godfather, Sally Callinbrano, was "a man of respect," as she put it.

A man of respect. It echoed and resonated in the boy's head.

Back then, being a member of La Cosa Nostra was a badge of honor to most everyone in the Italian American community. The Italian immigrants had been beaten down by the government, by corrupt police, by greedy landlords; they were overtaxed, put upon, and marginalized, and LCN had stood up for them.

The word *mafia,* with a lowercase "m," means "man of honor," someone who walks with his head high, shoulders back—proud. A fine thoroughbred horse might be referred to as *mafia.* Mafia, with an uppercase "M," has come to mean the organized crime families we know today.

Often, back then, when Italians had problems and were not getting justice from the government or the mostly Irish police, people turned to La Cosa Nostra. Disputes with landlords, abuse or exploitation at work, the rape of an Italian female—all could be settled by a local Mob boss. Thus, it was not at all unusual for Casso's mother to readily show deference to and much respect for Callinbrano, her beloved last born's godfather.

When Anthony graduated from Francis Xavier Catholic elementary school, his godfather gave him a $50 bill. When Casso received his Confirmation at St. Francis Church on Carroll Street, his godfather gave him his first pinkie ring (a staple for made men), a pear-shaped diamond and blue sapphire mounted on yellow gold. Unbeknownst to Casso, Callinbrano was cultivating him to be La Cosa Nostra. He saw promise in the young boy—a stoic seriousness beyond his years, a natural air of pride and defiance. Even back then Anthony had engaging, dark, penetrating eyes that showed no fear. Sally Callinbrano influenced Casso more than anyone else. For the young Casso, the world of organized crime was his destiny, the only road he was interested in walking.

CHAPTER 2

STREET SMART

Michael Casso lived in two radically different worlds. He was well connected to men in the underworld and men in politics as well. He was a member in good standing of the famous Mangano Democrat Club on Union Street, a few doors from the Casso residence at 319 Union, just off Fifth Avenue. This was a predominantly Italian neighborhood. Giant wheels of provolone and Parmesan cheese and rolls of aromatic sausage hung in shop windows. The smell of freshly baked bread and pizza permeated the air.

At the end of every workday at the rough-and-tumble Brooklyn docks—carrying heavy crates of all sizes with a hand truck—Michael Casso would come home from work, shower, and put on a suit, white shirt, and tie and go to the Mangano Democrat Club. In those days, every neighborhood in New York had a Democrat club. Here, power brokers in government and the private sector who controlled patronage could get together in an informal setting over a game of cards, coffee, a drink, and do business. A building contractor might be introduced to a landlord—a zoning law could be changed or altered. Here the wheels of commerce, business, and government were greased and ran smoothly, to the collective benefit of all those involved.

Yes, money was exchanged under the table, illegally, but these clubs were more about the facilitation of men's ambitions, hopes, and pla..., here things got done; here deals were made—this was how New York worked.

Here, too, judges came to let down their hair, play cards, have a drink, get away from the wife. They offered their much sought after advice, helped with the outcome of a case, discreetly took money for a favor or to throw a case.

Michael Casso cut a handsome figure. He was broad shouldered and thin waisted and wore clothes well. Quiet and reserved, he was good-looking enough to have been a movie star. People liked him. It was hard not to like him. He'd back down from no one, yet was always a gentleman—never looked for trouble. But if trouble came knocking, he'd meet it head-on. He and his friends—judges, and all types of city and state politicians, businessmen, civic leaders, union bosses—met at the club just about every evening. There were, as such, no tradesmen here, just the bosses. The club was capitalism at its best. On the ground floor of the club, there were a dozen round card tables and constant, friendly games of pinochle. With his mild manners and manly good looks, his keen sense of humor and inherent toughness, Michael Casso was always welcomed: he was the liaison between what went on in the club, the street, and organized crime. He facilitated deals. He made introductions. People grew to trust him explicitly. The trust he instilled in people was his entrée into the club.

Sometimes, during the warm weather, a few of the boys, mostly judges, would want to take a ride to Coney Island for some of Nathan's Famous hot dogs and fries. Michael Casso would accompany them because "Coney" was a rough place; all kinds of seedy characters peopled it, and Michael, or Mike as he was known, would make sure no one bothered any of the judges . . . his friends. These were soft, learned men; few, if any of them, had calluses on their hands—had any street smarts—but Mike Casso had an abundance of both, and he watched over his charges like a protective shepherd over sheep. Fact is, if Mike wasn't going with them, the judges wouldn't go at all.

The young Anthony Casso rarely went inside the club. It was no place for kids. But if his mother had a message for Mike or needed him, she'd send Anthony. Even at that early age, he understood the rudimentary workings of the club—how one hand washed the other, how respectfully his dad was treated. Again, like with his godfather Sally Callinbrano's club, Casso learned important subliminal lessons—about power, how men of power comported themselves, and that deals were sealed and bonded with a mere handshake.

————

Margie Casso, Anthony's mom, was an excellent homemaker, a wonderful cook, a doting mother, and a very nice lady. She loved her husband profoundly. Her children were her world . . . her sunrise and sunset. She couldn't do enough for any of them. She was loving and attentive—"the perfect mom," as Casso recently put it.

In the summertime, during the stifling July and August heat, she'd dutifully take her children to Coney Island, to Bay Sixteenth Street just in front of the famous Steeplechase and Parachute ride. This was an exciting, joyful place—the playground for all New York. For the young Casso, the smells, the sights, and the sounds were an ongoing cacophony of fun, laughter, and good cheer that literally flooded the senses. Margie Casso would bring delicious Italian hero sandwiches made on bread she baked herself, which were then washed down with ice-cold lemonade. Casso would frolic in the surf, build sand castles, and have mud fights with his brother. Sometimes, before they went home, Margie would allow the children to go on the rides that were everywhere they looked, the smell of cotton candy and the report of the .22 rifles from the shooting galleries a constant.

In school, young Anthony Casso was a mediocre student. He was much more interested in fooling around and making his schoolmates laugh and having fun than studying.

On summer Sundays, the Casso family would go on daylong outings, to Allendale Lake in New Jersey. Other Italian families joined them— Sally Callinbrano and his family, and members of the infamous Joe Profaci, Vito Genovese, and Albert Anastasia families. These men were the very epicenter of organized crime in New York, some of the toughest, most ruthless stone-cold killers La Cosa Nostra ever produced. But here on these Sunday outings in rustic New Jersey they were all devoted family men, concerned parents, fawning grandparents . . . loving husbands and dedicated sons. The amounts of food brought to the picnics was staggering; there were all kinds of pastries and vegetables, sausage and chicken and steak to grill, and huge bowls of salads washed down with homemade wines. Then homemade cheesecakes and cookies were served. The men played histrionic games of bocce, grimacing and arguing, waving their hands and shouting in one another's faces; the many children played boisterous games of tag, hide-and-seek, and softball. Their laughter filled the air. They would also have target practice with .22-caliber rifles. Casso especially liked the shooting.

The young Casso was a very good shot; he naturally took to firearms. He loved how sleek and well crafted they were; he cherished their deadly blue-black precision. He understood well their function—that they were carefully crafted tools to kill with, the ultimate equalizer and arbitrator.

Anthony Casso's being born and raised on South Brooklyn's streets had a profound, sobering effect on him on numerous levels. It aged and matured him beyond his years, and eventually garnered him a Ph.D. in street smarts.

The Mafia mind-set was as intricate a part of South Brooklyn as its traffic lights and sidewalks. Mob-related shootings and killings were not unusual. As well as its being the home base of the Genovese and Profaci crime families, Albert Anastasia held court here, created and ran Murder Inc. in the 1930s, had his club/office at 230 Fifth Avenue, just off Carroll Street, a mere stone's throw from the Casso residence on Union Street. Albert Anastasia was not only running the ILA Local 1814, he was outright selling murder contracts as though they were hot dogs at Ebbets Field. He sold between four hundred and five hundred of them in one decade alone, the price anywhere from five thousand to a hundred thousand, depending on the complexity and danger of any given job. These were not necessarily Mob-sanctioned murders of people *in the life*. Many of these killings were of civilians. For example: two businessmen were having a disagreement, and one decided to kill the other. Anastasia would gleefully provide the service—for a fee. Bodies, some with bullet holes, many with ice pick holes, were popping up all over the place, in the barren flatlands of Brooklyn's Flatbush and floating in one of the many bays and estuaries along Brooklyn's thirty miles of coastline.

Young Anthony Casso was privy to all this. He often saw Anastasia in the neighborhood, strutting about like a pompous king, in fancy hand-cut suits, driving a gleaming Cadillac—an impressive though disconcerting sight. He demanded and he received respect.

This was a way of life that Casso began to covet at an early age.

The Mob elite were at the top of the food chain. They controlled everything—commerce, construction, private sanitation, the docks, who lived and who died.

———

In 1954, Casso actually witnessed Joe Monosco's murder on Fourth Avenue. He was twelve years old. He also saw the killing of Donald Marino, who was shot to death on Fifth Avenue and Sackett Street. These were very traumatic, sobering experiences for the young boy. He, both consciously and subconsciously, learned that murder was a natural byproduct of the street.

Casso was thirteen when Frankie "Shoes" De Marco was gunned down and murdered in Costello's Bar on Fourth Avenue. De Marco had been with the Profaci family. Young Casso heard the shots and saw the blood, and he saw the dead bodies being carted off to the medical examiner's office by bored city workers.

Murder, Casso came to know firsthand, was a way of life, the end result of being "in the life," as he recently put it. Murder for the young Casso equaled business. Murder, in that neighborhood, in those days, was a way of life, as common as its cobblestone streets. Casso came to see murder as nothing more than a means to an end.

If you played the game, you had to be prepared to suffer the consequences.

"Kill or be killed. It's that simple," he says.

Casso learned that the key to survival on the street was to strike first and definitively. No matter how tough someone was, a bullet to the head won all arguments. In a very real sense, the concept of striking first, to kill or be killed, was seared into Anthony Casso's brain.

CHAPTER 3

FIRST BLOOD

The young Anthony Casso very much enjoyed hunting trips with his father and uncles in upstate New York, at the farm of mafioso Charlie La Rocca. Deer were plentiful and eaten with gusto, thought of as a delicious delicacy. It was a common sight in South Brooklyn during hunting season to see deer, one or two and sometimes even three, strapped and tied to the fenders and trunks of cars, their long purple tongues hanging lifelessly, their coats often dappled with snow. La Rocca's farm was on fifteen hundred acres near Saugerties, New York. Back then many made men bought homes all over upstate New York. Owning land was an Italian immigrant's dream come true. The fresh air and wide open space, the idyllic scenery, the growing of vegetables in the summer, and the abundant hunting in the winter were all added bonuses. It was a far cry from the South Brooklyn tenements. It was also a status symbol that meant you had arrived, that the American dream was yours.

As a boy, Casso loved to hunt. He had the necessary patience to sit still like stone, waiting for his quarry to come in range. He learned from Charlie La Rocca and his father, both seasoned hunters, to make every shot count, to not pull the trigger unless he knew he had a "kill shot."

"There's no reason to make the animal suffer," his father explained.

Michael Casso, who loved the outdoors, was a dedicated, avid hunter.

Everything he shot, they ate—deer, rabbit, duck, and quail. He bought Anthony his first gun, a .22 rifle. The boy loved and cherished that rifle. He'd clean it and hold it, clean it and hold it some more.

Often, on the spur of the moment, his father would decide to go hunting, and he'd say to Anthony, "We are going; we'll get up early and leave." Casso could barely sleep, he was so excited. His father would wake him at 4:00 A.M. and off they'd go, just the two of them. Anthony relished these times alone with his dad. They'd go to La Rocca's farm and could hunt all they wanted. When they were finished, after his father dressed what they'd shot, he'd set up targets and instruct Anthony on how to shoot, where to put a bullet.

The first deer Casso killed, however, was a traumatic experience for the boy. It was a large buck. The animal came out of a quiet stand of pine trees off to his left, walking slowly, warily sniffing the chilled air. In the distance Casso heard the sound of gunshots, as did the deer—and they both knew what the shots meant. Casso, hidden behind a moss-covered boulder, aimed carefully for the animal's chest—his heart, as his father had taught him—and slowly squeezed the trigger. The buck went right down—dead. Young Casso and his dad slowly approached him. The animal's blood reddened the snow, a slowly spreading circle of crimson red.

"Nice shot," his father said.

Soon the animal was dressed and strapped to the fender of Michael Casso's black Buick.

Back in Brooklyn, Mrs. Casso served up the venison for the family to enjoy.

This was the first time Anthony had killed a large, warm-blooded creature. He was fourteen years old. Though he was oddly upset by killing the deer, he didn't mention this to his father. It wasn't manly, he thought. He knew that hunters killed prey; that the strong survived; the weak were marginalized and put upon, fed from. It was very much like that in the street—"eat or be eaten," a South Brooklyn mantra Anthony often heard.

Still, the killing of the deer hurt him, and he never shot another one. He felt it was unfair. "If deer had guns, I would've been back out there, but of course they didn't," he explained.

Although Anthony did not do well in school mainly because he didn't apply himself, since he already knew his future would be on the street, he had a particularly sharp inquisitive intelligence, readily thought out of the box, and saw problems from both points of view. He was not at all reticent about expressing himself, but he was shy and soft-spoken, never boisterous or loud, a trait that would stay with him for the rest of his life. But once he warmed up to someone, he was open and gregarious, a good friend and a devoted son. Anthony, though, was always serious beyond his years.

As if he was born to suffer great tragedy. As if he was born to cause great tragedy.

————

Guns: Anthony Casso loved them. He took to target shooting whenever the possibility presented itself. Back then, in the mid-1950s, firearms were relatively easy to come by in South Brooklyn. Crates of them—pistols, rifles, even machine guns—were regularly stolen from the nearby docks and Idlewild Airport.

Anthony first practiced his marksmanship with the .22 rifle his father had bought him for upstate and Jersey outings. As he got older, he became much less conflicted about killing animals, and his interest in guns went far beyond using them to hunt and for sport. He knew them to be precision tools of a trade, and that trade was crime. The way a shoemaker used a leather knife, a carpenter a hammer, guns were the tools of the outlaw. Even then, Anthony knew that he was surely destined for the world of organized crime.

"That's what I wanted. That's what I went after. That's what I got," he said.

Anthony practiced shooting both with pistols and his .22 rifle. He found basements of abandoned warehouses where the report of the shooting could not be heard. He also practiced target shooting on warehouse roofs. Over time he became an excellent marksman, so good that he garnered a reputation in the neighborhood as a genuine crack shot with both handguns and rifles. As a youth, it was one of the things he excelled in. Any target he shot at, he hit. He could hit the ace of spades dead center at twenty paces, over and over. His acumen as a marksman grew so that men in the neighborhood who kept blue ribbon pigeons in rooftop coops, actually hired Anthony to bring down hawks that hunted and killed their champion birds. Using his .22, Casso managed to shoot down hawks that seemed, to others, like mere specks up there in the vast Brooklyn sky. Thus Anthony was first paid to kill a living creature.

Although he admired the hawks—their grace, their hunting ability, how they could effortlessly hang perfectly still in the sky, how they could dive-bomb and snatch fast-moving pigeons in midflight—Anthony still killed them without a second thought . . . any remorse.

CHAPTER 4

LAST STANDING

South Brooklyn was teeming with children. During the warm months—April though mid-October—the streets were filled with boisterous young people joyfully playing street games: stickball, Johnny on the Pony, Cork-Cork, Ringaleevio, jump rope, stoopball, flipping and trading baseball cards, and tossing nickels and pennies. In that this was, for the most part, an Italian American neighborhood, the families were usually very large. Six to ten children were the norm, not the exception. The Italians believed that the key to success in their new country was to have many children, that the odds for success increased greatly with each birth. Male children were especially desired for they would protect the family.

The streets were paved with gold was an often-repeated phrase for these people, and the more available to pitch in and help mine the gold, the greater the opportunity for success.

By comparison, Anthony Casso's family was small, but Anthony always had an abundance of friends, boys his own age. A group of them formed a gang of sorts and they called themselves "the South Brooklyn Boys." They hung out on Union Street stoops and in local candy stores. They had occasional turf battles—only with fists and feet—with other gangs, robbed the dairy delivery truck of milk and freshly baked pies, played cards, lifted weights, and talked about girls, the most recent neigh-borhood murder, and what Mob boss was the most powerful or danger-ous. Inevitably most everyone settled on Albert Anastasia, better known as "the Mad Hatter." The South Brooklyn Boys were not involved with any kind of serious crimes. Still, Michael Casso didn't like his son hanging around with these boys. He saw no good coming from it—"only trouble," as he told Anthony, which of course turned out to be fortuitously true. Casso's first of many arrests was because of the South Brooklyn Boys.

A natural leader, Casso already understood the importance of having allies—bonding with other gangs to present a more formidable defense. One such time, a nearby gang, the Day Hill Road Gremlins, headed by Casso's friend Danny Marino, had a beef with an Irish gang called the Seventh Avenue Micks. The Micks were a notoriously tough gang. These were all the sons of hard-boiled blue-collar workers, and being tough and able to dish out and take punishment were important attributes. Here fathers, both Italian and Irish, taught their sons *not* to turn the other cheek, but to stand up for their rights, to make sure that if they were in a fight that they were the last standing.

Another Italian American gang, the Jokers, from Fifth Avenue and Twentieth Street, also joined in on this battle. Most all these "gang wars" were among the different ethnic groups, the Irish, the Polish from Green-point and the far end of Park Slope into Greenwood, and the Italians for the most part. Most all the battles were fought over some real or imagined slight—the insulting of a female, a girlfriend, wife, or sister.

"Honor had to be upheld," Casso explained.

Anthony Casso became a notorious street fighter. He would take on anyone. He had inherited his father's laborer's strength, and he regularly lifted weights. He was short and square with excellent reflexes and a low center of gravity. He too was fearless, though he never bullied anyone. He didn't like bullies. Anthony was a bully slayer. He didn't care if the opponent was twice his size; what concerned him most was that he struck first—and hard.

The night Casso's gang, the South Brooklyn Boys, teamed up with the Gremlins and the Jokers was one of the biggest gang wars in South Brooklyn's rough-and-tumble history. Irish toughs from all over Brooklyn and Manhattan came to help their own. The running feud, hatred and animosity between the Irish and Italians was legendary, harked back many years, and the Irish jumped at the chance to "take a sock at a wop," as they put it.

It was early July 1956, a hot summer night. The fight went down a block from Prospect Park, at the Fourteenth Regiment of the New York National Guard armory at Eighth Avenue and Thirteenth Street. The Italians—nearly a hundred of them—met on Union Street and Fifth Avenue and, en masse, made their way south along Fifth. Anthony led his crew. They were all serious-faced and planned to put the Micks in their place, once and for all. They were a formidable sight, silently walking east, four and five abreast, muscular young men in their prime, intent upon violence, intent upon reddening Brooklyn's streets and sidewalks.

The unbridled hatred Italians and Irish had for one another began with the great migrations of the two peoples from Europe. They competed for work, housing, streets, blocks, neighborhoods, and the lucrative underworld rackets.

The war Al Capone—a neighborhood hero to these young toughs— had with Chicago's Irish gangs was legendary, as was the war the Italians had in New York with Irish gangsters Vincent Coll "Mad Dog," Eddie and Jack Diamond, "Big Bill" Dwyer, and Owny Madden. As history shows, the Irish gangsters were eventually decimated by the Italians . . . by the Mafia's jungle cunning and killing prowess.

They fought, too, because of females . . . an Irish girl becoming sweet for a dark-eyed, sexy Italian, or an Italian girl being charmed by an Irishman's blue eyes, beguiling smile, and glib ways.

The Irish immigrants had always had an advantage over the Italians. They came over first, they spoke English, and they managed to secure, by the late 1800s, most all the municipal jobs, which they jealously guarded. All these elements were in play that warm July night. The fight that night was no longer over a slight—the disrespect of a female. It was about every injustice ever suffered by both camps.

No one had a gun or knife. This war was fought mano a mano, up close and personal. The two groups met and clashed in front of the armory, on Eighth Avenue, diagonally across the schoolyard of P.S. 107. They came together in a furious swirl of angry fists and feet, pieces of pipe, and socks filled with rocks; they fought tooth and nail. The Irish were outnumbered and began to knuckle under—retreat.

This was a tree-lined, residential neighborhood, and the cops quickly got word of the fight. Suddenly the air was filled with the screams of sirens. Police cars, filled with mostly pink-faced Irish cops and detectives, came from every direction. They cut off the getaway routes. Anthony made for Prospect Park until a pig-nosed detective stuck a pistol in his face, made him freeze, and laid him flat on the ground, where he was roughly handcuffed and kicked a few times in his ribs, knocking the breath out of him. Paddy wagons appeared. Anthony was made to get in one. He was kicked in the ass as he stepped up to get in. Most all those arrested, not surprisingly, were the Italians.

Anthony was booked at the Seventy-eighth Precinct on Sixth Avenue. His father was called. The senior Casso soon appeared at the precinct, as always dressed impeccably in a suit and tie, now all grim-faced. He confronted his son.

"I warned you. I told you. When are you going to learn?"

Anthony, of course, had no answer.

He was arrested for the first time. It would be, to Michael Casso's dismay, the first of numerous arrests to come.

CHAPTER 5

READIN', WRITIN', 'RITMATIC

School and Anthony Casso didn't mix; they were as incompatible as oil and water. Anthony didn't like the regimentation; he didn't like being told what to do and when to do it . . . the conformity of it all. Plus he already knew his future would play out on the street, for better or for worse. It was, for him, an accepted fact—the way winter follows fall.

"The natural order of things," as he recently put it.

Anthony, for the most part, was not interested in what they taught at Manual High School on Seventh Avenue—science, history, shop, English—but he was fond of math. For Anthony already knew that money was always represented in numbers, and money was a thing he was most interested in.

Michael Casso was not pleased that Anthony wanted nothing to do with school—a higher education. He would like to see his last born become a professional, a lawyer perhaps, or a banker, an occupation in which he never had to break his back, callus his hands, or regularly come home with aching muscles. The senior Casso would certainly have preferred that Anthony not choose a life of crime, not become part and parcel of a criminal enterprise. But since he knew his son would not be a scholar, a straight-A student, he was wise enough to know that the path to success was not just through the regimentation of public schools. He had many friends who were amazingly successful and respected . . . and very wealthy. He would, he decided, expose Anthony to this other path, to let him make his own way, and support and encourage any decisions he made. He felt in his heart—indeed, knew instinctively—that Anthony would be successful. Anthony had the nerve, the strength of character, and the respect of family to make it in life. The only question was, would he get hurt, maimed, or even killed? Only time, the senior Casso knew, would tell. He had taught Anthony everything he knew: to always keep your word, to respect your elders, to respect the solidarity of family, to always be able to provide for your family, to keep your emotions in check, to never cry in front of your enemies, to finish what you start, to be a man, to walk with your shoulders back and your head high. They were best friends. A father could do no more.

Anthony's godfather, Sally Callinbrano, would play a big role in Casso's future. Sally had moved his headquarters from the Flatbush Avenue Extension Club to Monty's Bar on Carroll Street. He was more respected and powerful than ever. He would soon be running the Brooklyn docks and hold sway over ILA Local Union 1814.

CHAPTER 6

A VERY CLOSE SHAVE INDEED

It was now that a bold public murder occurred in the world of La Cosa Nostra that altered and reshaped the American Mafia in a profound way; it shook its very foundations and caused a bloody war that would last some twenty-two years and claim many lives.

The man murdered, a homicidal egomaniac, was an out-of-control liability to everyone in organized crime. To this day his real killers have never been identified. As a result of this book, however, and Anthony Casso's inside track on the true inner workings of the New York Mafia, the truth will finally be known.

Albert Anastasia, who had a stranglehold on the Brooklyn waterfront, had become known as the Mad Hatter for good reason. The founder of Murder, Incorporated, the head of a New York crime family, he had been killing indiscriminately for so long, unchecked, that he came to believe himself invincible, above both society's and the Mafia's laws, rules, and protocols.

When he ordered the murder of a civilian, one Arnold Schuster, a witness against the bank robber Willie Sutton, he boldly said that he "*hated* squealers."

This appalled everyone in Mafiadom—even its aristocrats—Lucky Luciano to Meyer Lansky. Anastasia's days were numbered. His violent end came on October 25, 1957. As was his custom, he was getting a shave in the Park Central Hotel in Manhattan, which of course, everyone in the Mob world knew; what few know is who actually pulled the trigger.

According to Casso, Vito Genovese—with the treacherous compliance of Anastasia's underboss, Carlo Gambino—took the contract and ordered the hit. He gave the job to Crazy Joe Gallo, Albert Kid Blast Gallo, and Carmine "the Snake" Persico, all tried and true killers. They met early that morning in South Brooklyn and were at the hotel barbershop waiting, keyed up and ready to strike, when Anastasia arrived. All three knew this job—the killing of the head of a family—was extremely important, that it would get them all made . . . that it would assure their reputation in the underworld.

The barbershop was one story below ground. Joey Gallo and Persico entered through the garage, wearing handkerchiefs over their faces, their guns in their hands hidden in baggy overcoats. Albert Gallo stood guard outside. Anastasia was reclining in a barber's chair, fifth one down the row from the entrance. It faced a wall of mirrors. There was a steaming towel—to soften the bristles and open the pores in preparation for the straight razor shave—covering his hard countenance. He was totally unaware that death was silently approaching.

Both Persico and Gallo had on soft rubber-soled shoes. They understood that Anastasia was a very dangerous man, a seasoned, extremely experienced killer who knew intimately the beat and rhythm of murder—its whispers and footsteps. But Anastasia heard nothing now.

"Keep your mouth shut if you don't want your head blown off," Persico whispered to the owner, Arthur Grasso, who remained silent.

Persico and Gallo moved toward the reclining Anastasia. Gallo gently pushed the attending barber out of the way. Without further preamble they quickly drew out guns and released a fusillade of deafening shots.

Anastasia, a physically powerful man, jumped up and went to grab his assailants, growling loudly as he moved, animal-like, but he was confused and went for their mirrored images as they continued to mercilessly shoot him, leaving him in a heap of broken bones and torn up flesh, bleeding profusely. Dead.

———

Back in South Brooklyn, the hit team was greeted and praised by Carlo Gambino, who assured them that they would all be made when "the books were opened." No money was paid for this hit. The young Anthony Casso learned all the details from his godfather, Sally Callinbrano, who was soon put in charge of ILA Local 1814. Not one of those who knew the true identity of the killers said a word. These were the days when no one talked, when *omerta* was still taken seriously.

Sally Callinbrano now controlled the South Brooklyn docks. He decided who worked, who didn't, and who would secure a coveted "no-show job"—that is, to be paid for work never done, a classic Mafia setup. Sally wanted to provide a no-show job for Anthony on the docks, but Anthony was not yet eighteen and could not yet join the union. Sally arranged to get Anthony a forged birth certificate, stating that he was eighteen. With that, Anthony was able to become a bona fide union member in ILA Local 1814.

Thus, at seventeen, Anthony already had a no-show job thanks to organized crime. Every week he picked up a check for hundreds of dollars for work he did not do. He was already all about beating the system, stealing whatever wasn't nailed down, taking advantage wherever possible. Casso soon managed to secure another no-show job, this one with interesting fringe benefits.

A Genovese family "friend," Ray Muscarella, was the manager of Tony Bennett. Bennett was hot in 1959. Money was rolling in from both personal appearances and popular recordings. The Genovese family had their sharp talons in him. The few hundred dollars Casso received from all the money Bennett was generating was a drop in the bucket. Not only did Anthony get a check for $250 every week, but he could sign for meals at Monty's Bar and Restaurant on Carroll Street . . . both lunches and dinners. Casso, always magnanimous and generous, began bringing all his friends for meals, and Ray Muscarella was soon forced to put a stop to the free food.

Anthony also earned money from having a booth in the San Gennaro festival in Manhattan's Little Italy. He ran a nickel-pitch game where patrons threw nickels into glass containers to win prizes. While he ran this booth, his father was in charge of a dice game in an alleyway. The festival had been a Mob-controlled enterprise since its inception at the turn of the twentieth century, and only people who were connected managed to secure lucrative booths. All members and friends of the five families had their fingers in this sweet pie. It was a yearly tradition, as controlled by the Mob as the Fulton Fish Market and the Brooklyn docks. Anthony, with these "easy money" situations, was effortlessly benefiting from one of the many tentacles organized crime has. He was already part of the system. He was "connected."

Sally Callinbrano and Christie "Tick" Furnari, a Lucchese capo who took a shine to Casso, and his own father all collectively saw in Anthony certain qualities that are mandated to become a bona fide member of La Cosa Nostra. He was stand-up; he had proven over and over that he had courage in battle; he had proven that he could keep his mouth shut; he showed the proper deference and respect not only to made men but also to his own family—his mother and father.

Anthony was quick to smile and make jokes, too—he had a likable side people readily warmed to. He was tough and confident and sure of himself, but he also had a stoic, sober maturity beyond his years.

Already Anthony was very aware of clothes. He knew how to look good. With his lucrative no-show jobs, he had the money to buy expensive shirts and slacks and shoes, sharkskin suits, and well-cut Italian leather jackets that were soft like butter. By carefully observing the dress, manners, and physical carriage of mafiosi Casso respected, he had made what he saw his own, made what he saw a part of whom he became. Anthony had matured into a handsome, dark-haired young man with an engaging smile that lit up his whole face. Though he had a pockmarked countenance from a serious bout with acne, females quickly warmed up to him. He was polite and somewhat shy, a gentleman, never loud or a braggart, which further drew the opposite sex to him. Anthony now had his own car, a 1958 black Chevy convertible, which he proudly tooled around the neighborhood in. He had also taken to regularly carrying a gun with him, a short-barreled .32, easy to conceal and deadly at close range. For Anthony, the gun was the ultimate arbitrator; by having a gun with him, he knew he could readily control who lived and who died. With two swift movements, he could kill an enemy . . . pull the gun out, pull the trigger. By now, he was a bona fide crack shot. When he pointed a gun and fired, he hit what he aimed for.

Anthony had been dating a neighborhood girl named Rosemarie Billotti. Her parents, decent, hardworking Italian Americans, owned a candy store. They were very fond of Anthony and thought of him as a son. Anthony's destiny, however, was with Lillian Delduca.

Lillian and Anthony began dating in earnest in the winter of 1960. He took her to nice dinners, the movies, drives out to Long Island, and sometimes to the city. He always had money, which he freely spent; he well knew that if you wanted the finer things life had to offer, you had to have money . . . the more the better. They also went to Coney Island with other couples, and there enjoyed the bounty of innocent fun Coney had to offer. Whenever he shot at the different shooting galleries, he'd win a prize, some kind of stuffed animal for Lillian. He could repeatedly shoot out candle flame after candle flame at twenty paces. Anthony hit whatever he aimed at. He had become a deadly shot.

CHAPTER 7

IRRATIONALLY VIOLENT

It was the spring of 1961. The renewal of life was in the air, returning to South Brooklyn. Buds were opening and flowering in Prospect Park. Birds chirped gaily. Butterflies danced in the first warmth of the year. Children were returning to playing boisterous street games after a long brutal winter. In most all the backyards throughout the neighborhood, Italian Americans were happily planting tomatoes and basil and all varieties of vegetables. Coveted fig trees brought over from Italy as mere cuttings were being unwrapped, their winter tarps carefully removed and put away for the fall. Front yards filled with flowers. Here, people had pride in and took good care of their homes. Wherever you looked, stoops and sidewalks were carefully swept and cleaned. Statues of saints that adorned many front yards were cleaned and freshly painted.

This place, South Brooklyn, was a safe neighborhood to bring up children. Here women could walk the streets unmolested, without fear. There were few burglaries. The fact that so many mafiosi—"the boys," as they were known—lived here ensured that the level of street crime was minimized.

That was, of course, except *their* crime. Interestingly, however, La Cosa Nostra did not commit crimes where they, their mothers and fathers, their wives and children, lived. They did not, as the saying goes, "shit where they ate."

But they definitely killed people where they lived without reservation or hesitation, almost as though murder, for them, was a God-given right. Brazenly shooting someone to death and leaving him where he dropped was the norm, not the exception. This would eventually create a publicity nightmare that would cause both intense press and police scrutiny and would be a contributing factor in LCN's eventual decline. The crime families never seemed to get— still don't—that it was not okay to shoot people to death publicly whenever they chose.

Anthony now always carried a gun. He was collecting bookmaking money, as well as the loans that he had put out in the street, and he sometimes had to be heavy-handed. He also had interests in two different South Brooklyn after-hours clubs; by being associated with LCN, Anthony had automatic license to open these after-hours clubs. They were in commercial spaces on the second floor of buildings. There were doormen who would not let you in unless they knew you. The cops knew about them but were paid off and so left them alone. There was music, dancing, and drinking till the wee morning hours. They were a lucrative source of income. Whatever Casso made, a portion was kicked up to his mentor, Christie Tick Furnari.

In 1960, Anthony met Paul Castellano for the first time—a fortuitous occasion that would affect his future. A good childhood friend of Casso's, Lee Mariano, who was in Castellano's crew, managed to get Casso a plum no-show job for the Japanese Shipping Company. When this was protested by Anthony Scotto who was then leading the ILA Union, Castellano stepped up and told Scotto that Casso was keeping the job. And he did. Castellano, a tall, thin cadaver of a man, was Carlo Gambino's brother-in-law—Carlo was married to Paul's older sister, Catherine—and he wielded much power.

———

The incident occurred in the spring of 1961, in broad daylight. Cas Anthony so was driving on Brooklyn's busy Fifth Avenue. He kept a .38 pistol in an innocuous brown paper bag under the front seat of the car.

Junkies, in those days, were relatively rare, but there were some in this South Brooklyn neighborhood. It was the heroin addicts who committed neighborhood burglaries, who stole women's pocketbooks and ran with surprising speed. The junkies were loathed and despised by virtually everyone.

As Anthony drove along that beautiful spring day, he spotted a tall skinny junkie named Bobby Bebop harassing a woman with a child at a bus stop on Fifth Avenue, just off Carroll Street. She was a local girl Casso knew. Bebop, the man harassing the girl, was "a junkie creep," as Casso said. Anthony had nothing against him as such, but he didn't like what he saw—this low-life guy bothering a nice girl. Casso—and most all made guys—hated rapists and child molesters. He parked on Fifth Avenue, grabbed his gun out of the paper bag, stuck it in his pants, and got out of the car.

"Leave her alone," Casso told Bebop.

"What's it to you?" Bebop asked.

"Leave her alone," Anthony repeated.

Bebop pushed Casso. The argument escalated. Bebop showed no fear. Why should he? He had an uncle, Carmine Bovie, who was a captain in the Genovese crime family. The argument moved to Carroll Street. The junkie pushed Casso. Sitting on a stoop there, reading a newspaper, was Ralph Salerno, a made guy, an uncle of Carmine and Alley Persico.

The dangerous psychopath who lived inside of Anthony Casso now suddenly showed himself. Without hesitation he pulled out his .32-caliber pistol and fired—*Boom!*—the shot resonating loudly on the quiet residential street. Bebop moved his head just in time. Anthony fired again, and again; they were so close that, miraculously, the junkie was able to avoid the bullets with little more than flesh wounds. Ralph Salerno witnessed all this. Of course, the whole neighborhood would know all about it soon. The junkie, tall and gangly, fell over some trashcans. Casso had three shots left. He aimed and shot Bebop three times, hitting him, and left him there like that, glad he'd done it . . . but not quite sure why he'd done it. Nevertheless, for better of for worse, it was done.

In no time the jungle drums that resonate throughout Mafiadom spread word of what Anthony Casso had done—why and how he'd done it.

Thus, Anthony Casso's reputation was forever chiseled in stone for all in the underworld to see and know.

———

Bobby Bebop the junkie was taken to Methodist Hospital, gravely wounded but not dead. He had lost a lot of blood. Doctors told his family and hard-boiled detectives out of the Seventy-eighth Precinct on Sixth Avenue that he might not make it.

Casso knew he was in serious trouble, and he first naturally went straight to his father, who took him to see his godfather, Sally Callinbrano. Neither Callinbrano nor the senior Casso reprimanded Anthony. What they did was make sure he got out of town until this thing blew over and they had a chance to make it right—make sure street justice was served.

Anthony had been dating a neighborhood girl named Rosemarie Billotti. Her parents, Nick and Annette Billotti, owned a popular candy story at 687 Union Street. It had a hot jukebox with all the popular hits of the day including "Runaround Sue," "That'll Be the Day," "All Shook Up," and the kids danced up a storm. The Billottis, who were very fond of Casso, had known him since he was a kid wet behind the ears. They hoped he would one day settle down with their daughter, but that was not in the cards.

The Billottis heard, like everyone else, about what Casso had done, and they offered to let him hide out in their rural New Jersey summer home until things cooled down.

In those days, justice could readily be bought. The South Brooklyn NYPD, for the most part, was as crooked as a pretzel. Deals made and money passed under the table was business as usual.

It didn't take long for the police to come knocking loudly on the door of the Casso home. They had an arrest warrant for Anthony. Polite and friendly, always a diplomatic gentleman, Michael Casso well knew how the game was played and he was cordial and friendly. He told Detectives Gallo and Sullivan that he had no idea where his son was.

"What's all this about?" he asked, wide-eyed and innocent.

"He shot a guy three times on Carroll," Gallo said. "Thinks it's the Wild West."

"I'm sure there's some mistake."

"We're sure there's no mistake. The victim is critically wounded. If he dies, your son will be facing murder charges."

"My God . . . like I said, I'm sure there's some mistake," the senior Casso repeated.

"Like I said, we're sure there's not."

"Soon as I hear from my son, I'll have him go to the precinct."

"Good. We'd appreciate that," Gallo said, handing Michael Casso a card.

They shook hands, all of them knowing already that this would be resolved in the Mangano Democrat Club down the block, that the NYPD didn't care about some wayward junkie being shot. This was about money in a paper bag, a payoff, not justice. Here scales of justice were controlled with the delicate weight of hard cash—of graft, the odious currency of corruption.

The only question was how much?

Calmly, slowly, Michael Casso put on a shirt and perfectly cut suit and tie and strolled over to the Mangano Democrat Club. He had been developing contacts and nurturing friends there for over twenty-five years, and he'd now use those resources judiciously.

He believed in his heart that his son was destined for greatness. He just wished the boy would learn to control his temper and not be so quick to resort to violence.

———

Through friends, Michael Casso soon learned that Detective Gallo out of the Sixth Avenue station was looking for $50,000 to "throw" the case. This was an outrageous sum of money to ask for, and the Cassos didn't have that much hard cash on hand. Anthony was young, spending lavishly on women, clothes, good times, jewelry, and gambling, and he did not have that kind of dough. Plus, everyone felt the amount was far too much—unfair.

As the lengthening days of spring slowly passed, Bebop got better. He remained in critical condition for nearly a month. He wanted revenge. He and his older brother, with their uncle's blessing, would find Anthony and kill him, he vowed vocally and loudly from his hospital bed.

This shooting was frequently talked about and discussed throughout

LCN. It was the kind of spontaneous shooting that warranted attention. It was the kind of incident that got the interest of the bosses.

One such individual was Vincent "the Chin" Gigante, who later became known as the "Odd Father" for his brilliant portrayal, over a twenty-five-year period, of an insane, out-of-control buffoon, when in truth he was one of the most cunning, ruthless Mafia bosses in its long sordid history.

Chin, now a capo, sent out word to Anthony Casso that he'd pay the fifty grand to get him off the hook and into his fold. Casso was already clearly established as a rising star in the underworld and the Chin wanted him in his camp, his *borgata*. The Chin was not yet head of the Genovese family, but it was a position he coveted. It was the Chin who had been dispatched by Vito Genovese himself to kill Mafia prince Frank Costello in 1952. Though the Chin was foiled in his attempt to kill Costello in the fancy lobby of the Majestic apartments on Central Park West, it became his initial claim to fame in the underworld. Costello, however, got the hint and retired from the rackets, healthy, wealthy, and wise.

Now, carefully, discreetly, word was sent to Anthony that he should come to a meeting in the Village—Genovese territory—to discuss his problem with the law. This area, commonly referred to as Greenwich Village, was once part of Little Italy—Italians filled its tenements, most all the shops catered to Italians. However, over the years, Little Italy kept shrinking to the point that now the area was known as Greenwich Village and not part of Little Italy anymore. Anthony soon met with the Chin's brother, Mario Gigante, who told him they'd front him the fifty thou. Casso stared at Mario, who had the hard jawline, overreaching brow, and deadpan eyes inherent in most Mob guys' faces.

"Why?" Anthony asked.

"We know," Gigante said, "you're good for it, and we know you're an earner and we'd like you with us."

Rather than make a quick decision right then, Anthony politely thanked Gigante for his offer and said he'd let him know. They had dinner and parted as friends. Casso returned to Norwalk, New Jersey, not sure about what he should do.

On the one hand, it was nice to be wanted, but he was not sure about the Genovese family—their contacts, their political connections, the wisdom of its head, Phillip Lombardo—or about being inducted into it . . . he was also hesitant about having to be beholden to Chin Gigante.

Clandestinely, Casso went to see his godfather, Sally Callinbrano, in a small, out-of-the-way Italian restaurant, called Stella's, in Coney Island; it was collectively decided to resolve this problem another way. By now, Callinbrano's hair was all white, thinning, but perfectly barbered and combed straight back. As always, he was in a beautifully cut suit, his hands well manicured, his diamond pinkie ring glistening.

"You go back to Jersey. You stay there till we put this to rest," Anthony was advised.

———

Michael Casso knew the best way to get his last born out of this jam was to go see the uncle of the guy Anthony had shot. Michael Casso knew Carmine Bovie and was relatively certain he could put this to rest with him. He knew that Bovie would not want his nephew to take the stand and be a rat, even though he'd been shot numerous times.

Meanwhile, the junkie Casso shot was released from the hospital, and, true to his word, he and his brother went looking for Casso. He had it in his head to kill Casso, and who could blame him? Casso was not yet *made* and in light of what he'd done, he was fair game. These two brothers boldly went to the after-hours clubs Casso had an interest in—one was on Seventh Avenue and Eleventh Street, the other on Ninth Street and Fifth Avenue in Brooklyn. Casso was partners with Anthony "Blackout" Marciano, whose brother Lu Lu, a made man in the Gambino family, under Paul Castellano, was a close friend.

The junkie Casso shot not only came looking for him, saying he was going to kill him, but also showed people in the clubs a sawed-off shotgun, saying, "I've got this for the motherfucker."

A sawed-off shotgun is only good for one thing . . . killing human beings.

Of course, Casso soon heard what was happening. He immediately left the sanctuary of the Jersey hideout and went to Brooklyn, murder on his mind. He could not find the junkie or his brother, but he left word in several places that *he* was now looking for *them*. Anthony knew it could not seem like he was hiding from the guy he shot.

Michael Casso knew that he had to act quickly and decisively or the situation would become worse; he could very well lose his son to either state prison or the city morgue. He would not let that happen. A meeting—"a sit-down"—was set up. Michael Casso went with Sally Callinbrano, who knew Bovie well. Bovie, a large bald-headed man with broad shoulders, was not happy.

"Where," he demanded, "does your son get off here—pulling such a stunt? He very nearly killed my nephew, shooting him like that . . . what, six times? Jesus."

"Anthony knew the girl's mother," Michael said, his voice strong, his dark eyes boring into Bovie's triple-chinned face.

"It is well known," Sally Callinbrano put in, "that your nephew is a junkie . . . he has a reputation in the neighborhood as a troublemaker."

These, Bovie knew, were true words. He also knew his nephew was a no-good bastard. All his life he'd been getting him out of jams. He drew a long, deep, exasperated breath and took a more conciliatory tone. Soon a deal was made. Casso would allow himself to be arrested and the nephew would not ID him. This plan, fused with Michael Casso's judge contacts ensured that Anthony would walk.

The money, ten grand, was soon paid to Bebop. Casso and his father appeared at the Seventy-eighth Precinct. Detective Gallo detained him and put together a hasty lineup. The junkie, as planned, said he "wasn't sure." Detective Gallo, knowing what was up, made him choose Casso, and he was duly arrested.

"Think you and your father are cute?" he asked Casso as he booked and printed him. "Do the right thing here, Casso, or you're going away. Hard time; a lot of it. Take that to the bank, got me?" the detective said.

Here, now, Anthony learned a very good lesson, one he would always remember and use over and over in his career of crime. Justice, the police, could be bought and sold like any other commodity—bread at a bakery, fish in the fish market, a sandwich at a luncheonette.

Anthony spent the night in jail, hating the loss of his freedom, the smells, the filth, the cops who held the keys. Jail, for him, was anathema . . . made him a failure—a bona fide loser.

Late the next morning Michael Casso bailed his son out. Anthony did not go looking for the junkie and the junkie didn't come looking for him.

When, several months later, Anthony appeared in court and the junkie took the stand, tall and gaunt and pale, he said—gritting his teeth—that he could not identify Anthony as the shooter, that he had told Detective Gallo that at the precinct. The judge, a friend of a friend of the Mangano Democrat Club, immediately dismissed the charges against Anthony, then admonished the assistant D.A. for even bringing the case to his courtroom. Anthony walked out of court a free man as Detective Gallo and his partner glared at him. Anthony had beaten the system. But this was not the end of Anthony's battles with the law; it was only the beginning.

CHAPTER 8

WHEN YOU STEAL WITHOUT HURTING ANYONE, IT'S A LOT OF FUN

Oddly enough, Anthony Casso did not shy away from hard work. His father instilled in him a responsible, dedicated work ethic that stayed with him all his life. As well as the underworld activities he was involved in, he now went to work at the docks at 8:00 A.M. every day, working alongside his father and older brother, Michael, till 4:00 P.M. After work he would go home, shower thoroughly, have dinner with his family, then go hang out with close friend Lu Lu—a made guy with the Gambino family—at Morrisey's Bar at Fifth Avenue and Sackett Street.

For these men, for mafiosi, select bars and clubs were their offices, their conference rooms, the places where they met, strategized, planned crimes, divvied up profits from different rackets, settled disputes . . . and ordered murders.

Casso always dressed impeccably, his hair well barbered, his nails carefully manicured. He also kept his car amazingly clean. He was in fact obsessively clean, another reason he hated jail cells—they were dirty, filthy.

Casso was partners with Lu Lu's brother, Anthony Blackout Marciano, in the after-hours clubs. Already obsessed with making money, Casso was not afraid to sweat or take chances to earn it. He was intent upon making the American dream his . . . and his family's. He well knew that all his grandparents had left Italy with nothing but what they could carry, hoping and praying for a better life for themselves and their offspring. In the old country they all heard that the streets in America were paved with gold, and they were only too happy to break their backs and endlessly strain their muscles for some of that gold.

Casso very much wanted to buy his father and mother a beautiful upstate retreat with a lot of land and running brooks where they could retire, where his dad could fish and hunt and enjoy life to his heart's content. That, for Casso, was an important goal. He often fantasized about surprising his father with the gift, of driving to the estate—setting it up by saying it was a friend's and they could use it—then handing him the keys.

"Dad, this is yours," he'd say.

In time, he was sure, that would come to pass. Now was the time to put his back to the millstone, focus his energies, and work—make money, lots of it.

Casso was intent upon being made, upon rising quickly up the ranks of LCN's ladder—surely one of the most dangerous, precarious ascents in this world. This was his future. This was his dream. This was what he was after come hell or high water.

He imagined he'd be made by the Gambino crime family. They were the largest family with the most crews. He thought, too, that he'd end up as part of Paul Castellano's crew. Paul was well connected to Carlo Gambino via marriage. His wife was Carlo's sister, Nina. Paul was also an astute businessman, a classy guy. Casso thought Carlo Gambino was an excellent boss. He blended with the woodwork, never bullied or yelled—kept himself out of the public eye, off police radar. He was also, Casso knew, responsible for the killing of Albert Anastasia, which was no small thing. Carlo had been Anastasia's underboss. Anastasia was a loud and vulgar bully who flaunted his wealth and didn't know how to handle real power. Gambino was, as the Sicilian saying goes, *quiet like a lamb, but dangerous like the lion.* Casso thought that he merited respect. There were other bosses Casso admired, but he felt he'd one day end up in the Gambino family. However, he was also close to Lucchese capo Christie Tick Furnari, a silver-haired, good-looking man who had known Anthony since he was a kid.

CHAPTER 9

LARCENY-HEARTED

Anthony Casso was a born thief. However, he never stole from poor people, only those who would not miss what he'd taken. Always on the lookout for a good score, he noticed that there were trucks filled with easy-to-sell items—jeans, TVs and appliances, imported dresses and fancy foods, makeup, razor blades, leather jackets, and so on—all over the Brooklyn docks. He made friends with the drivers, who agreed to readily give up their loads for $10,000 cash and say they were hijacked at gunpoint. They'd meet at a prescribed place, and the driver would hand over the keys to the truck and be given a bag full of money, no one the wiser. They'd get in the cab and drive, whistling as they went. This was profitable and "fun," as Casso put it. "No one was hurt; all involved profited." When he had control of the stolen goods, he'd sell the loads to an assortment of men, *fences,* connected to different families, always at a huge profit.

Anthony's father's friends, Long John and Joe Profaci, controlled the piers, but Casso didn't let that stop him. He figured they weren't personally losing anything, that all was fair in love and war.

Casso, always the black sheep, never followed the tail in front of him. He had balls and imagination and thrived on the challenge of beating the systems of both the straight and crooked worlds. He believed, though, that when you gave your word, shook someone's hand, that was cast in cement, and you had to honor the agreement—another trait he inherited from his father. Casso never told either Long John or Joe Profaci that he wouldn't rob the piers. He figured that as long as no one was hurt, it was okay—what he took would not be missed.

Anthony used to lie awake at night, thinking of various scams from numerous points of view. He now decided that, instead of working just with the lowly truck drivers, he'd approach the guards who watched over the piers, who controlled what came and left, who guarded the henhouse.

The guards were much more wary and circumspect than the drivers, but cash on the barrelhead is the ultimate persuader and they agreed. Like this, the young Casso managed to steal several rigs a week without strife or fuss. He had to bring other guys into the scam, he became so busy. One of these individuals was Frankie DeCicco, who in years to come would be the underboss of the Gambino family under John Gotti.

The guards did so well working with Anthony that two of them bought homes. Anthony also developed contacts with shopkeepers up and down South Brooklyn who gladly, indeed gleefully, bought the boun-ties of swag he had to offer. The shopkeepers did so well with the always well-dressed, handsome Anthony Casso that they smiled broadly when they saw him walk into their stores, offered him coffee, tried to fix him up with their daughters and nieces. He became known as the Robin Hood of Fifth Avenue, a title he enjoyed, for he felt it was what he was about. It was an illusion that would stay with Casso all his life. The more he made, the more he spent—on a better car, clothes, fancy restaurants. Casso always kept his word, kept his mouth shut, and was a gentleman, though a natural danger emanated from him, like waves of heat from sunbaked stone.

The neighborhood wise guys all liked Anthony. He comported him-self with pride . . . a chin-up, shoulders-back stoicism that was pure ma-fioso.

———

On a summer evening in 1965, Gambino capo Long John came to see Casso at Morrissey's Bar. There was someone, he said, he wanted to "scare back into the fold." Long John was a tall, rugged man with dark eyes. Knowing Casso was an excellent shot, he said, "I want you to be there when he leaves for work at 7:00 A.M. and put a couple of shots real close to him but don't hit him, see . . . okay?"

"Sure, I'll do it," Casso said.

"I'll make sure you'll be clocked in before 8:00 so no matter what you'll've got a solid alibi, see."

"Perfect."

For the first time Anthony would be firing a gun at a human being at the behest of a made man.

Anthony did not ask why Long John wanted this done. He would do the deed without question. First Anthony scoped out the man's house. It was a residential street near Greenwood Cemetery. Anthony found a perfect place to lie in wait for him behind a thick cluster of bushes, and when the mark left his home for work, Anthony was in position. He had stolen license plates and, using magnets, attached them to cover his real plates—easy on, easy off. A little after 7:00 A.M., the mark left his house, a two-story redbrick home, and headed for his car.

Holding a long-barreled .38 revolver in comfortable combat position, Anthony fired three well-placed shots in rapid succession, shooting out the mark's headlight and car window and putting a hole in a wooden post. Anthony then drove straight down to the docks. There he threw the .38 into the water and got rid of the stolen license plates. He then went to work, where he had already been clocked in. Anthony did not know who the man was—that didn't matter. All that mattered was that he did what was asked of him.

The mark, as planned, came running back to Long John. The desired effect had been achieved. Casso refused to take any money for what he'd done. A favor returned, he already knew, could be far more valuable than a few thousand dollars. Plus he now had a bond—an ally—with Capo Long John that would serve him well for years to come.

CHAPTER 10

THE OPPOSITE SEX

Anthony Casso loved women and women loved him right back. He was usually dating several women at once. He always had new clothes, his pockets filled with cash. He was generous and spent freely. He also had a keen sense of humor and loved practical jokes just as much as he had when he was a schoolboy. Even as Casso grew older and became deeply immersed in all the nefarious business of the Mafia—especially murder—he'd never lose that playful sense of humor; he'd always be a fun-loving kid . . . a practical joker.

Most of the women Anthony dated were neighborhood Italian American girls, but he also dated Irish girls. The Irish females more readily bestowed their favors upon him . . . but Anthony's persistence and charm eventually won over most all the women he pursued. Because of his after-hours clubs, he came into contact with many women.

One of his more regular girlfriends was Rosemarie Billotti. She loved him and hoped to marry him, but he never thought of her that way. Her parents' candy store was still a popular hangout, packed with young people every night. Good dancers came there to tear up the black-and-white linoleum floor and warm up for bigger, more popular dances all over Brooklyn—at Prospect Park, Coney Island, and New York's famous Roseland, on West Fifty-first Street. Anthony was not a dancer; he was shy, and he felt it wasn't consistent with his image as a serious-faced mafioso. Though Casso was not yet made, he had the walk and talk and dress down pat.

As much as Anthony enjoyed playing the field, he wanted to settle down—he wanted a family, a nice home away from the underworld hurly-burly of South Brooklyn. He came to view South Brooklyn as a place to do business, hold court, and plan and plot, but not a place to live, to bring up children. It was, back then, very different from the safe, upper-class enclave Park Slope has become.

———

As with most Italian Americans, family was important to the Mafia. All revolved around it. An interesting dichotomy was—indeed, still is—how so many ruthless, coldhearted mafiosi were loving, doting husbands, fathers, and sons. Anthony Casso seamlessly fit right into this mold.

But he would not settle down with the wrong woman just for the sake of being married. He wanted his marriage to last forever; he wanted a life partner.

He took "Till death do you part" quite literally—like his mother and father's marriage and his grandparents' union. Casso did not believe in divorce.

There was one woman in his life whom Anthony thought of as a potential wife, and that woman was Lillian Delduca.

CHAPTER 11

TRUE LOVE

Anthony and Lillian had known each other all their lives. Each was brought up on Union Street, she in number 673, he in 719. They had always been friends, had gone to the movies, taken the subway to the beaches at Coney Island, and enjoyed rock-and-roll shows at the Paramount and Fox theaters hosted by Allan Freed. Lillian was a tall, thin attractive woman with a small waist, a perfectly proportioned body. She had large thick lips and big fawn-shaped eyes, and she moved sensuously like a female who was supremely comfortable in her own skin.

Lillian was Italian American; all her grandparents had emigrated from southern Italy. Though Lillian had three brothers, Anthony had always watched over her as though she was family . . . his sister. He knew her to be "a nice Italian girl," and he felt an obligation to protect her.

Both Anthony and Lillian were born in 1942, he three months her senior. They each quit high school and went to work early on. As the months and years went by, they became closer and closer still. Anthony became more and more drawn to her, seeing her as a life mate, the mother of his children. She had, he knew, a huge heart, and was unusually giving and caring. One incident that brought home to Anthony just how magnanimous Lillian was happened in Prospect Park on a terrible stormy night. A torrential rain fell. Anthony was forced to drive slowly. Suddenly Lillian screamed. "Stop!"

"What?" he asked.

She opened the door and jumped out of the car like a madwoman. Anthony went after her. There was a shivering German shepherd on the side of the road. Without fear Lillian petted it, hugged it. The dog whimpered like he knew her.

"I have to take him home," she announced.

"You can't—he's filthy," Anthony said.

Ignoring him, Lillian put the soaking wet dog in the car. It shook. Everything got wet.

"What are you going to do with it?" he asked.

"Take care of him," she said, and she made Anthony take her and the dog home. She fed him and washed him thoroughly in the tub. The dog soon fell asleep. Anthony couldn't get over her big heart. The next day Lillian found a good home for the wayward shepherd.

———

Unbeknownst to Lillian, Anthony used to go to the subway station on Fourth Avenue and Union Street in the late afternoon and watch her walk home from work. She was always well dressed and kept her eyes straight ahead . . . *the perfect lady*, he thought.

Anthony began pursuing Lillian with serious romantic attentions when they were in their early twenties. At first she resisted his entreaties. She felt he was a dedicated playboy, a ladies' man, and would never change. She knew too that he had had a relationship with Rosemarie Billotti, and perhaps most important of all, Lillian knew Anthony was involved with La Cosa Nostra. This made Lillian wary, for she also was aware of the difficult life wives of made men lead, that it was a very dangerous occupation—that for reasons she knew nothing about, could never know, he might not come home. She knew, too, that there would be many nights when she slept alone, regardless of how cold it was outside. That being a member of LCN was a 24/7 occupation.

Lillian also wanted a family with a man at the head of the table, there for their children, there for her. She had been born and raised in the neighborhood and knew the ways of the street, its inherent brutality. She knew, too, that Anthony would not change, that he was destined for a life involved with organized crime. She therefore spurned his early efforts to turn their friendship into romance. But he was not the type of man who took no for an answer. The more she said no, the more he wanted her.

She explained her reasons.

He told her how much he cared.

"Plus," she said, "you're always seeing a lot of women."

"That'll all stop."

"I doubt it," she said, bemused by his sincerity.

"For real."

"Yeah, sure."

"Lil, I want to settle down, have children, a beautiful home— with you. With only you. I love you," he said sincerely, for he truly did love her.

It went on like this for quite some time. Anthony wanted Lillian and would not rest until he had her. He came to believe they were destined for each other. He began showing up at the Wall Street office where she worked as a secretary, wanting to make sure she got home okay, wanting to make sure she knew how much he really cared. He was tenacious.

In the end Anthony persevered. In the winter of 1968, Lillian said yes; they were married on May 4, 1968.

The wedding reception, attended by many made men from all the five families, took place at Mob boss Joe Colombo's wedding hall on Roosevelt Avenue in Astoria, Queens. It was the happiest night of Anthony's life. Lillian Delduca was a beguiling, beautiful bride. They were, everyone said, a very handsome couple.

Anthony had the woman of his dreams . . . a woman who would always stick by him, a woman he could trust implicitly, who would always watch his back.

That evening was an enchanted fairy tale come true; both Anthony and Lillian looked forward to their lives together, believing theirs was a blessed union that would bring much happiness.

CHAPTER 12

BENSONHURST

The Cassos rented a nice one-bedroom garden apartment at 175 Bay Thirty-fifth Street, just off Bath Avenue. It had a large country kitchen and a sunny garden and was in a new two-family redbrick building. Anthony and Lillian enjoyed their new Bensonhurst neighborhood, which, like South Brooklyn, was a large Italian American enclave. Only several blocks away from their apartment was Eighty-sixth Street, a bustling shopping mecca with many food stores catering to the Italian American community. Bensonhurst was also home to many mafiosi—all ranks from all the five families lived here.

Lillian and Anthony's parents often visited the promising young couple with boxes of Italian pastries and sweets in hand.

Anthony came and went as business dictated. Lillian understood that his "work" was done at unconventional hours, and she didn't question him. Their relationship thrived. They often made love, but Lillian did not become pregnant. She was a good cook and an excellent homemaker. Like Lillian, Anthony was a neat freak, and everything in their home, from the toaster to the kitchen faucet, shined like it was brand-new.

Casso was pleased . . . he was a happy man. He had a loving, loyal, idyllic wife and was surrounded by dedicated family and good friends. He also headed a crack breaking-and-entering (B&E) crew and an efficient hijacking team. Money came rolling in. Lillian and Anthony talked about having children and buying their own home. Because all of Anthony's income was illegal, however, he knew he had to be careful about purchasing real property—that he would have to show where the money came from.

One of Casso's best friends was Carmine "the Snake" Persico, the head of the Persico faction of the Profaci crime family. On weekends Anthony and Lillian used to drive up to the Persico farm in Saugerties in upstate New York and spend the weekends. Both dedicated animal lovers, Anthony and Lillian rode horses; they ate home-cooked meals with the Persicos, and often the men would target practice at an outdoor range the Persicos had set up. Anthony was consistently the best shot—with revolvers, automatics, or rifles.

He now refused offers to go hunting. He was an "animal lover," as he puts it, and would not shoot to death helpless creatures that could not defend themselves, though he had no such qualms about killing people.

For the longest time, Anthony had wanted to buy his parents—especially his father—a country retirement home. In the fall of 1970, with the help of some friends, Anthony located the perfect place. It was in Roxbury in upstate New York, just north of the Catskills. The grounds had a lake and streams his dad could fish, and over twenty acres of rolling hills and forests he could hunt to his heart's content. The stone and wood house had four bedrooms with a big stone fireplace, a barn and guesthouse. After all the paperwork was done, Anthony paid for it with cash. He felt it was the best money he ever spent. It made him feel ten feet tall. After having the place cleaned thoroughly and the grounds manicured and landscaped, Anthony told his father a friend of his had loaned him a house where they could spend the weekend hunting and fishing.

By now Michael Casso was sixty-two years old, physically fit and lean, and still a dedicated outdoorsman. When Anthony and his father arrived at the house, it was late morning. The leaves on the trees had turned to brilliant reds and hot butter yellows. Birds chirped. White, cottony clouds slowly moved across a clear blue sky. After showing his dad around the house and property, Anthony—a mischievous smile playing on his face, barely able to control his joy—took out a set of shiny new keys.

"Dad," he said, "the place is yours—yours and Ma's."

Stunned, Michael Casso stood there, speechless. "Anthony, you're kidding?" he finally managed.

"No, Pop, it's yours. Here," he said, handing him the keys.

Father and son hugged, both thick-armed and broad-shouldered, both with tears in their eyes.

"This is," Michael Casso said, "the nicest thing anyone has ever done for me."

———

Michael Casso was a happy man. What his son Anthony had done, the way he had done it, told him a world of what his last born was about: thoughtful, giving, caring—a truly dedicated son, his best friend.

What more could a man ask for? Michael had been very concerned about Anthony—his going to jail, being hurt on the street, his becoming cold and callous and distant, but none of that had come to pass.

All that fall the Cassos packed, joyfully planning to move to their new home, to finally get away from South Brooklyn and enjoy the bounties of the great outdoors. They planned a huge garden for the spring, tomatoes and basil, zucchinis and eggplants, garlic and parsley and cucumber, all there for the picking. They planned to spend Christmas in their new home that year, the fireplace burning, the whole family present.

Life, for the Cassos, held much promise.

CHAPTER 13

THE CARLOS

Anthony and Lillian Casso became friendly with a couple, Dante and Nina Carlo, who lived next door to them, at 173 Bay Thirty-fifth Street.

The Carlos, like the Cassos, were Italian Americans. Dante Carlo, like Anthony, came from South Brooklyn, and he was also a sports fan. Oddly enough, Casso was very fond of watching tennis on TV. The Carlos had two teenage children, Doreen and Philip.

The Cassos began coming over to the Carlos' home for Sunday dinners. The two families bonded. It didn't take long for the Carlos to learn that Anthony was "connected," which meant nothing to them. Many men in that neighborhood during those years were connected. They asked no questions. Anthony volunteered no information.

Around the Carlos, Anthony felt relaxed and at ease; he could be himself. Dante Carlo had nothing to do with crime, LCN, the streets. He was a civilian with a straight nine-to-five job in importing and exporting bristle for hair and paintbrushes, a vice president at Frederick H. Cohen and Company on John Street in Manhattan. Nina Carlo, a particularly attractive brunette who had a striking resemblance to Elizabeth Taylor, owned a beauty salon in the neighborhood.

Sunday meals in the Carlo home were a joyful time with much laughter, food, the telling of jokes, the eating of sumptuous meals—pastas, gravy meats and salad, stuffed artichokes, and sweets. Nina Carlo made a pasta sauce Anthony was very fond of. After dinner, drinks were served. Lillian was fond of crème de menthe, and after a shot or two her tongue and lips would get all green and she'd tell jokes.

The Carlos and Cassos got along so well that they began vacationing together; they went to Miami Beach, Gurney's Inn in Montauk, Long Island, for long weekends, and to different hotels in upstate New York. Casso also took them to the Persico farm several times.

Anthony always insisted on paying for everything. He was generous to a fault. If Anthony liked someone, as he did the Carlos, he couldn't do enough for them. If he didn't like someone, it was a good idea for that person to head for the hills.

As good and kind as Anthony Casso could be, he could also be "cold and mean like a rattlesnake and amazingly calculating," as a former associate recently put it.

Yet, Anthony's friends and family thought the world of him.

CHAPTER 14

DREAMS

December 16, 1970—nine days before Christmas—was the worst day of Anthony Casso's life. He had been up late the night before, plotting and planning myriad crimes. He was now enmeshed in the production and execution of many different schemes. Some panned out; some didn't. He ran a crackerjack hijack team and had guards and drivers giving him tips about loads to steal—what they had inside, when and where they'd be. He also headed an amazingly successful "bypass crew." Their modus operandi was to find banks with vulnerable safes in their basements. Back in the days before banks had Saturday hours, they'd begin working on Friday nights, breaking holes through cellar walls that they had free access to, then into the vaults. Once inside the vaults, they'd break open the safety deposit boxes, stealing all kinds of valuables—bearer bonds, stocks, cash, gems of all sorts. By the time the bank reopened on Monday morning they'd be long gone.

Casso made contacts with men who bought the stocks and bonds and with fat-cat fences who paid cash on the barrelhead for the gems and jewelry. These were men who existed on the outer edges of all organized crime families. They were secretive and innocuous and dealt with anyone in organized crime who brought them just about any stolen item. They paid cash, no questions asked. Casso was highly professional and always careful, and he was making money hand over fist. His reputation on the street as an earner grew by leaps and bounds. He was a rising star in the always changing underworld. But he was still not made by any family. Carlo Gambino, the *capo de tutti i capi,* was still refusing to open the books. Gambino was concerned with the quality of men who were being proposed to be made. Rather than hurt people's feelings and egos, and create bad blood where there was none, he kept the books closed. It was all about, in Gambino's mind, quality control. One weak link, he knew, could break the chain that bound La Cosa Nostra together.

One of Casso's biggest problems became what to do with all the cash he was accumulating—where to put it, hide it, keep it safe. He resolved this by having trusted family members and friends rent safety deposit boxes under their own names and then hand the keys over to him, a simple solution to a complicated problem.

Casso regularly worked with men from different crime families. Unbeknownst to the police and the public at large, it was normal for Mob guys to interact with different LCN members. They were all about making money, and "networking" with one another opened many more doors. What LCN was about really was *organized crime* in a very real, tangible way.

Casso liked his new neighborhood. Scores of men he did business with lived and worked there. One of these was Anthony Spero, a respected captain in the Bonanno family who held court in Dutchy's Luncheonette, which he owned, on Bay Seventeenth Street and Eighty-sixth Street, and a bar—the 1717 Lounge—just across the street.

Spero bought a lot of the hijacked goods Casso deftly stole with his partners, Frankie DeCicco and Junior "the Irishman," who were both stand-up guys and stone-cold killers if need be. Not once did they ever use violence in hijacking trucks. But they often had to use violence, extreme violence, when collecting money. One such time was when they sold two loads of color TVs to guys from the Colombo crime family— Matty "the Horse" Ianniello and Jimmy De Bartolo. When Anthony and his guys went to collect the money due at another luncheonette on Eighty-sixth Street, Jimmy said, "Sally Dee"—a made guy with the Colombos—"said to tell you that the cops got the loads. There's no money."

Casso was not willing to be robbed by these guys, not willing to be bullied by them . . . he'd die first. If word got out in the street that you could take what was his, that you did not have to respect him, he knew he might as well pack it up and find something else to do, retire from the life. He said, "I don't have my money by tomorrow, I'm going to blow your brains all over the counter. You go tell Sally Dee that."

This was a ballsy and somewhat arrogant thing to do, but Casso was so well politically connected and respected by all, and was clearly in the right here, that the next day the agreed-upon amount was duly paid.

Another time, a similar incident occurred, though this time someone was killed, and the body count around Anthony Gaspipe Casso began in earnest.

Again, it involved hijacked goods, this time a big load of athletic equipment. A soldier from the New Jersey DeCavalcante family took the load. When he was supposed to pay, he too said the cops got the load, dismissing Casso and his crew as a bunch of punks. He refused to even meet with Casso for weeks. Finally, he agreed to a meeting in midtown Manhattan. Anthony and Frankie were there, as well as Junior Maguire, a tough Irishman who was part of Casso's crew.

They met at the corner of Thirty-fourth Street and Lexington. The De-Cavalcante soldier pulled up in a Caddie. He told them to get in. Thinking he was cute, he went and parked on the block of a nearby police station, the Seventeenth Precinct on East Fifty-first Street. He was a weasel-faced, dark-haired man. Casso recently explained what happened next: "So I was in the front seat. Junior was in the back. Frankie stayed there on Lexington.

"This guy believed because he was connected he could screw with whoever he wanted; that he had some God-given right to do whatever the fuck he pleased. It's not like that, even on the street. Maybe more than anywhere else, keeping your word is important, is a matter of life and death. All my life, I met bullies like this prick, and I always hated them. So he's sayin' that the Jersey City cops got our load, that it's outta his hands; there's no money. And I'm sitting there trying to reason with him—trying to save his life, but he's thinking he can do whatever he likes. I'm getting mad; I'm thinking he needs to be whacked. The next thing I know my ears are ringing . . . really ringing. Junior just upped and shot him in the head. In a second it was over—pop, done. We got outta the car and just casually walked away and that was that.

"Yeah, we lost the money of the load, but the message went out loud and clear and no one fucked with us from then on. What I mean is, what I mean to say is that the publicity we got would prevent others from popping up down the road and trying to steal from us. In the long run I think we earned more . . . in a backward kind of way, granted."

―――

Casso wanted to be made. He wanted the respect—being at the top of the food chain—that comes along with getting straightened out, but the books were still closed.

December came. Christmas in the Casso home had always been a big deal, a warm happy time filled with good cheer, the giving of gifts, much love, laughter, voluminous amounts of food served for hours on end . . . and an endless array of colorful sweets. For Italian Americans Christmas Eve and Christmas Day also represented the birth of Christ, their Savior and spiritual inspiration. Christmas was, for them, the most important holiday of the year—a milestone in their lives.

In 1970, the Cassos were planning to celebrate both Christmas Eve and Christmas Day at their new home in upstate New York. All of Michael and Margaret Casso's belongings were carefully packed and ready to be moved. They were leaving the neighborhood they'd lived in all their lives. Anthony had arranged to have friends with a moving truck come and get their things. As pleased as Michael and Margaret were that their dreams were coming true, they both knew they'd miss friends and the old neighborhood terribly; still, they looked forward to their new home with its twenty acres of pristine land, streams and ponds and forests, the wonderful garden they'd have. Michael planned to plant cuttings from fig trees brought over from Sicily. When Anthony thought about his parents' new home, that he had bought it for them, it brought a smile to his chiseled, handsome face.

―――

Early in the morning of December 15, Anthony was home in bed with Lillian, sleeping soundly. Their bedroom was in the back of the building away from the street, and it was unusually quiet; little sound from the outside world reached it. The only noise was that of the wind pushing against the windows.

The mid-December silence was suddenly shattered by the phone ring-ing, loud, insistent, demanding. Anthony looked at the night table—it was 4:00 A.M. It could only be bad news, he knew, but he had no idea just how truly bad it would be.

It was Anthony's mother. "Papa woke up with pains in the chest, he doesn't look good, he—"

"I'm on the way," Anthony said. He quickly got dressed and was out the door in a flash. He knew the fastest way to the old neighborhood was the Belt Parkway. He sped over to it and headed toward South Brooklyn, going faster and faster, weaving around cars. Luckily he wasn't stopped by the police. He got off the elevated Gowanus Expressway at Hamilton Avenue. The streets of South Brooklyn were quiet and still. Anthony reached Union Street and came to a loud, screeching stop in front of number 719. He ran to the entrance and bolted up the stairs, hearing his mother's wails and plaintive pleas. He found his mother standing over his father, who was lying on the bed. Michael Casso was a sickly gray color, foam and spittle gathered around his mouth.

"Dad—Dad!" Anthony yelled.

Nothing.

"Pop! Pop, open your eyes," Anthony demanded.

Nothing still. He wasn't breathing.

"You called for an ambulance?"

"They're on the way—"

Anthony knew it was a heart attack, and he knew what to do. He im-mediately began rhythmically pushing down his father's thick, barrel-like chest with the heels of both hands. Up and down—hard—as he gave him CPR. He did this for what seemed like an eternity. Sweat covered his face. His heart raced. His father was dying and he could do nothing.

How could life be so cruel?

His hands and arms grew tired, ached, but he would not stop; he'd die before he stopped. His mother wailed, "Michael, Michael." Minutes that seemed like hours slowly slipped by. Anthony thought about the new house.

God could not be that cruel, to steal his father away now . . . surely not!

Paramedics from Methodist Hospital arrived. Grim-faced, they checked the vitals. No heartbeat, no pulse. They shook their heads in dismay.

"Do something," Anthony ordered. "Help him!"

Prompted by Anthony's threatening, demanding tone, they quickly put Michael on a stretcher, strapped him in, and swiftly carried him down the stairs, with Anthony following close behind, helping them to negotiate the turns in the stairwell. Anthony got into the ambulance with his mother. With the sirens wailing, red lights spinning, they sped to Methodist Hospital, the place where Anthony had been born.

Now Michael Casso was a pale blue color, silent, unmoving. An efficient team of doctors and nurses met them at the ambulance port and hustled Michael Casso inside. It seemed like they knew what they were doing. Christmas decorations adorned the disinfectant-smelling emergency ward; there was a waving Santa Claus, Christmas cards, tired, blinking lights.

Anthony paced back and forth, consoled his mother, and paced some more, fervently praying, promising God all kinds of things, money for the church, if only he'd help.

Soon, a tall thin doctor approached them. "I'm sorry. I have bad news," he said, forlorn, eyes cast down. Margaret Casso began to cry uncontrollably.

"We did all we could. He's gone. I'm sorry," the doctor said in a practiced, modulated, sickening tone.

———

After Casso lost his father, he was a changed man. He grew quiet and morose, rarely smiled, and was distant from the world, his friends— even Lillian. His eyes seemed to darken. He walked differently. He aged notably in those chilly December days after his father's passing. The keen sense of humor he always had left him. He seemed like a stick of dynamite about to explode. He recently explained, "My father was the best man I ever knew. He was also the best friend I ever had. He was a man's man—honorable, tough . . . always there for his family and friends. Anyone who knew him loved him, respected him. All his life all he ever did was work hard to provide for his family. Never missed a day's work. He'd give you the shirt off his back.

"For him to die like that—so suddenly, so young. Just when they were leaving Union Street to move into that house he loved so much, that was unfair. He deserved better."

BOOK II

STONE COLD

CHAPTER 15

MAKING BONES

Balding and thin, Sam the Jew was an adept hustler. He'd pretty much do whatever it took to make a buck, including sell drugs, hijack merchandise, kill anyone who got in his way. He had made a good contact with South Americans who were regularly bringing over tons of high-grade grass. He was an associate of Lucchese capo Christie Tick Furnari.

Sam the Jew thought he was protected from rip-offs, from being compromised, when he learned from a contact in the Brooklyn District Attorney's Office that one of his customers was a police informant. He knew he had to move quickly and decisively. He went to see Christie Tick at his Fifth Avenue hangout and told him about his problem. Since Christie was getting a piece of this juicy pie, he said he'd take care of it. In turn, Christie looked to Anthony Casso to take care of Sam the Jew's problem. He was not called "the Jew" out of any kind of anti-Semitism. It's only that there were not many Jews still doing business with La Cosa Nostra, and it was just a moniker that he had picked up over the years.

Anthony didn't like anything about Sam the Jew: his walk, his talk, his shifty manner. But all of that had nothing to do with the request Christie put on the table, knowing the answer.

"Will you do it?" Christie asked.

"For you, of course," Casso said, always looking to build bridges and make loyal allies.

"Good. The Jew'll set him up. You work it out with him, okay?"

"Okay," Casso said, thinking that if Sam was as tough as everyone said, he'd have killed the snitch himself.

Casso met with Sam at a bar on Fourteenth Avenue and Eighty-sixth Street, the 19th Hole, so called because of the proximity to the golf course in the Dyker Heights section of Brooklyn, Casso's regular haunt.

Speaking in little more than a guarded whisper, and sitting at a darkened table in the back of the place, the smell of hard whiskey and hard men hanging in the air, Sam the Jew explained that he could readily get the snitch to a designated place, but he could not be there when "it happened."

"Why not?" asked Casso. He was suspicious . . . always suspicious.

"I gotta have an alibi. Too many people know I know him, know about our relationship . . . leasta which is the cops . . . so I'll leave him there with you, go to this place in Brighton Beach where I hang out so people see me. So I have an alibi."

"So, you got it all worked out," Casso said.

"Yeah, I do. Fly with you all right, Anthony?"

"Sure," Casso said, staring at Sam, not liking his thick oversize glasses, his birdlike countenance, his protruding Adam's apple.

Casso turned to Ronnie Esposito, a made guy in the Bonanno crime family. He had an after-hours club on Fifteenth Avenue and Seventy-ninth Street, in Dyker Park, which bordered Bensonhurst in the east and Bay Ride in the west.

"I got a piece of work to do," Casso said, "and I'd like to do it here."

"When?"

"During the week."

"All right. Be better late, though."

"Good . . . I'll let you know when," Casso said, and it was done, typical of how mafiosi kill people—swiftly and simply.

Casso contacted Sam the Jew. Wednesday night was agreed upon. The mark would be brought to the club near midnight, thinking there was a hot all-night poker game going. Casso also asked Junior Maguire to be there, to help clean up and get rid of the body. Contrary to common belief, killing within the fraternity of the Mafia can very well be a communal affair. Casso's involving several people who had nothing to do with the murder—or the reasons for it—was the norm, not the exception. The code of silence, *omerta*, was still very much practiced; people of the underworld, for the most part, trusted one another.

This was of course before the federal government learned how to cleverly and slowly use the RICO (Racketeer Influenced and Corrupt Organizations) Act statutes, like a sharp scalpel, to take apart the Mafia—its bosses, captains, and soldiers—piece by piece, bone by bone.

Before long, the government would learn how to turn them on one another.

———

Wednesday night, at the prescribed time, Sam the Jew showed up at the club with the unsuspecting mark. Casso and Junior Maguire were already there. Ronnie Esposito would be the lookout. They met at the bar, in the finished basement. Green tables and comfortable chairs filled the sparse, wood-paneled room. There was a tired bar and bartender on the right. They ordered drinks. Soon Sam said he had to use the john. Tall and gaunt and vulturelike, he left. As if by magic, the bartender disappeared.

Casso had a snub-nosed .38 revolver in his belt. At close range it would be lethal. Casso had an unlimited source of clean guns. Roy DeMeo, an associate in the Gambino family, managed to regularly steal shipments of guns from Kennedy Airport. Guns coming in from Switzerland, Italy, Germany, Australia, and Israel assured that La Cosa Nostra was well armed.

Casso was planning to shoot the mark in the side of the head. He was not nervous at all. He put it like this: "For me it was just business. I didn't know the guy. I'd never seen him before. He had to go. That's all I knew. That's all I needed to know."

Like most street guys, Casso was a consummate actor. He could readily show a friendly face when murder was on his mind.

Not only was Anthony Casso relatively young, but so were Ronnie Esposito and Junior Maguire. These were not experienced, seasoned killers —they were young Turks sharpening their teeth and claws, finding their way in their chosen world. The mark was becoming more relaxed, talking freely, expressively using his hands. Casso slowly reached for the pistol, his hands dry, his heart rate normal, a cool but deadly cucumber.

For Casso , he was doing what he'd been training to do since he was a boy, what he'd been thinking about doing and had seen done numerous times.

Casso learned early on that, no matter how physically tough someone was, a bullet to the head put a person down as if he were a meek lamb. A gun was the ultimate arbitrator. It made whoever was holding it the baddest motherfucker on the block. Casso now saw the spot, just above the ear, where he'd put the bullet. He focused. The moment arrived. All his senses were heightened. In one swift movement, so very comfortable with the gun in his hand, its weight, its balance, Casso fluidly—like the strike of a cobra—drew the weapon, put it to the man's head, and pulled the trigger.

Bang.

He hit his mark. The man went down like a wet bag of cement. A thick finger of blood pulsated from the sudden dime-sized hole Casso had put in his head. It was over and done in a split second, little more than the bat of a long-lashed eye.

"Get the blankets," Casso told Junior, who for some reason had become unhinged by what he'd just seen. He was, to Casso's dismay, farting repeatedly.

"Stop it," Casso said.

"I'm sorry, I can't," Junior said.

Calm and cool, Ronnie Esposito came in. "All clear outside," he said.

Junior Maguire, continuing to break wind, bent to help clean up the copious amount of blood. By now, the mark's heart had stopped and the bleeding had ended. They wrapped him tightly in some old army blankets and used rags and hot water to wash the blood off the floor. Junior Maguire tried to pick up the body, but he was farting so much, Anthony pushed him aside and picked up the body himself.

Aside from the strength Anthony had inherited from his father and grandfathers, the years he had worked on the docks had made him unusually strong. He was thick-chested and broad-shouldered, short and square and bull-like.

Now he picked up the corpse and carried it. Outside, Ronnie Esposito made sure the coast was clear. That done, he gave Casso the thumbs-up sign. Casso put the dead guy in the open trunk of his car, which was parked on Seventy-ninth Street, a quiet tree-lined residential block. It had been snowing for several hours now and the street had a pearly white blanket. Casso got behind the wheel, calm and cool and collected—oddly aware of all his surroundings—as though each of his senses had been heightened by some powerful drug. But Casso was drug free. He was now high on the omnipotent power of murder, of controlling life . . . of deciding who lived and who died.

The others quickly and efficiently cleaned up the blood and within a matter of minutes there was no trace of the man who had just lost his life there.

Casso calmly drove southeast to Avenue U, took a left, and made his way to the Marine Park area, a desolate, barren flatlands back then, perfect for the disposal of old appliances, refrigerators, stoves, washing machines—and bodies.

Because of the snow, Anthony drove slowly and carefully. When he passed Coney Island Avenue, another car slid into a lamppost. Casso dropped the body off at East Thirty-fourth Street, got back in his car, and went home, feeling no kind of guilt or remorse—no pangs of conscience whatsoever, he'd done what he'd been born to do, fulfilled his destiny.

Lillian was sound asleep. She knew nothing about where her new husband had been, what he'd done. Lillian, like Anthony, came from a neighborhood in which the Mafia culture was well known and understood by all, and in this culture women did not question their men. Casso slid into the bed next to his wife. Without meaning to, he woke her and they were soon making love, soft and gentle, with only the sound of the frigid Brooklyn winds pushing against the windows, rattling them.

———

Made men had seen this murder, and word now discreetly spread through LCN that Anthony Casso had done the deed, coldly and efficiently. He was now one of them—a bona fide killer of men.

Casso next killed in 1973. He and crime partner Frankie DeCicco were ripping off diamond dealers all over New York State. One of the guys who was working with them—fingering potential victims for them—was robbed by an "associate" of theirs.

This was a no-no and had to be swiftly and severely dealt with. Casso and DeCicco tracked the guy down and shot him to death in broad daylight on Brooklyn's East Sixth Street and Avenue T. Anthony crouched in a combat position and, holding the gun with his two hands, shot the fleeing man from half a block away and left him there—dead.

"It was about principle," Anthony explained. "The opportunity presented itself and we took it. Nothing personal."

Again, Casso had killed—and he felt nothing but that street justice had been served.

CHAPTER 16

THE BURN BAR

Diplomacy—making allies and building bridges connecting different *borgatas*, crews, within the five New York families—was one of Anthony Casso's strong suits. He made friends everywhere in the wide-ranging fraternity of La Cosa Nostra. And all of Anthony's "friends" made money, for another of Casso's strong suits was that he was "a born thief." He had an innate sense of just how to do any given piece of work, and he had the balls to do it. His crew would study the job like dedicated scientists looking through a high-powered microscope. Anthony had honed his B&E crew to a razor-sharp edge. They were the "best of the best," as he puts it. The gang now consisted of Anthony, George Rush Zappola, Junior Maguire —an expert in all things technical—and Frankie "Beansy" Melli.

Indisputably, Casso was the boss. Through the fast-moving changing months of the early 1970s, the gang met daily to carefully plot and plan many different scores.

Through a friend in the jewelry business, Casso learned about the burn bar, an extremely high-powered torch that burned at over 3,700 degrees Fahrenheit. In seconds it could cut through any kind of steel, any kind of safe. It enabled his gang to cut open any safe they encountered. Among law enforcement, especially the FBI, the gang became legendary. They also remained anonymous.

If more guys were needed for any given job, Casso would bring in either Frankie DeCicco, Joe Sis, Dee Fonse, Jackie T., Nicky Narducci, or Otto Heidel. They robbed all kinds of merchandise off the docks, from airports, from both the Canal Street and Forty-seventh Street diamond centers, from payrolls at Wall Street firms, and from gold refineries and banks.

Especially banks.

There was no safe they couldn't get into.

Now Anthony woke up close to noon each day. His "business" was done during the wee hours, when the straight world slept, and he slept when he could, to his own clock.

Violence was rarely, if ever, used in any of the burglaries Casso plotted. They were all about guile, not hurting anyone, and avoiding confrontations, though the threat of deadly violence was always there, real and tangible, if needed.

Through contacts in the Gambino family, Anthony was also on the payroll of the Japanese Shipping Company as a forklift driver, receiving a check of $500 a week for a job he never did—an added bonus of being "connected."

Money came rolling in. Anthony was already a wealthy man, but the American dream, he felt, was not yet his. He was intent upon having for himself all the bounty that life had to offer, no matter what the risk, come hell or high water.

Within the underground fraternity of LCN, Anthony Casso's reputation continued to grow. Each of the different bosses he knew wanted him in their families because he was a terrific moneymaker, and a piece of whatever he earned would automatically be theirs, as is the way of LCN. Anthony was now thickly associated with Lucchese capo Christie Tick Furnari, who of course received part of Casso's gang's take.

Casso wanted to be made—he had wanted that since he was a boy— but the Mafia Commission still had the books closed tight. In truth, Casso wasn't sure which family he would ultimately align himself with. Each of the families had its good and bad points. For example, the Gambino family was the largest, the Lucchese family controlled the unions and the docks, and the Genovese family was politically connected. Anthony and Chris Furnari had a special bond and trust.

When and if there were disputes with made men and Gaspipe, as he had become known, or any in his crew, Christie Tick would come to any sit-down on Casso's behalf. Casso did not like this new moniker, but he accepted it. He, therefore, had the full weight of the Lucchese family behind him, in the form of a stoic, serious, thin-lipped man who resembled Dean Martin. By the same token, Gaspipe was so liked and respected by so many capos that a dozen different men would gladly come to bat for Anthony Casso.

———

Anthony often thought of his father. Good memories of him were part of his daily thoughts, although the last images of him, Gaspipe trying to resuscitate him, would never leave Anthony—they were seared into his brain. Not able to deal with the loss, Casso sold the house in upstate New York and ultimately bought his mother a home on Sixty-fifth Street in Bay Ridge, Brooklyn.

Soon, Lillian became pregnant. Anthony was very pleased. A child would help fill the huge hole in his heart and soul made by his father's sudden death. Anthony and Lillian talked about buying their own home, but as always with outlaws who acquire wealth illegally, Casso had to find a way he could account for the money. What the Cassos ended up doing was putting their new home, which was not that expensive, in the name of a relative.

CHAPTER 17

CASSO'S CREW

One of the key elements to Gaspipe's B&E crew's amazing success, the millions of dollars they stole, was a van. Not just any van, but one completely outfitted for battle. The bulletproof windows were dark and specially treated so if cops looked in, they'd only see a false view of depth. The locks could not be opened except with a key; they'd automatically jam if they were tampered with.

Inside the van was a completely outfitted locksmith shop. Junior Maguire's specialty was opening locks, and his expertise was invaluable. The van also had a cooler for cold drinks and food and a chemical toilet like that on a boat. There was a cot as well as blankets, pillows, and several pairs of binoculars. Casso used a particularly talented mechanic he knew on Pennsylvania Avenue in Brooklyn for this job. He was not a member of La Cosa Nostra but one of the thousands who worked on the perimeter of organized crime, fed from it, and made a living from it, by providing a service that could be found nowhere else.

A typical score would go down like this: Once the gang located a bank, they'd carefully scope it out, keeping it under tight surveillance for days at a time. One of the gang members would park the van near the bank, get out, lock the door, and walk away, making onlookers think it was empty; in reality two gang members were left to do the surveillance.

They'd clock the traffic and the cleaning people, noting when they came and left and even the plate numbers of their vehicles. Once the gang was ready to move, Casso and Junior Maguire would change the lock on the bank's front door, bring the original lock back to the van, use it to duplicate the key, cut and then put back the original lock.

"Once we had the key, we owned the bank," Casso explained. They'd then enter the bank and take numerous photographs of the alarms and the vaults, the whole setup. Armed with this invaluable information, they'd meet at Frankie Beans's finished basement in his house in Bensonhurst, where the eight-by-ten black-and-white photos they'd taken and developed were posted in logical sequence on a large blackboard. It was now that the steps of the actual heist were laid out, carefully, methodically. The gang would actually buy the same alarm system as that in the bank, sometimes traveling out of state to get it, so they could practice on the safe in preparation to dismantle the bank's alarm while actually in the bank.

They would then decide the best way to get into the different vaults, through a wall or vault door. Once inside the vault, with the help of the burn bar, they'd cut open the bank's safe, where its cash was usually kept; they'd then open as many safety deposit boxes as possible, not having any idea what kind of treasure they'd come upon—diamonds, all kinds of gems, gold bars, drugs, stocks, bonds, and lots of cash. It took arduous hours to punch holes in the safety deposit boxes, but the treasures in them were well worth it.

———

Gaspipe's crew robbed a Chemical Bank in the Canal Street jewelry district, *knowing* that many of the area's jewelers kept their precious stones in the bank's safety deposit vault instead of in the jewelry exchange or their own vaults. In that one job the crew made $10 million. Casso explained the score like this: "It was an experience of a lifetime. It's a wonder drug. An amazing high every time you punched another safety deposit box. No one box is the same."

For Casso it wasn't just the money he was after. It was the thrill—planning the job, successfully pulling it off, and, most important, beating the system.

Turning what the crew stole into cash was, unto itself, a large undertaking. But the crew had half a dozen reliable fences who'd readily take what they had, no questions asked. There were times when it took three whole days for all the loot to be gone over, value assessed, and the money paid.

Gaspipe and his crew also traveled to other states to rob banks for LCN groups. They'd take their key-cutting equipment and the burn bar and do the job, always applying the same careful surveillance and methodical tactics.

The Lucchese family was very happy to have Gaspipe in their fold. His B&E crew became famous—admired, respected . . . talked about in revered whispers; they were that good.

CHAPTER 18

A BLESSED EVENT

nthony and Lillian Casso's first of two children was a healthy baby girl they named Jolene. She was born July 12, 1971. Anthony loved being a father. He couldn't get enough of his little girl. He held her for hours on end, talked to her, smiled and cooed, and showed a happiness he hadn't experienced since his father's death.

Both Anthony's mom and Lillian's parents often came to visit their granddaughter. Anthony wished his father, too, could hold her, be a part of her life, but that was not meant to be. Anthony was still bitter that his father never got to know and see his grandchildren.

———

With the consistent success he had on the street, within the wide umbrella of LCN, Casso continued to garner more respect, make more connections, and his reputation continued to grow.

One would think that because Casso was now a father and had a loving and dedicated wife, he'd be less mercurial on the street, control his impulse toward violence, but just the opposite happened. He became more volatile, more apt to kill first and ask questions later.

Aside from the Carlos next door, all the people Casso interacted with were LCN or LCN connected. His B&E crew now consisted of his best friends and trusted confidants.

Both Anthony and Lillian often went to functions that included only LCN: weddings, birthdays, funerals, and all kinds of celebrations. Theirs was a close-knit society. They stuck together.

———

Thirteen-year-old Doreen Carlo often babysat for the Cassos. She was reliable and trustworthy and loved children. Both Lillian and Anthony were very fond of her and paid her well.

Lillian and Nina Carlo became close—best friends. They often went shopping together. When Lillian went to visit Nina's sister Rosemary in Mill Basin, Brooklyn, she liked the neighborhood so much—its quiet tree-lined streets, the well-tended homes, the excellent shopping nearby—she told Anthony she wanted to buy a house and live there, not in Staten Island as they had planned. Anthony agreed. They began house shopping and soon bought a two-story redbrick home in Mill Basin. The Carlos were saddened to lose the Cassos as neighbors, but they stayed good friends for a while. The Cassos continued to come to the Carlo home for Sunday dinners. Nina and Dante Carlo still knew little about Anthony's business and they liked it like that. When Anthony's reputation reached the Carlos via mutual South Brooklyn friends, it still didn't affect their friendship. It was hard not to notice, however, the absolute deference and respect Anthony received when they went to fancy Italian restaurants in Bensonhurst—Tommaso's on Eighty-sixth Street or the Villa on Twenty-sixth Avenue—and when Russi Scavelli, Nina's brother-in-law who owned a supermarket in Brooklyn Heights, was shaken down by a Mob-connected private sanitation company, Anthony heard and immediately put a stop to it. He asked for nothing in return.

"My pleasure," he said.

Neither Anthony nor Lillian was happy with the first house they bought in Mill Basin. The rooms weren't spacious enough, and the stairs to reach the front door were too long. The Cassos began looking for a different home, wiser and more aware of what their needs were, but they still had to account for their income. Casso's answer to this age-old dilemma for outlaws was to turn to another outlaw—one Burton Kaplan. He was a tall, thin, tough, wily man—a throwback to the amazingly tough Jews of days long gone by—Meyer Lansky, Micky Cohen, Arnold Rothstein, Abe Relis, Dutch Schultz, Bugsy Siegel, Monk Eastman, and the like. Over the years, Casso had done a lot of business with Kaplan. Kaplan was a particularly cagey, cunning individual who would do just about anything to turn a buck. He sold drugs, he sold clothes, he sold swag, he murdered people.

Casso asked Kaplan if he'd put the new, second house under his name. He agreed. How could he not? Casso had gotten Kaplan, a degenerate gambler who thought himself shrewder than he really was, out of numerous jams over the years with Mob guys from other families, extended him credit on drugs he fronted him and on loans he gave him, and made sure he earned money. Casso had saved his life several times. In view of all of this, Casso was relatively certain Kaplan would never betray him. A mistake.

Kaplan well knew Gaspipe's reputation on the street—that he had no compunction about killing someone, that he thought more about his reputation than people's lives. Casso, therefore, felt secure when he went to Kaplan and asked him if he'd help Lillian put the second home in his name. Casso proposed giving Kaplan $450,000 cash, which would be deposited in Kaplan's business account, Progressive Distributors, located on Bay Fourteenth Street. Kaplan would then issue, they agreed, a check to cover the purchase. The $150,000 balance could be secured with a conventional mortgage. This was supposed to be for a "short time only," as Casso recently put it.

"After a year or so he was supposed to have this title transferred back to Lillian . . . but he didn't."

What Kaplan did do was use the title to secure a large $2 million loan at the Capital Bank in Florida, thinking Anthony would never be the wiser. Kaplan was still dealing in huge shipments of grass and only planned to use the Casso deal as collateral for a short while, but as time went by circumstances changed and the deed was never returned to Lillian's name, causing Casso and his family a world of grief.

———

Another good source of money for Casso was marijuana. In the spring of 1971, Casso made a good grass contact through a mutual friend of his and Vic Amuso's named Oscar, who lived in Florida. He also met a boat captain out of Sheepshead Bay with a seventy-foot trawler.

In the middle of the night, he was rendezvousing with another boat, filled with tightly packed bales of grass from South America, beyond the twelve-mile limit. Casso would take thousands of pounds on consignment and pay the amount agreed upon when due. He always kept his word. Even though selling drugs was frowned upon by the full Mafia Commission, many made men earned a lot of money from drugs. Though Gaspipe wasn't made yet, he was working directly under Christie Tick, now the underboss of the Lucchese family.

Grass was the least dangerous of drugs, and most people in the government didn't care who was selling or buying it. But Casso was soon selling kilos of cocaine and heroin, too. Casso himself was drug free, never even smoked a joint. Drugs, he believed, made one sloppy and irresponsible—stupid. But he had no qualms about selling them. For him, it was just a matter of money. Joe Kennedy felt no compunction about selling alcohol, though he did not want to be around alcoholics. It was a similar situation with Casso. He also made sure to religiously give his mentor, Christie Tick Furnari, his just share. Furnari gladly took the money and looked the other way. Casso was still not sure what family he'd join. They all wanted him, and made overtures to him, but he was leaning toward the Lucchese clan.

Casso fronted Burton Kaplan several hundred pounds of pot at a time. He also fronted grass—heroine and cocaine—to an up-and-coming mafioso named Sammy Gravano, out of Bensonhurst, as well as to Gerard Pappa, Roy DeMeo, and Gene Gotti out of Canarsie, Brooklyn, men who years down the road would become infamous even among members of LCN. Casso rented a warehouse in Sheepshead Bay where he stashed the grass, amazed at how lucrative the business was.

Money came rolling in.

Gaspipe's fortune continued to grow. Between his B&E crew, loan-sharking, drug dealing, no-show jobs at the docks, and interest in five after-hour clubs, Casso was a wealthy man. But he wanted more. He bought three shrimp trawlers to bring more grass over from South America, and trucks with secret compartments to transport the grass. He even bought a 707 cargo plane to bring drugs over from South America. For himself, he bought a fancy twenty-five-foot luxury speedboat and kept it at the King's Plaza Marina in Mill Basin. He loved that boat and being on the open ocean with the fresh air and sun on his face. For him the boat represented part of the good life, the American dream he was always so intent upon making his own.

How he wished his father was still alive to enjoy the boat, to go fishing from it, and to cruise the waters off Brooklyn, happily moving up and down the Hudson and East rivers, as Casso did.

Often, in his mind's eye, he saw his smiling father landing a fish, muscles rippling, a broad smile on his handsome face. Anger would suddenly darken Casso's eyes. The muscles in his powerful jaw would bulge.

Life is cruel, he'd fatalistically say to himself, fighting hard to make the images go away.

CHAPTER 19

A BACKSTABBING BACKSTABBER

"If all the fish in the sea kept their mouths shut, they'd never get caught" is an often repeated mantra in the world of organized crime.

The men of Gaspipe's B&E crew were so successful for so long that word of their exploits resonated in the world of La Cosa Nostra.

One of the gang members, Frankie Beansy, was friendly with actor James Caan. Beansy told Caan about the burn bar, how professional Casso's crew was, their many successful jobs, all the money they were making. Caan in turn went to a director he knew named Michael Mann. Mann liked what he heard. They collaborated and wrote a script for a film; the eventual result was the hit cult film *Thief* starring James Caan. The FBI also got word of Casso's exploits, and, using a rat for information, agents arrested Gaspipe in the fall of 1972.

As Anthony was driving home on the Belt Parkway with Jolene and Lillian in the car that evening, they were suddenly surrounded by unmarked FBI vehicles, dark-colored Plymouths with blackwall tires driven by stone-faced agents. Spinning red lights adorned the roofs. They made Casso pull over to the shoulder. Guns drawn, deadly serious, they surrounded Anthony's car, scaring the hell out of Lillian. Jolene was sleeping. Anthony was not about to put up any kind of fight. They pulled him from the car and cuffed him.

The agents kept hearing how dangerous Gaspipe was, that he was a psychopathic killer, and figured this was the best way to bring him down—with his wife and child there.

"You didn't have to do this," Anthony said, but he was told to "shut the fuck up," and whisked away, leaving Lillian numb with shock and fear, her hands trembling.

Not only was Gaspipe arrested that day, but crew members Joe Brewster and Junior Maguire were, too. Casso put up the bail money and was soon back out in the street, seething mad, intent upon not going to jail. His career was just beginning. There was no way he would allow the feds to put him away.

Gaspipe was genuinely liked on the street and had the respect of most everyone in his world. Since he was a kid, he'd been building bridges in the vast secretive community of LCN. Casso now tapped one of the many contacts he had nurtured. His name was Greg Scarpa—a fierce war captain in the Colombo crime family, who was known by a select few to have good friends in law enforcement . . . in the NYPD, and the FBI.

Casso knew the only way to fight fire was with fire so he set out with a vengeance to do just that. Through his attorney, Michael Rosen, he learned that the government had a snitch, Bobby Dennish, who told them about Gaspipe's B&E crew's exploits and about a bank they robbed in South Brooklyn, a Chemical Bank on Union Street.

Casso went to see if Scarpa could help. Scarpa was a big, strapping, dark-skinned Italian, a genuinely tough man. "I love the smell of gunpowder," he said after shooting to death a rival in the long-lasting Colombo/Persico war. His right eye had been shot out in an attempt on his life. He was one of those rare individuals who knew how to play both sides of the proverbial fence—Greg Scarpa was a highly prized informant for the FBI, as well as a respected made man.

For thirty-five years Scarpa brilliantly played both roles. No one in LCN knew he was an informant; that would have been an automatic death sentence. In 1972, however, word on the street was that he had crooked feds in his back pocket working for him, which turned out to be true.

Anthony Casso met with Scarpa in his social club on Bath Avenue in Bensonhurst. The two men liked and trusted each other. They hugged and kissed on the cheek. Deadly serious, they sat down, and Casso laid out what he needed. Scarpa listened knowingly, said he'd get back to him . . . that he was sure he could help.

Two days later, true to his word, Scarpa called Gaspipe. They met for dinner at Mary's on Eighty-sixth Street. Scarpa said that, according to FBI agent Anthony Vescone, the witness was Bobby Dennish, and he was stashed in Topeka, Kansas. Casso managed to send word to Dennish that if he threw the case, did not ID him or the others in court, he'd take care of him.

Shocked and unnerved that his whereabouts were known, Dennish agreed to Gaspipe's terms. How could he not? The government brought the case to trial, and because Casso had gotten to the witness, he won the case and walked out of the courtroom a free man, his head high, shoulders back, classic mafioso, inexorably moving toward his amazingly violent destiny. The government knew that Gaspipe had gotten to the witness, but there was little prosecutors could do.

After cleverly beating the bank robbery case, Gaspipe's reputation on the street was bolstered considerably. He had kept his mouth shut and, using guile and guerrilla tactics, beat the government. But he knew he was now under scrutiny, being trailed and watched.

Casso learned a good lesson because of this case—it was vitally important to have law enforcement people in your corner, on payroll, giving you tips. That was, Casso came to realize, an essential ingredient to have in play if your life was devoted to breaking the law—all laws, in all places, all the time, as you saw fit.

With a laserlike intensity and focus Anthony Casso set out to find crooked cops and FBI agents and make them part of his operation. He would, in fact, have great success in this enterprise. He would become the go-to guy for anyone in the families to get the inside track on what the cops and the feds knew.

Gaspipe put out the word to all those in blue that they could make cash for good information—no questions asked—that they'd be protected and treated honorably. Two New York City detectives were soon on Gaspipe's payroll. They provided Casso the names of informants and facts and details about investigations into LCN, and they would kill at the behest of Gaspipe. Their names were Stephen Caracappa and Louis Eppolito. Caracappa was thin and gaunt and rodentlike. Louis Eppolito was heavy, barrel-like, and round-faced.

Gaspipe paid NYPD cops and detectives excessively well. He kept his word and protected their identities. Thus it didn't take long for Gaspipe to have cops from all over the metropolitan area, including New Jersey and Connecticut, on his payroll. Finding crooked FBI agents was another matter, but Casso had his friend Greg Scarpa constantly feeding him information directly from an agent he was very close to.

Scarpa and Casso did more and more business together, hijacking valuable trucks and stealing all kinds of goods from Kennedy Airport. The Colombo family was hoping that when the books were opened, Gaspipe would join them. Scarpa offered to sponsor Casso; he politely declined.

———

Wary about FBI surveillance, Casso started to have meetings and discuss business on his boat. He was one of the innovators of having sit-downs on boats. Gaspipe and whomever he was talking to would cruise around the Great Jamaica Bay, up and down its estuaries, the noise of the engine making any kind of recording impossible. It was the ideal meeting place. Casso also used the boat to plot and plan new bank robberies and heists. He had a passion for that kind of job—it gave him a thrill that no other crime could match . . . except certain murders.

More careful than ever, Casso passed on anything that was "iffy," as he put it.

Casso also used the boat to socialize. He took the Carlos on rides, to see the Coney Island fireworks on Tuesday nights. Lillian's mother, Josie, also enjoyed the boat. Anthony would take her and Lillian to the Statue of Liberty, circle it and Ellis Island, then cruise up the two rivers surrounding Manhattan, the East and Hudson rivers. He especially enjoyed taking them for elaborate lunches at fancy waterfront restaurants. Anthony spent money like he had an unlimited supply of it. Anything Lillian wanted, he was only too happy to get for her. As all Mafia wives, she didn't question Anthony about his business. She didn't ask. He told her nothing. This arrangement, "don't ask, don't tell," was the classic unspoken understanding—indeed law—between LCN couples, though it was very obvious to Lillian that her slow-moving, stoic, handsome husband was deeply involved in La Cosa Nostra . . . because he was shown much respect and deference wherever they went.

———

It was now 1974. The drums of LCN's jungle were resonating with a new sound, an ominous, different beat, caused by rumors that the Commission was going to finally open the books and allow new members into the fold, a historic date in the history of the American Mafia. The books had been closed some twenty years. Carlo Gambino finally agreed to open the books because the ranks were thinning. Men who had been trustworthy and loyal deserved to be promoted—deserved to be officially welcomed into the fold.

In an age-old custom that harkened back to Sicily and the very roots of La Cosa Nostra, word of who would be sponsored was sent to every Mafia family in the country with this question: "Does anyone anywhere have good reason why so-and-so should not be *made*?"

CHAPTER 20

STRAIGHTENED OUT

The event that Casso had been waiting for all his teen and adult years was at hand. It was the spring of 1974 and Anthony Michael Casso of Union Street, Brooklyn, was going to be *made*.

Emissaries, captains, and underbosses from each of the five families were dispatched to go see Casso and talk with him about joining them.

Casso listened attentively to everyone, both what they had to say and how they said it. This was an important, potentially life-and-death decision, and Casso turned it over carefully in his mind. Each of the families had its good points, but Casso's mind kept going back to the Lucchese family. He was extremely close to Lucchese underboss Christie Tick Furnari and the respected family head, Tony Ducks Corallo—an old-school mafioso who was extremely well connected politically and had control of numerous unions.

Casso was not interested in power as such. What he wanted more than anything was to have his own crew and the freedom to do things his way. Casso was about making money and staying out of jail, and he felt under the Lucchese umbrella he'd always be able to be his own man, call the shots, and he would have the loyalty of Furnari and Corallo behind him.

Casso saw the Lucchese family as a very well-conditioned lightweight fighter—rippling with muscle, lean and mean, nimble and fast and lethal when necessary, able to knock out an adversary with either hand. The bond that Casso had developed with Christie Tick, however, was really what made the Lucchese family so appealing. He knew that the Lucchese family would allow him the freedom he needed to develop new schemes and scams. He viewed the other families as cumbersome and muscle-bound.

Casso was made at Salvatore "Tom Mix" Santoro's City Island waterfront home in the Bronx. Santoro was the consigliere of the Lucchese family. It was a Friday, a particularly nice spring day. Tony Corallo was there as well as Tom Pappolio, Vinny Beans, Christie Tick, Paul Vario—portrayed in *Goodfellas* by Paul Sorvino—Joe Beck, several other men who were to be made. All were dressed formally in sharp, superbly cut suits, with silk ties, shirts, and socks, and handmade Italian shoes. The sharkskin silk suit Casso wore that day sold for $3,000 at George Richland's on Eighty-sixth Street in Brooklyn. There was a huge pear-shaped diamond pinkie ring worth $40,000 then—over $175,000 today—on his right hand. The stone was the size of a macadamia nut. This was a solemn, serious event, a rebirth—a formal dedication to a life of crime, blood, murder.

After today the family would always come first, above wives and children, mothers and fathers. All roads would lead to the family. All roads would lead away from the family. The family would be the epicenter of the world.

Life.

Air.

Sustenance.

There was no turning back now.

There was a wooden table in the center of the room. It was ten feet long and four feet wide, made of glistening mahogany. It would be a hard, mute witness to the deadly serious events that were about to play out here. In the center of the table was a knife and a loaded blue-black pistol, each there to symbolize the most important tools in this trade, the essential elements, the fuel that drove the engine of organized crime—deadly force.

At the appropriate time, when Tony Corallo, a short, jowly individual who wore granny glasses, gave the solemn nod, the ceremony began.

Gaspipe walked to the right side of the table. He faced Tom Mix Santoro, Tony Corallo, and Capo Tom Pappolio. Vinny Beans, also a capo, stood to Casso's right. Casso felt ten feet tall. All his life he had waited for this moment. This was his one true goal, what he had always wanted . . . the Mob version of a doctorate degree, a coveted seat on the stock exchange. He stood there formally, stiffly, deadly serious, his dark eyes seeing all, shoulders back, head high.

For the thirty-two-year-old Anthony Casso, *this* was his family. These were his people. This was where he was comfortable, at peace—among his own. He was not one . . . he was many, part of a secret army.

For the rest of America, indeed the whole world, these men were notorious criminals, murderers, treacherous cunning wolves who would tear out your throat in a second. To Casso, they were role models, men to emulate and be like.

Now, officially, for all to know and see, Anthony "Gaspipe" Casso proudly stood at the hard wood table with the gun and knife and a picture of Saint Peter, formally becoming one of them, irreversibly bonded to them; their history and their future would soon irrevocably be his.

Solemnly, the ceremony began. Vinny Beans intoned the oath, as Casso repeated, *"Io, Anthony Casso, voglio entrare in questa organizzazione per proteggere la mia famiglia e per proteggere i miei amici."* (I, Anthony Casso, want to enter into this organization to protect my family and to protect all my friends.)

He was then ordered to never betray the family or break his vow of silence, with the express understanding that he would burn in hell for eternity if he did such a thing, that the only way he could leave this brotherhood was through death.

Vinny Beans asked him which finger he used to pull the trigger of a gun. Casso indicated his right index finger. Vinny Beans pinpricked that finger and allowed glistening droplets of blood to drip onto a picture of Saint Peter. That done, Vinny Beans lit the saint on fire and put the picture in Casso's hands. Unblinking, unfazed, Casso held the burning paper in his extended, cupped hands. The saint burned longer than normal. The fire blistered Gaspipe's hand. He didn't so much as bat an eye. The brief ceremony was suddenly over. Anthony Casso was now a *sgarrista,* a bona fide member of the Lucchese crime family.

One by one, they all came over to him, kissed him on each cheek, hugged him, and congratulated him. It was done.

Gaspipe was "straightened out," a made man, officially in the exclusive membership book of La Cosa Nostra.

———

After each of the new members were made—there were seven in all—the group, as is the custom, all went out to eat and celebrate. They went to Louie's Fish Restaurant on City Island Row and had a hearty meal "in a quiet fashion," as Casso put it. That done, everyone went their separate ways.

Tony Corallo assigned Casso to be part of Vinny Beans's borgata. Their headquarters was a private club on 116th Street between First and Second avenues in Manhattan, and the 19th Hole on Brooklyn's Fourteenth Avenue, right across the street from Dyker Park, on the outskirts of Bensonhurst, the epicenter of Mafiadom.

Casso left his home the next afternoon a happy man, part of a secret, dangerous society.

———

The following night Casso went to the 19th Hole, Christie Ticks's place, a Mafia watering hole and hangout. Many men hugged and kissed Casso, congratulating him. Plans were made. Schemes hatched. Near 2:00 A.M. Alley Persico came in, the man who killed Albert Anastasia. Gaspipe was at the bar. The two men had known each other since they were kids.

"You think they did you a favor?" Persico asked. "They didn't do you a favor. You're worth your weight in gold. *They* should celebrate that they got *you*."

"Nice of you to say," Casso said.

Persico had wanted Gaspipe in his crew.

———

Lillian knew nothing about Anthony being made.

CHAPTER 21

RISING STAR

Anthony often had dinner at the famous Rao's restaurant on 114th Street. It was near capo Vinny Beans's hangout and there was always a table put aside for Vinny and his crew in the small, fifteen-table restaurant. Vinny was a gray-haired, old-school, well-dressed capo. Casso enjoyed not only the authentic Neapolitan cuisine at Rao's but the A-list celebrities who frequented the place every night. He saw such movie luminaries as Warren Beatty, Jack Nicholson, Marlon Brando, Sidney Poitier, Francis Ford Coppola, Barbra Streisand, Robert Redford, Paul Newman, and on and on.

It seemed, curiously enough, that the actors were more impressed with La Cosa Nostra big shots than the Mob guys were with the actors. The Mob guys, the actors all knew, didn't make believe they killed people—they really did kill people. Yet here they were, in the flesh.

Now that Casso was officially made, many more opportunities to make money were presented to him, and Casso heartily embraced them all. Few, though, readily offered more potential in profit, with the least amount of personal exposure, than drugs.

By the fall of 1975, Casso was the secret owner of four trawlers and a 707 cargo jet. The trawlers would pick up the drugs—marijuana and coke—in Colombia and move north through the Atlantic where the loads were taken off the boats in different Far Rockaway inlets Casso had scoped out. Business was so good that Gaspipe had to rent a larger warehouse off Kings Highway and buy more trucks to transport the loads all over the country. For the most part, Gaspipe was never near the drugs. He paid people to take chances; he stayed away from the actual stashes.

Gaspipe carefully nurtured a solid relationship with the stoic Colombian kingpins. He kept his word; he had cash ready when he said he would.

Some of Casso's best clients were the infamous Roy DeMeo, Sammy Gravano, Gerard Pappa, and Burton Kaplan . . .

DeMeo had a well-oiled crew of devoted psychopaths working for him: Joey and Patty Testa, Freddy Di Nome, Anthony Senter, Henry Borelli, Chris Rosenberg, and Roy's cousin, known as Dracula because he bled the assembly line of bodies passing through the place, and he resembled Bela Lugosi. DeMeo and his crew got rid of tons of pot every month. Money came rolling in—often in $10 and $20 denominations. Gaspipe made a contract with the head man, "a guy named Mario," in an armored truck depository on Old Richmond Road in Staten Island. Gaspipe would bring him $5 million in small bills and receive $5 million in brand-new cellophane-wrapped $10,000 packets issued by the Federal Reserve—clean money, nice and neat and tidy. Although DeMeo had no qualms about killing for money or killing for sport, he always paid Gaspipe on time and met his obligations. In years to come, DeMeo would be the subject of a bestselling true crime book, *Murder Machine.*

DeMeo—a homicidal psychopath—was one of the most prolific, brutal murderers ever to be made. Even the Gotti brothers steered clear of him and his crew. As a younger man, DeMeo had been a butcher. When he turned to murder as a source of income, he used his knowledge of how to butcher meat to take apart a body, severing joints and sinews, making the getting rid of it that much easier. When he was done, there'd be six neat pieces—the limbs, torso, and head; he affectionately called it "disassembling."

Although Albert Anastasia, the lion of the Brooklyn docks, had begun selling murder as a product in the 1930s and 1940s, Roy DeMeo took a page from Anastasia's handbook and improved on it. A large, very powerful, dark-haired man, DeMeo feared no one, yet he gave Anthony Casso a wide berth and was always straight with him.

Roy, like Gaspipe, had been made in 1974, inducted into the Gambino clan and assigned to the crew of Nino Gaggi, still another Bensonhurst resident. Gaggi lived on Cropsey Avenue and Bay Twenty-second Street. He was the kind of man who put money before reason, and it was he who looked the other way and allowed DeMeo to become an out-of-control killing machine who would cause far more grief for the Gambino family than he was worth. Greed, the age-old nemesis of reason, is what drove Nino Gaggi.

Gaggi reported directly to Paul Castellano. Although Castellano told Gaggi to reel DeMeo in, that DeMeo should stop selling murder to "every Tom, Dick and Harry," Castellano liked the money generated from DeMeo and he did not enforce this as forcefully as he should have.

Another resident of Bensonhurst, Sammy "the Bull" Gravano, was a nasty piece of work. As a youth, he was a member of the notorious Brooklyn street gang known as the Rampers (a derivative of "rampage"). He, like DeMeo and Gaspipe, was a genuine born killer. Gravano was five feet, six inches, had a weight lifter's exaggerated muscles and thick neck, and was an early devotee of anabolic steroids. Gravano was first associated with the Colombo crime family, worked under Shorty Spero, a former boxer with a dour disposition and a perpetual chip on his shoulder. It seemed that Gravano was destined to be made by the Colombos, sponsored by Spero, but as it happened he was taken into the fold of the Gambino family.

Eventually, he'd rise to become underboss of the family and the most infamous informer of all time, responsible for the convictions of forty-three members of LCN, including John Gotti himself. He, too, would write a number one *New York Times* bestselling book *Underboss*, coauthored by Peter Maas.

Gravano would publicly admit in open court to nineteen murders, but people in the know, one of whom is private investigator John McNally, adamantly say that Gravano was directly responsible for forty-four murders. McNally says he has voluminous evidence to back up this claim. Gravano, like DeMeo, met all his obligations when dealing with Gaspipe. He, like DeMeo, respected Gaspipe, knew his reputation, and didn't try to fuck him. He understood that doing that was a one-way trip to the morgue. Both men, Gaspipe and Gravano, prospered, and they had a good relationship. Interestingly, another of Casso's best customers was Gerry Pappa, another ice-cold killer known also as "Pappa Bear."

Pappa, like Gravano, had also been a member of the Rampers as a youth. A fierce street fighter, he was one of the baddest badasses Brooklyn had ever produced—as tough as rusted barbed wire. Pappa had stick-straight, jet-black hair and steady, blue-gray eyes. He was also made in 1974, inducted into the Genovese crime family. Pappa was an assassin. When the Genovese family needed someone suddenly dead, Pappa often got the job. Cunning and treacherous in the extreme, he personally killed thirty-seven people. He would sometimes dress as a woman to fill murder contracts. Casso fronted him grass, heroin, and cocaine, and Pappa always paid, like the others, what was due Casso without excuse or delay. They prospered. To date there is no book about Gerry Pappa.

Burton Kaplan was very unlike DeMeo, Pappa, or Gravano, a criminal of a different mold. He was one of the few Jewish gangsters Gaspipe dealt with. Casso fronted Kaplan all the narcotics he wanted. Kaplan moved huge amounts of drugs, but because he was a degenerate gambler he was often short or late with the money due. Casso, knowing he would always get what was due him, cut Kaplan some slack and the two men prospered. Like this, Gaspipe supplied much of the eastern seaboard with marijuana, coke, and heroin. There would be four books featuring Kaplan's exploits in years to come—about how he very cleverly backstabbed Anthony Casso.

Drug dealing was, of course, all "off the record," for the Mafia Commission frowned severely on selling narcotics. Therefore, Gaspipe not only had to keep an eye on law enforcement but on organized crime as well. La Cosa Nostra members who were selling drugs could very well end up dead. Men who were part of LCN and newly arrived from Sicily were known on the street as zips, and they were often brought across the water to kill indifferently.

———

Gregarious and outgoing, it didn't take long for Lillian Casso to become friendly with the Scavelo family, who lived next door to the Cassos on East Seventy-second Street. The Scavelos had an attractive eighteen-year-old daughter named Carmella, who babysat for the Cassos. Carmella was raped by a zip, who was arrested for the crime. When Gaspipe learned about the rape—the sadistic details regarding what the zip had made the young innocent Carmella do, that he had threatened to kill the girl's family—he took the law into his own hands. He found the zip when he was out on bail, had him abducted, had his genitals mutilated, then killed him. The last thing the zip saw was Gaspipe's face, a slight smile playing across it.

CHAPTER 22

MIA FIGLIA

For Gaspipe, as well as most La Cosa Nostra, a rapist was the lowest form of life, at the very bottom of the totem pole of crime. Even in the hardest prisons anywhere in the world, rapists are put upon—assaulted, even beaten to death. This is not an accident. All men, in all prisons, in all places, have mothers, wives, daughters, and nieces, and a rapist becomes the universal nemesis of all these men.

For Italians—particularly for Sicilians—the hatred for rapists is literally in their blood. From time immemorial the Sicilian people were attacked and conquered by just about every nation in Europe. These included the Norsemen (the Vikings)—thus blue-eyed and blond-haired Sicilians—Greeks, Turks, French, and Moors; all came to Sicily because it was the breadbasket for the Mediterranean. All manner of fruit and vegetables grew in great abundance. The island nation was also strategically located to control the ships going and coming from Europe, the Middle East, and North Africa.

The Moroccans especially held the delicacy of Sicilian women in great regard. They were a dark-skinned people, the Sicilians white. For Moroccans, the buying and selling of human beings was the norm, so in addition to stealing Sicily's bountiful crops, they regularly stole Sicilian women and girls, who were sold off at slave blocks across Morocco and Algeria.

When each of the different conquering countries came to Sicily, they were immediately upon Sicily's females. Rape was a way to terrorize, control, and subjugate the peoples being conquered. Rape was a way for any given nation to plant its collective seed in Sicilians' very souls. In a sense, just as a conquering nation might plant a flag on the coast, so the soldiers of these attacking, warlike nations planted their seed in Sicilian wombs.

This bred into the Sicilian psyche a seething, burning hatred for those who would dishonor and terrorize Sicilian females. The actual rape sometimes was only the beginning of the pain caused by the incident, because if a Sicilian female became pregnant by the rapist, she was forced to carry her pregnancy to term; the church would not allow such pregnancies to be aborted—compounding the pain and turmoil of the victims many times over.

One incident of particular note, known as the Night of the Sicilian Vespers, happened in 1282. On that fateful date, March 30, the Sicilian men had had enough. Every man and boy old enough to fight on the island of Sicily banded together for revenge against French soldiers who had come to Sicily for its treasures. That night, across the broad expanse of the island nation, ten thousand French soldiers were camped.

At midnight, when bells sounded at the Church of the Holy Spirit outside of Palermo and all across Sicily, Sicilian males came forth for one purpose and one purpose only—and that was pure revenge.

Murder.

The drawing of blood.

Justice!

Revenge!

While the French soldiers slept and milled about, enjoying the fresh, sweet air and the cloudless night filled with glimmering stars, the Sicilians attacked with a quiet ferocity that would shock all of civilized Europe. They not only killed every last Frenchman but also cut off their genitalia and stuffed them in the Frenchmen's mouths, and left them there like that.

The French never came back to Sicily; they wanted nothing more to do with the barbarous Sicilians. Though the island country was never attacked again—except when the Allies invaded in 1943—it was ruled by myriad European nations.

"Enough was enough!" the Sicilians had proclaimed so loudly that the message resonated from Saudi Arabia to Norway.

When, therefore, Italians, united by Garibaldi over a twenty-year period ending in 1871, emigrated to America by the millions (4.5 million) between 1890 and 1924, they brought with them an innate, very personal hatred for not only the crime of rape, but indeed for the rapists themselves, for it was not just the Sicilians who were assaulted, raped, and brutalized—most all of the peoples of southern Italy suffered at the hands of conquering nations.

Early on, at the turn of the nineteenth century, the Italians quickly learned to protect their own, especially their women. Just as in Sicily, any man who raped an Italian female would end up dead, more than likely stabbed to death.

Like all LCN members, Anthony Casso hated rapists. Through all his childhood years in South Brooklyn he had come to loathe them, as one would sewer rats. The thought of someone raping Lillian or his daughter, Jolene, could make his blood boil. But this was not only relevant to his immediate family, this was relevant to any friend, relative, or neighbor Casso had. By now Casso was literally in charge of an army of killers. All he had to do was point and nod his head and someone would be dead; no explanation was asked for or given.

When, then, Mill Basin neighbors of Anthony complained that one Angelo Sigona had raped their daughter, Lucy, Sigona's days were numbered; the clock was ticking. Anthony liked this family. As was his nature, when he was fond of someone, he would go out of his way to protect them, to make sure they were not exploited. In this sense, Anthony very much came from old-school Mafia. Within twenty-four hours of Casso learning what happened, Sigona was killed. As he got into his car one lazy summer night, he was shot numerous times. Casso did not want anything in return. It was truly his pleasure to kill the rapist. And the family whose daughter had been raped never even knew for sure that Casso was responsible for the killing.

CHAPTER 23

ANTHONY JUNIOR

A s busy as Anthony had become, with all the money he was making, it wasn't enough. It was never enough; he wanted more. He needed to show legitimate sources of income to be able to spend and not worry about the feds. His intention was to start legitimate businesses—"fronts"—and toward that end, he opened three Italian restaurants/pizza places he called Capri's. One was in Frederick, Maryland; another in Johnstown, Pennsylvania; and another in Altoona, Pennsylvania. Anthony also bought a pizza place on Eighty-sixth Street in Brooklyn, just a few doors north of the infamous 19th Hole, which Anthony would eventually buy from Chris Furnari. Christie Tick was endlessly amazed at what a good moneymaker Anthony was, and he knew Anthony would go far in their world. He thought of Anthony as a loyal son.

Naturally, enough, Casso took to spending money like there was no tomorrow, as though it grew on trees in the backyard. He took Lillian on frequent vacations—to Saint Thomas, Bermuda, Florida, the Caribbean, Las Vegas. They regularly went to the finest restaurants in New York City and saw all the popular Broadway shows, especially the musicals *A Chorus Line, Cabaret,* and *Pippin.*

Lillian soon became pregnant again. Anthony hoped it would be a boy, a male child he could teach all he knew about life, the street, and human nature. If, he reasoned, his son wanted into LCN, he wouldn't stop him, but he certainly wouldn't encourage such a thing.

A lawyer. He hoped if he had a son, he would become an attorney. The lawyers he knew made all the money and wrote laws to protect themselves.

His prayers were answered, for Lillian gave birth to a healthy baby boy in 1974. They named him Anthony.

———

For Anthony Gaspipe Casso, life was good. Between Casso's B&E crews and his drug business, one would think Casso would have been happy . . . satisfied. But just the opposite proved true. For him, it wasn't just about making money. Rather it was about beating the system, getting over on those who would arrest him and put him away for life—steal him from his beloved family. It was the age-old war between the outlaw and the sheriff—a perverse take on the classic Robin Hood tale.

Surprisingly, considering the chances he took, Anthony was extremely generous with money—he would readily help out a friend or family member; he donated excessively to Saint Bernard's Church in Mill Basin and anyone he deemed righteous. The parish priest often visited the Casso home and Lillian made sure he left with money—one time $10,000. Anthony gave waiters and waitresses ridiculously large tips. He'd gladly reach in his pocket to help someone down on their luck. All anyone had to do was politely ask.

Casso regularly bought $5,000 bottles of wine at fancy Manhattan restaurants such as Bravo Gianni's on the Upper East Side, "21" Club on West Fifty-second Street, and Regine's on Park Avenue. Money was no longer an obstacle. He had so much cash on hand, he was forced to rent supersized safety deposit boxes in banks he carefully checked into beforehand, wanting to make sure they were "foolproof"—he did not want to be robbed.

CHAPTER 24

BAD APPLES

Casso was now making so much money that he was able to buy not only material items galore and more real estate, but also NYPD detectives, Suffolk and Nassau County cops, and FBI agents.

One such FBI agent was Doug McCane. He supplied Casso with the status of numerous federal investigations into organized crime. Casso paid well for this information, and always in cash.

Wisely, decently, Casso gladly shared what he knew with other mafiosi, indebting Mob guys to him from every family—making friends, building bridges, a constant role that Casso played while on the street; he was the quintessential snake oil salesman.

Drugs—even Casso couldn't get over the enormous profit in them, the insatiable demand for them. No matter how much coke and grass and heroin he imported, it was never enough. He likened what he was doing to the bootleggers of old. If the government didn't have the common sense to legalize, regulate, and tax drugs—as it did with alcohol—why shouldn't he prosper from it? He knew that many of the greatest fortunes made in America were the results of crime.

However, Casso realized that the sheer volume of drugs he was bringing in would inevitably cause problems. His insurance policy was crooked cops, and he regularly milked them like fat cows with full udders. If there was an ongoing investigation of Gaspipe's operation, they'd let him know. Casso made millions for himself.

The beginning of the end of the drug business came from, not surprisingly, a rat, though the identity of the rat was a surprise. He was a Mob wannabe by the name of Paul Bennett. He had rigged the drug-transporting vehicles with cleverly hidden compartments to avoid police scrutiny—discovery. When he was busted selling ten pounds of pot, he basically gave up Gaspipe's operation, at least what he knew about it, and the Coast Guard and Maritime Police were alerted.

Sure enough, the next load coming in ran into trouble. A fifty-seven-foot trawler, *Terry's Dream,* was coming directly from the northeast end of Colombia. It had a full load of high-grade marijuana, called wacky weed—twenty thousand pounds of it—with a wholesale value of $5 million. The crossing had gone well; the weather had been ideal. The boat entered the U.S. jurisdictional waters, the three-mile limit, without being challenged. As planned, it proceeded to pass under the Jamaica Bay drawbridge. However, the bridge master became suspicious of *Terry's Dream* and started making phone calls from his conveniently located crow's nest position on the bridge. *Terry's Dream* slowly continued on to a Far Rockaway inlet, where it docked and was met by an unloading crew and four trucks. Using hand trucks, men quickly began to unload the fifty-pound bales of grass and stash them in the trucks.

Of course, Casso wasn't there. When Casso seemed to be cruising around in one of his boats, he was really carefully scoping out the coastline, looking for good drop spots. He really enjoyed these outings. He viewed himself as a crafty pirate, making the best of a profitable situation that had been handed to him on a silver platter.

The boat captain transporting the drugs that night preferred cloudy skies—the less light the better. But on this night the sky was clear, the boat clearly visible there at the mooring docks.

As soon as a Coast Guard ensign saw what was happening, he lay low and called in the police; soon *Terry's Dream* became *Terry's Nightmare* as cops and federal agents surrounded the inlet, guns drawn, quickly rounding up everyone. The proverbial shit had hit the fan.

———

With FBI agent Doug McCane's help, it didn't take long for Casso to find out how the bust went down, and who was responsible. He dispatched killers with a grudge to put an end to Paul Bennett.

This murder gave Casso no kind of thrill at all. He was not some kind of antisocial psychopath who derived thrills or chills, a feeling of omnipotence, by killing people. It was all about business, getting rid of loose ends. In a matter of days, Paul Bennett was murdered as he left his home, shot to death right outside it on Avenue N and East Forty-first Street. Bennett had no idea that he'd been fingered by an FBI agent, had no idea that he'd been marked for death.

Casso did not use a Lucchese hit man to kill Bennett; he instead gave the job to Roy DeMeo. Roy had a vested interest in the pot shipments—he'd been making millions of dollars because of them—and he gladly killed Bennett.

"The fuckin' rat," he told Casso. "My pleasure."

That was not the end of the killing, however, just the beginning. Next, the captain of *Terry's Dream* and his son David were brutally murdered. They knew too much and were talking to the feds, Casso heard, and they had to go.

Again, these two murders were about business, money, and staying free, yet the method of death seemed more than the practical application of the Mafia protecting its interests.

When the son of the captain of *Terry's Dream* was cornered in Fort Lauderdale, Florida, Gaspipe was there. After hearing what he had to say—garnered while being beaten and battered—Gaspipe shot him and had him buried alive in the Everglades off 595.

People in La Cosa Nostra soon heard what Gaspipe did. *Fuck with Gaspipe and you'll pay dearly* was the message Casso wanted delivered to the world—and so it was.

Conversely, an associate of Casso's, "Hollywood" Joe Barbara, who oversaw the shipments from Colombia, was killed by the Colombians, shot in the head and dumped into the sea; someone had to pay for the lost twenty thousand pounds of pot.

It is actually kind of amazing how Mob guys talk and brag about their deeds and crimes . . . their murders. At face value, one would think they'd be a tight-lipped fraternity, but more often than not they blab up a storm, and so all in organized crime soon learned about the burying alive of the captain's son.

"Street justice," Casso said. "Betray us and you pay with your life."

For Gaspipe, it was like taking a dump and flushing the bowl.

CHAPTER 25

FAMILY AFFAIR

Michael Delduca was Lillian's youngest brother Ralph's only child. A troubled youth with drug and attitude problems, Michael seemed destined for trouble—if he didn't find it, it would find him.

Anthony was very fond of the boy, however; he had known him all his life and thought of him as a wayward son. Michael, a small-framed, frail youth, put on a tough front. He wanted to be respected, to make the Brooklyn rough-and-tumble, ready-to-rumble way of life his. He was not tough—he just thought he was.

Anthony had repeated talks with Michael, sitting him down and endlessly lecturing him, though nothing he said or did seemed to matter. Anthony took him for rides on his boat, took him fishing, bought him clothes, and generously gave him spending money, yet still Michael found trouble—he got into fights, got arrested, got into trouble in school . . . did drugs.

Michael was often on Anthony's mind, and because he held family in high esteem, no matter how busy he was, he always had time for the boy. For Anthony, the blood bond that stitched and wove family together was unbreakable. He felt personally responsible for the well-being—and protection—of not only his own family, but Lillian's family as well. This even held true for the family members of his friends.

Thus, for Anthony, the bond and solidarity of family was, in a very tangible way, like a religious commitment—a holy bond to be devoted to, to be held in high esteem and respected.

Michael Delduca was murdered on an uneventful weeknight. He had been in a bar on Thirteenth Avenue and Seventy-first Street, Colombo capo Greg Scarpa's neighborhood. It was the latter part of 1975.

Michael got into an argument over a pot deal with his older cousin Sal—a relative on his mother's side of the family. An out-of-control psychopath, Sal took Michael into a hallway, as though to talk to the boy, but then he put a gun to Michael's head and pulled the trigger, shooting the boy to death and leaving him there in the hall.

Sal was connected to and sold drugs for the Colombo family, so he figured he was above reproach or discipline—a fatal mistake. When Anthony learned of Michael's murder, he was furious. Casso's getting angry was an odd, unsettling sight, for he would not raise his voice, scream, yell, or break things. On the contrary, he'd become quiet and morose; his face would set into a granite mask, and his jaw muscles would bulge and quiver slightly.

What, more than anything, gave Casso's anger away, however, were his eyes—they'd grow distant, black and cold and unseeing.

Even before the sixteen-year-old Michael Delduca had a proper wake, funeral, and burial, Casso went and saw Capo Greg Scarpa, one of the most feared, genuinely dangerous war capos in all Mafiadom. As protocol dictated, Gaspipe, Scarpa, and other made men of the Colombo family sat down in Scarpa's Bensonhurst club.

"I'm here," Gaspipe began in a calm voice, "because my wife's nephew, her baby brother's sixteen-year-old son Michael, was killed by Sal." He let his words sink in. He continued. "I want his head," Anthony said, every word immediately backed up by his already legendary reputation.

Joe Peach spoke up for Sal.

"Anthony, we are very sorry for your loss but everyone knew that kid Michael was trouble. Sally was trying to keep him in order, keep him outta trouble all the time, but the kid wouldn't listen, would never listen—"

"Listen to me carefully," Casso stopped him, his voice little more than a growl. "Sal has to go; either you do it or I will—simple."

Again, the Colombos tried to save Sal, talk Casso out of having him killed. Casso, his face rigid and immobile, answered with one word: *morta* (dead).

To demand something so emphatically from Greg Scarpa was a ballsy thing to do. A stone-cold killer, Scarpa now stared at Casso. The two men respected and liked each other. Scarpa, who knew that Casso was in the right, decided not to get in the way of his request.

"We are friends," he said, "and in friendship, I'll make sure to take care of this."

And on that note the sit-down ended. The Colombos really had no choice in this matter. Casso had every right in the Mob world to demand—and get—Sal's death. They all hugged and kissed on the cheek, as was the age-old custom. Greg Scarpa dispatched a hit team from his crew. Michael Delduca's killer was shot to death on Fourteenth Avenue—left where he dropped . . . just as Michael had been. Justice had been done, swiftly and irreversibly.

When Lillian learned this she felt better, the whole family did. The need for revenge seemed to be a genetic trait in Italian American blood.

Casso, too, felt better that his nephew's killer was dead. He would not have rested otherwise.

When Michael Delduca was lowered into the ground of Greenwood Cemetery just south of Prospect Park, Anthony held his wife, Lillian, tight and cried along with her, tangibly feeling her grief and pain and loss. As cold and detached as Anthony Casso could be, often would be, he had an unusual capacity for empathy, to feel the pain and heartache and loss of others.

———

Lillian never asked the details of what happened to her nephew's killer, and Anthony did not volunteer the information. She knew, though, that the deed had been done, that her husband had made sure to right this terrible wrong, without needing to involve the police, courts, or jail.

It was 1977 and Lillian's thirty-fifth birthday was coming up. Anthony resolved to do something "special" for her. His love for Lillian was deep and wide and all consuming. As well as being husband and wife, Lillian and Anthony were helpmates and friends . . . partners in life.

Yes, Anthony fooled around with other women now and then, females he met in fancy restaurants, Russian women who flocked to the 19th Hole knowing there were wealthy mafiosi there, but Lillian he held in high esteem; he trusted only her—a rare thing for Anthony, because he trusted few.

Anthony decided to take Lillian and their good friends to Las Vegas for a week for her thirty-fifth birthday, a surprise. He invited Consigliere Chris Furnari and his wife; Vic Amuso and his wife; and the guys from his crew he was the closest to and all their wives. He took the best suite at the famous Dunes Casino, which he recently explained was paying $100,000 a month to the New York Mafia back then.

"A few times a year," Casso said, "I went and got the money and brought it back. Different guys from different families would rotate."

The business of making money fueled and drove LCN like a well-tuned Ferrari engine.

Dressed to the nines in formal wear, Anthony and Lillian entered the Dunes's amazing dining room. Anthony had reserved a sumptuously laid-out table—a work of art unto itself. A pretty woman dressed all in white played a white harp on a gondola in the water near their table . . . Lillian's favorite song, "What I Did for Love."

Before Lillian knew it, they were surrounded by their friends, all yelling, "Surprise!," nearly bowling her over she was so caught off guard. It really was a surprise. Lillian had had no idea. Anthony was so tight lipped and had such a finely tuned poker face that he could readily fool his own wife.

Lillian had a grand time, one of the best times in her life. The food, wine, and champagne were all the best—first class. Money was no object. Whatever doubts Lillian had about Anthony—his being away so often, infidelities—were washed away. His love, dedication, and devotion to her were irreversibly proven. No man who wasn't mad about his wife could be so considerate, caring, and dedicated.

The truth was that Anthony not only treasured Lillian, but he also treasured the life he had with her. Lillian was an excellent homemaker and a devoted mother and wife. Anthony had, he was sure, found his soul mate, and he considered himself very lucky. He valued Lillian as a rare woman and often gave quiet thanks to the "high power" for her. Lillian also had a sharp mind and good business sense. When, for example, Lillian heard that the Fortunoffs' home—this being the family that owns Fortunoff's department store—on East Seventy-third Street was for sale, Lillian negotiated the price to $600,000 . . . a very good deal.

By now Anthony could claim the $600,000 legitimately and they bought the property.

CHAPTER 26

CRIME PAYS

Anthony Casso was the most successful earner of La Cosa Nostra, hands down. In late 1980, Lucchese consigliere Christie Tick, the only boss Casso ever had and to whom he was unusually close, sat Casso down in the 19th Hole. Christie said, "I'm thinking it's time you became a capo . . . have your own crew."

Since a consigliere is only allowed to have one man under him, Casso had always "stood" with the family administration, directly under Christie. Now all that would change. As a captain Casso would have—and run—his own crew; he would be responsible for what everyone in his crew did, keep them on leashes, mitigate the clash of personalities, the cutting up of different scores, the carrying out of killings, the squabbles over wives and girlfriends and bruised egos. It was a position Casso did not want, along with the responsibility, the obligations, the nitpicking, the having to worry about what the twenty-odd guys under him were doing.

No, none of that was for him.

"I appreciate," Casso said, "what are you saying, but I'd rather stay where I am. I'm happy." He could readily see the disappointment on Christie's face. This was, he knew, a nice gesture on Christie's part, a big step up for Casso.

"This is," Christie said, "a good opportunity for you to move up, Casso. You've got more on the ball in your pinkie finger than five guys put together. I'm thinking . . . Casso, I'm thinking one day you'll lead the family. We need someone like you who understands the traditional and the modern ways of doing things. Consider this."

Casso, flattered by Christie's words and the sincerity behind them, which was evident in his eyes and on his jaded face, slowly shook his head. "I'm happy where I am for now," he repeated. "Why not elect Vic?" he suggested. They both knew that Vic Amuso was a far cry from Casso, that Amuso did not have nearly what Casso had going for him.

"That's what you want for sure?" Christie asked.

"Yeah, for now for sure," Casso said, and it was done.

It didn't take long for word to get around LCN that Gaspipe had turned down being a captain. When Frankie DeCicco and John Gotti of the Gambino family heard, they thought Casso was crazy.

Crazy, because the opportunities that would open to Casso as a captain would be many—but Casso stayed where he was and Vic Amuso was soon a captain in the Lucchese family.

CHAPTER 27

THE FORBIDDEN FRUIT

There was just too much money in drugs for La Cosa Nostra to pass it up. The selling of drugs was still very much a cardinal sin for made men to have anything to do with, yet most all of the families did—especially the Bonannos, which was one of the main reasons they, the Bonannos, were outright banned from the Mafia Commission.

Drugs, the bosses felt, wisely knew, would automatically cause excessively long prison terms to be handed down, tempting men to make deals to get themselves out of trouble.

For the most part, it was all about greed. There were literally tons of money to be made via LCN's conventional rackets—hijacking, shylocking, robberies, shakedowns, fixed bidding, union infiltration, murder, and so on—yet the mafiosi could not, it seemed, keep away from the selling of drugs . . . the forbidden fruit.

Anthony Casso was no exception. It didn't take long after the first drug bust along the Brooklyn-Queens border for Casso to have a whole new drug operation set up and running smoothly, generating millions. Now loads of grass were being brought into New York by way of the Bronx City Island inlets, then taken by truck to a Brooklyn warehouse—an old pickle factory with an inside loading platform—on Ralph Avenue, just off Kings Highway. Trucks were backed onto the platform and the grass was quickly unloaded into a hidden room with a secret wall, which could be moved by hand, provided one knew exactly where to push. In this hidden room there were long tables and special lights to treat and dry the bales of pot that got wet in crossing the often rough Atlantic. Now, too, rum would cleverly be added before the drying so fungus would not ruin the pot. A fifty-pound bale of pot at four hundred per pound wholesale was worth twenty grand retail. This operation ran successfully for months, but Gaspipe, always on the lookout for bigger—and better—opportunities, made a contract with a larceny-hearted man who ran the night shift at a small airport in Fort Lauderdale, Florida. Casso arranged to have Colombian cocaine barons fly a small plane up from Bogotá—filled with bricks of high-grade cocaine for a fee of a million dollars cash per load. This scheme worked flawlessly for many months, with no difficulties. Everyone prospered.

In addition, wanted Colombian drug barons traveled to the states on these clandestine flights to take welcomed safe haven in Florida.

Gaspipe always kept his word. He never even thought of having any of the Colombians kidnapped and held for ransom. This, he knew, could be very profitable, but he consistently played it straight, on the up-and-up. Casso put it like this: "We were honest with everyone, and everyone knew that about us from coast to coast and abroad—whatever you had coming to you, you got, no problem."

His reputation as a straight shooter spread; his earning power became legendary in LCN.

The FBI and the New York organized crime strike force kept hearing about Gaspipe, all the money he was making, the many pies he had his manicured fingers in. Agents began to trail Casso to try to get something on him, but he proved to be unusually "bright and resourceful" as a retired agent in the know recently put it. "He was," he said, "a wily son of a bitch. We were never able to record him."

Casso was again selling voluminous amounts of drugs to Sammy Gravano (Gambino), Roy DeMeo (Gambino), Gerard Pappa (Genovese), and Burton Kaplan.

Because of Gaspipe's pristine reputation in the underworld, he made still more contacts with "biggies" in the drug business and soon was doing business with an international heroin ring based out of Marseilles, France, with associates in Afghanistan and Sicily. Through the Lucchese domination of seaports all over the country—especially in Jersey and Brooklyn—

Casso managed to get shipments of heroin into the States, bringing millions more into the bursting Lucchese coffers and his own bulging pockets.

Casso bought more real estate, opened more businesses. Interestingly, one of Gaspipe's best customers was infamous Gambino soldier Sammy the Bull Gravano. He moved more drugs, all "off the record," than any of Casso's other LCN customers.

Again, Casso's biggest problem became where the hell to safely stash all the money he was making, and he was forced to rent more and more safety deposit boxes. The money itself became a concern for him. His pockets filled with $100 bills, Casso spent a fortune on shopping trips. FBI agents who were now tracking him began checking how much he actually spent. He'd spend $20,000 or $30,000 at the drop of a hat. He purchased the finest suits, shirts, shoes, ties, and coats money could buy. He was always dressed superbly, and he cut a very handsome, dashing figure in Brioni, Armani, and Hugo Boss suits, a $25,000 cashmere overcoat folded neatly over his powerful left arm. He became the mobster most talked about, pointed at, admired—a man of respect everyone wanted as a friend. If Casso became an enemy, you had to leave town or you were quickly dead. Unlike John Gotti, however, Casso didn't flaunt himself. He stayed out of the public eye and as far away from the media as possible.

Gaspipe garnered such respect within LCN that members of other families regularly came to him with new schemes, rip-offs, and murders that had to be done. Not just the killing of LCN enemies—those who would compromise it and defy it—but made men who had "turned bad" and become informers.

Thus, Gaspipe became the Mafia's in-house sweeper—enforcer. He got rid of its bad apples quickly and efficiently, few the wiser.

He soon became known as "Mafia royalty," a new breed of mafioso that impressed his cohorts, awed his adversaries, and stymied law enforcement. Though he didn't officially have his own borgata, when Casso came to sit-downs, he was treated with the deference owed a respected boss. He was a nine-hundred-pound gorilla, a wise, wary mafioso.

"Gaspipe," his inherited moniker, became a household word within LCN's community, and Anthony Casso hadn't even begun. He was just warming up.

BOOK III

LA VENDETTA

CHAPTER 28

INSIDE INFO

FBI agent Doug McCane, an innocuous-looking man with short gray hair, blue eyes, high cheekbones, and thin lips, became more and more helpful to the Lucchese borgata, to Casso and La Cosa Nostra indirectly. By way of the Bronx, then Harlem to Brooklyn, McCane sent information to Casso.

The rule of thumb when dealing with crooked agents and cops was for one Mob guy—in McCane's case it was Lucchese capo Vinny Beans—to deal with the individual, to nurture and make payoffs and develop "a meaningful bond," as LCN put it. This not only insulated the other members of any crime family from exposure, but lulled the crooked officers into a false sense of solidarity and insulation.

For more than twelve years, Agent McCane let the Luccheses know when indictments and subpoenas were coming down, enabling LCN members to make themselves scarce or have a crack criminal attorney playing quarterback even before an arrest was made or a subpoena was served.

This kept Mob guys out of trouble, avoided potential indictments and arrests, and hugely frustrated law enforcement efforts.

McCane also let the Lucchese family know who was a rat, and if the rat was in hiding exactly where he was hiding—basically delivering a death sentence. Casso acted very quickly on this information, immediately dispatching hit teams to find and kill the rat.

Often, the hit victim was thought to have been stand-up and righteous, for no one ever suspected his duplicitous police involvement—like, for instance, Colombo capo Greg Scarpa, a bona fide informant for the FBI while acting as a capo for the Colombo crime family. He deftly played both sides of the fence.

Casso came to be thought of as a paranoid psychopath by most all of LCN and the FBI's Organized Crime Bureau, when just the opposite was true: he was eliminating malignant growths, he felt, with the efficiency of a seasoned surgeon. He offered no reasons or excuses. Once McCane identified a made man as an informer to the Luccheses, Casso made sure he was dead, no questions asked, no quarter given, no excuses accepted.

He became feared, a kind of modern-day King Lear, but all he was doing was cleaning house—"Taking out the garbage," as he put it.

When recently asked just how many people were killed because of Agent Doug McCane, Casso said, "Thirteen, fourteen . . . maybe fifteen. Yeah, fifteen."

Casso also had two Suffolk County detectives on the Lucchese payroll who were each routinely paid $200 a month by Lucchese capo Sally Avellino. Casso, personally, never had any contact with these detectives. Any dealings he had with them were through Avellino. When recently queried about these detectives, Casso said, "I heard that both are now retired; one may have been a black guy, and one passed on."

Burton Kaplan likewise had a contact with two crooked NYPD detectives via a relative on his wife's side of the family. These two black-hearted individuals would end up causing a firestorm of trouble not only for themselves but also for the NYPD. Their eventual arrest and trial would spark no less than five books, one by famed author Jimmy Breslin; a motion picture; and several television dramas. Their names were Louis Eppolito and Stephen Caracappa, and they would eventually kill, at the behest of Casso, who always referred to them as "Fat and Skinny," eight people.

Interestingly, the symbiotic relationship Gaspipe had with cops worked both ways. For example, a New York lieutenant detective named Louis Tusso had a fourteen-year-old daughter who was sexually abused by two older guys connected to the Genovese family. This happened in a private home on Ocean Parkway, just near Coney Island. They got away with what they did. The lieutenant went to Casso. Casso in turn went to Chin Gigante. A short time later, the two rapists, John Napoli and Peter Jordan, were shot to death.

Gaspipe seemed blessed. He had King Midas's touch fused with the luck of the Irish. Everything he touched seemed to turn to gold; he blissfully went about his life of crime unencumbered by the feds or the NYPD OCCB—the Organized Crime Control Bureau task force. Casso was careful not to flaunt his success, his riches, his unequal position in LCN. He stayed low-key; he was all about understatement.

Casso's role models were the old-timers—Tommy Lucchese, Lucky Luciano, Vito Genovese, Joe Profaci, and, more recently, Carlo Gambino.

Shortly before Gambino's death in 1977, Casso had met Carlo at his modest Ocean Parkway home. For him it was like meeting the pope. As always in LCN, a man's reputation proceeded him and Carlo treated Casso with respect; he gave Casso a bottle of homemade red wine.

"I hear," Carlo had said in his soft voice, "good things about you. Too bad you chose to be elsewhere, but we understand."

Casso came away very impressed, for Carlo was a perfect gentleman; he was considerate, respectful—modest. He dressed plainly. He walked softly but he carried a big stick, indeed, everyone in LCN knew.

Don't flaunt power; don't flaunt wealth were the subliminal messages Casso took away from Gambino.

CHAPTER 29

KENNEDY AIRPORT

As the cruel, vicious winds of the winter of 1978 blew across the flat expanse that is Kennedy Airport, a classic case of the insidious control La Cosa Nostra had over the comings and goings of commerce at Kennedy Airport began.

For the New York Mafia, the airport was like a big candy store. Through the infiltration of made men and men who were connected to LCN, as well as men who worked in the unions controlled by the Mob, LCN had an inside track on all valuables coming into the airport. These included firearms, cash, gold coins, minks and other furs, all types of jewels, and expensive food (caviar, wines, champagnes, truckloads of alcohol). If something valuable was coming into Kennedy Airport in 1978, the Mob knew about it. They had a virtual monopoly on pilferage at the airport. However, no one family had an absolute lock on the airport, though the Lucchese and Bonanno families did have a stranglehold on it. These two families managed to keep the peace by sharing equally in scores.

Certainly, one of the most profitable robberies ever pulled off at the airport was the famous Lufthansa Heist. A huge amount of money, in excess of $5 million cash, was being flown to Germany to pay American soldiers. Along with the $5 million, there was $875,000 worth of jewels.

Word went from one man to another to another to another, working its way up the food chain of the Lucchese family until it reached Jimmy Burke. Burke was associated with Paul Vario's Lucchese crew. It's a long convoluted story how this robbery was planned and executed; suffice it to say in the early morning hours of December 11, 1978, a team of twelve men descended on Kennedy to rob the military payroll. The head of this crew was Jimmy Burke. Burke was a bona fide killer. He'd sooner kill a human being than swat a fly. He was a hard, tough Irishman, a two-fisted gangster. The great Robert De Niro would excellently portray him in the hit film *Goodfellas*, based on the book *Wiseguys* by Nick Pileggi. Burke would have been made and might very well have had his own crew if he hadn't been Irish. With the speed and alacrity of a special forces army operation, Burke and his band managed to catch all the guards unaware, bind over a dozen employees, and carefully get in and out of the safe holding the cash. They knew exactly what they were looking for. They picked and chose duffel bags filled with money. By the time they had finished, they'd absconded with some forty-four bags of cash without a shot being fired or anyone being seriously hurt. They were essentially responsible for the largest heist in the annals of crime history.

The problem with the so-called Lufthansa heist was that too many people knew about it. Fifteen different men were directly involved in the robbery. Scores of other men knew about it, and they told their girlfriends, wives, and families; it was really no secret who was responsible for this news-making robbery.

Paul Vario managed to strike a deal with the Bonanno family and they got a percentage—so there was no strife or friction between the Luccheses and the Bonannos.

But greed, according to what Casso recently divulged, spun its insidious web over all who were involved, and Paul Vario gave the go-ahead to kill just about every participant in the robbery, some thirteen men. Bodies were popping up all over Brooklyn: on street corners, in sanitation trucks, in landfills that ran along Brooklyn's Belt Parkway. Henry Hill, a bottom-feeding wannabe, Casso says, ended up giving information to the police and the FBI that ultimately allowed whoever was left alive in the robbery to be arrested and prosecuted. Jimmy Burke died in jail. Paul Vario died in jail. Yet not one penny of the money taken from the Lufthansa terminal was ever recovered.

———

Always on the lookout for new scores, new sources of income, Casso soon came upon the most lucrative of schemes, a new racket that would generate far more money than drugs or bank robberies or both put together. It involved the Russian Mafia out of Brighton Beach, Brooklyn, and, for LCN, was like taking candy from a petulant baby, as Gaspipe thought of it, smiling . . . bemused.

CHAPTER 30

NEWFOUND WEALTH

L illian Casso gleefully renovated their new home on Seventy-second Street. Money was no object. The Cassos hired a noted architect, who was friends with Lucchese war capo Fat Pete Chiodo.

If, in reality, Lillian Casso wanted pure gold faucets in the three bathrooms of the home, that would not have been a problem. Anthony Casso's new scheme involved the stealing of $950 million.

It all began with a tough and clever gang of Brooklyn Russians—Marat Balagula, Evsei Agron, and Boris Nayfeld. When the Long Island faction of the Colombo family tried to move in on the Russian rackets, Balagula came to the Lucchese family with his hat in his stumpy hand, looking for help.

Marat Balagula was a unique piece of work, a very clever businessman, a tough, wily Jew. He owned restaurants, health clubs, and hundreds of gas stations all up and down the East Coast, 125 gas stations and truck stops in New Jersey alone. The Jersey stations were run by his brother, Leon.

Marat Balagula, who also lived in Mill Basin, Brooklyn, had a huge, overdone, ostentatious home on the water, attesting to his enormous wealth, as is the Russians' way. If you have it, flaunt it was their credo, just the opposite of Carlo Gambino's.

Balagula also dealt arms in Sierra Leone and sold heroin and "blood diamonds" out of Africa. Although it was highly successful, the Russian

Mafia, or Organizatsiya at that time, couldn't hold a candle as a lucrative enterprise to the Italian Mafia with its tight structure, precise organization, and smooth operation.

When, then, the Colombo crime family began to put the squeeze on Marat and his cohorts, Marat wisely asked to see Christie Tick at the 19th Hole. A meeting was arranged.

Casso, working directly under Christie, was there. After complaining about the Colombos, how greedy and gruff they were, Marat made Christie an offer, a percentage of the take. The two men haggled for a while, and an agreement was reached, but not before Christie said, "Here there's enough for everyone to be happy . . . to leave the table satisfied. What we must avoid is trouble between us and the other families. I propose to make a deal with the others so there's no bad blood."

This, Marat knew, was a smart move, and he readily agreed to Christie's proposition.

"Meanwhile," Christie added, "we will send out word that from now on you and your people are with the Lucchese family. No one will bother you. If anyone does bother you, come to us and Anthony will take care of it. You have any kind of problems on the street, Anthony will take care of it . . . okay?" he said.

"Okay," Marat readily agreed, a happy man. This was a huge sweet pie that could readily feed many. Two cents of every gallon of gas sold would go, from then on, to LCN instead of federal and state tax coffers, a staggering amount when one considers the volume of gas sold—billions of gallons a month.

Over the ensuing days, the Lucchese bosses had a sit-down with the leader of the Colombo family—Vic Orena—and the Genovese clan, Chin Gigante; they both readily agreed to the deal and appointed made men from each respective family to act as bagmen and collect the family's share. As time went by, Vic Orena asked that the Gambino family be brought on and all agreed.

Chin Gigante appointed Danny Pagnano, Orena appointed Vic Orena Jr. and Franky "the Bug" Sciortino. Christie Tick appointed Lucchese capo Frankie Lastorino, while newly self-appointed head of the Gambino family, John Gotti, appointed Fat Tony Morelli and Tony Pep Trentacosta. The Bonanno family was still officially on the outs, not part of LCN's community and not included in this—or many other LCN schemes.

Once a day, made men would show up at select gasoline terminals for their money, and like Swiss clockwork, the cash was handed over to them, no questions asked. Everyone was astounded by the huge amounts of money—millions upon millions.

Anthony Casso and Marat became friends. They dined with their wives in the finest restaurants; they went on outings on each other's boats. Casso very much enjoyed going to Marat's chic, expensive Odessa nightclub on Brighton Beach Avenue, where he was treated like an honored king—the best food, the best drink, gorgeous Russian women with mile-long legs and high cheekbones who gladly gave their favors to Gaspipe, who gladly accepted their charms. Casso's obvious power, for these status-obsessed women, was an aphrodisiac.

Marat also had extensive contacts in the diamond business, a bonanza for Casso, who was still masterminding thefts of millions of dollars in diamonds.

Money, money, money—it was all about money . . . the thrill of taking it at will. For some men, big-game hunting gave this thrill; for Casso, planning and pulling off lucrative robberies was big-game hunting.

One such robbery had a particularly sad ending: Casso and his crew robbed a Chase bank on the corner of Baxter and Canal streets, in the very heart of the Bowery diamond district. They knew there would be a lot of diamonds, of course, but they were stunned speechless by the amazing amount of flawless, gorgeous stones, a virtual treasure trove of precious gems. After the robbery, one diamond dealer from the Canal Street Exchange committed suicide; he'd been wiped out and hadn't wanted to live any longer.

Gaspipe then proceeded to sell the same diamonds he stole back to the dealers he robbed in the Bowery diamond exchange—insidiously amazing. As the go-between, Casso used his friend, Big Frankie Heart, Chin Gigante's right-hand man, to facilitate the numerous under-the-table transactions.

"I made," Casso recently explained, "Big Frankie a wealthy man with that one heist alone."

This, too, further bolstered Casso's growing, sterling reputation within the tight circle of LCN's community.

Gaspipe *was* a Mafia household name.

CHAPTER 31

THE SEEDS OF THE WINDOWS CASE

Gerard Pappa had a severe high-cheekboned, triangle-shaped face and thick, jet black hair. As a youth, Pappa was the head of the Rampers street gang. As mentioned earlier, Sammy the Bull Gravano was also a member of the Rampers, and he was a close friend of Pappa's. In fact, Gravano would name his son Gerard in honor of Gerard Pappa. As an adult Pappa was a ruthless businessman—he would murder someone for being late in paying back borrowed money just to teach a lesson—just to enhance his reputation. He had been one of Gaspipe's best customers in the drug business—they made millions together. Good-looking, treacherous, and paranoid, Pappa was a particularly dangerous man.

Pappa, like all Mob guys, had his well-manicured fingers in many pies. One pie was Arista Windows at 99 Scott Avenue in Brooklyn. With his partner, Peter Savino, Pappa wanted to make replacement windows on a large scale for city-owned projects. Because the Luccheses had control of Local 580, the architectural and ornamental union, and could manipulate what window company would install hundreds of thousands of windows in city-owned projects, Pappa and Savino approached Christie Tick and Gaspipe, and a mutually rewarding agreement was struck. The

Lucchese family would put up $500,000 start-up money, to buy a warehouse building and get it up and running.

While this building on Scott Avenue in Williamsburg was being renovated in the spring of 1980, Pappa murdered two men there and buried their remains in the foundation. One was Shorty Spero, a nasty capo in the Colombo crime family—this was to settle an old score. The killing, however, was not sanctioned, and Pappa would end up paying for it dearly. You cannot kill a Mob guy and get away with it, period. Especially a captain.

The second victim was Richard Scarcetta, a loudmouthed punk who bullied and insulted most everyone he came into contact with—a known "first-grade prick," as someone who knew him well recently put it.

Pappa had such disdain for Scarcetta that he made sure he was buried in concrete just below where the toilet bowl was placed, so that every time someone crapped or peed, it was directly on his face.

Pappa involved one Bobby Farenga in these two murders. Farenga, who helped Pappa dispose of the bodies, was another Mafia wannabe. He lived on the fringes of LCN and was a bit player. He could be likened to a jackal that just managed scraps that others left behind.

———

On June 16, 1980, Gerard Pappa was shot to death in Dutchy's Luncheonette on Fifteenth Avenue in Brooklyn by a Colombo hit team. Years earlier, Pappa had murdered Colombo captain Shorty Spero, and now the time to pay the piper had come. Little Dom and his nephews Nick and Joey pulled it off. Knowing how hard Pappa would be to kill, that he was always armed, very fast and very game, they were hiding in the luncheonette's rear kitchen when he arrived; they approached him from behind and shot him in the head with a sawed-off shotgun, literally blowing his head to pieces. Pappa never knew what hit him. What he had done so many times to so many people had just been done to him.

Nevertheless, the windows business went on; a deal was cut so four of the families—Colombo, Genovese, Gambino, and Lucchese—could prosper, and prosper they did. They cleaned up by rigging bids and controlling every single thermopane replacement window installed in city-owned housing projects and buildings—millions of them. Everything went smoothly for years. The Mob had again created—through guile, fear, and intimidation—a moneymaking tree that showered them all with legitimate cash through Arista Windows, and other front corporations they set up. No fuss, no violence, no one the wiser.

Yet, this enterprise would end up sending a busload of Mob bosses to jail. It was, in a very real sense, the beginning of the end for a long list of LCN superstars. This simple window price-fixing case would end up completely destroying Anthony "Gaspipe" Casso's life.

CHAPTER 32

THE SECRET SWEEPER

The first chilly winds of the fall of 1982 brought with them the plans to kill one of the Mafia's most feared murderers—the homicidal maniac Roy DeMeo.

Gambino boss Paul Castellano had had enough of DeMeo. He had created all kinds of problems for Castellano: he brought the reckless Irish gang—the Westies—into the Gambino fold; he helped Gambino capo Nino Gaggi murder two made men in the Gambino family, Jimmy and his father, James Eppolito (uncle and first cousin of "Mafia cop" Louis Eppolito); he recklessly sold murder contracts; he brazenly sold drugs; he helped Sammy Gravano kill a New York City cop named Peter Calabro by supplying hit man Richard "the Iceman" Kuklinski. There were also rumors swirling about with the fall leaves that DeMeo was about to crack, that he was going to become a rat. He had all kinds of major felony charges against him, state and federal, and was facing hundreds of years in prison. People in the know felt he was about to "flip."

In mid-November of that fall, Castellano summoned war capo John Gotti and Gotti's right-hand man, Frankie DeCicco, to his ostentatious home in the exclusive Todt Hill section of Staten Island. The house was a big white residence with a sweeping view of the fast-moving Narrows and Bensonhurst, Brooklyn, beyond—the mean streets where Castellano had been born and raised. Castellano had summoned Gotti because he was the only one in the family who could take out DeMeo. Gotti was dangerous, ruthless, and cunning—all attributes that would be necessary to kill Roy DeMeo.

DeMeo, everyone knew, would be a very hard man to murder.

Sitting at the kitchen table, after espresso and anisette had been served, Castellano began talking about DeMeo.

"He," Castellano said, "is out of control. He has to go. I want you to take care of it. Quick as possible. He's been nothing but trouble. I never wanted to make him. Nino badgered me all the time and wouldn't stop. I trusted Nino. Now we have this out-of-control psychopath to deal with. He's selling murder contracts like hot dogs. I want you, John, to take care of it. Nothing messy, just do it."

"I'll take care of it, Paul. Don't worry," Gotti assured Castellano, and soon Gotti and DeCicco were on their way back to Brooklyn.

Gotti was overjoyed. He wanted to dance a jig. With DeMeo out of the way, he'd be able to do what he'd been planning on doing all along—kill Castellano and take over the family.

However, even the treacherous, overtly violent John Gotti feared Roy DeMeo. The whole Gambino family did. All of La Cosa Nostra did. Everyone knew that DeMeo and his crew had killed over two hundred people, that they bled bodies in the bathtub of the apartment in the back of the Gemini Lounge and regularly cut up bodies into pieces to help get rid of the corpses. Everyone knew DeMeo was surrounded by loyal killers, one more dangerous than the next.

This would be no easy task.

———

After trying to kill DeMeo through the fall and into a particularly brutal, very cold New York winter, Gotti and Frankie DeCicco weren't able to pull it off.

Castellano wasn't happy. He now had trouble with the law, too, and the last thing he needed was Roy DeMeo cooperating with the authorities. A long jail term for Castellano, at his age, would mean he'd surely die in prison—away from his family, his doting wife, Nina. Many on the street say that Paul Castellano should never have been made head of the family, that, yes, he was a good businessman, a good moneymaker, but not a good Mafia boss. He didn't have, they say, the street savvy, the killer instinct, the finely tuned senses to know who to trust and who to keep at arm's length, who to kill before they kill you . . .

In early January, Frankie DeCicco and John Gotti returned to Paul's home. They told him how hard-hitting DeMeo was, that he, DeMeo, knew better than anyone all the moves and dance steps to committing a killing. He knew what could lurk in shadows what a following car meant, the body English, the fast stiff gait of death approaching, the hidden hands that held cocked, always obedient guns.

"I'm disappointed, but not surprised," Paul said.

"But I have an idea," DeCicco quickly put in.

"What's that?" Paul said.

"We'd like permission to go to someone we think can pull it off."

Deadpan stare—"Who?" Paul asked.

". . . Gaspipe," John said.

Paul stared at John and DeCicco for long, tense moments with his oversized poker face.

"He's got the Testa brothers in his pocket," John added.

". . . Okay," Paul said. "He's a good man," he added, as if to convince himself. Castellano knew Casso and did like him and respect him . . . trusted him.

"So be it," he said.

———

A meeting between Gaspipe, John Gotti, and Frankie DeCicco was set up at the 19th Hole. Now, for the most part, Gaspipe conducted all his business from the 19th Hole. It was under FBI and Organized Crime Bureau surveillance, but Gaspipe made sure the locks were changed regularly and that someone was always inside so the feds couldn't bug the place. Gaspipe knew well the power of taped conversation and was always scrupulously careful. All the years he was in LCN, no law enforcement agent ever managed to record anything he ever said, a rare distinction, further proof of just how wily Gaspipe truly was. He always spoke in hushed whispers, his cupped hand about his mouth; if he spoke in a car, the music was very loud; when doing business in the 19th Hole, he always sat close to the loud jukebox. Gaspipe believed no place was safe to talk freely and was constantly aware of the fact that he might be recorded.

They met on January 5, 1983, in the back of the 19th Hole. Casso made sure the popular jukebox was playing. Speaking in hushed whispers and with age-old hand movements, nods, and winks brought over from southern Italy and perfected in Brooklyn, Frankie DeCicco explained why they were there, how Paul knew . . . what he had said—the difficulties they had taking DeMeo out.

None of this surprised Casso. LCN jungle drums had been saying as much for a while. Seeing no downside to the killing of Roy, Casso readily agreed. Roy was disliked by all of LCN. People did business with him but didn't like him. Roy DeMeo was bad news.

He said, "Tell Paul this is a favor."

They shook hands, hugged, and kissed, as is the custom.

———

Gaspipe next did the logical thing—he went to the Testa brothers, Joey and Patty, trusted confidants of Roy DeMeo. They, with Anthony Senter, were DeMeo's best guys. Gaspipe had gotten to know them well over the years, as they moved tons of grass he had brought over from South America. They met at a diner on Avenue U. Gaspipe succinctly laid out what he wanted. They listened intently. They all knew if they didn't throw their hat into the ring with him, they'd soon be dead. There was no other way. This was a one-way street.

"When it's done," Casso said, "you'll be with me. The Lucchese family."

"Straightened out?" Joey asked.

"Yes," Casso nodded.

Anthony Senter could not be made, they all knew, for he was not a full-blooded Italian, though he looked very much like Joey Testa, more so even than Joey's brother Patty. They were each six feet tall and had high cheekbones and full lips.

They readily agreed. They, too, knew this day had been coming, that Roy was destined to die for a laundry list of sins.

"And afterwards, we're okay?" Joey asked.

"No one's going to come looking for us?" Anthony asked.

"You're good. You have my word," Casso said, and it was done.

January 10, 1983, Roy DeMeo went to a meeting at Patty Testa's house in East Flatbush. It was a freezing cold day. Brutally chilled winds blew off the nearby Atlantic. Brooklyn felt like Siberia. The sky was low, mean, gray.

It was a good day for murder.

All keyed-up, a very dangerous, heavily armed Roy DeMeo left his home at 9:30 that frigid January day. He told his wife, Gladys, he had some "legal papers to sign." He drove to Patty Testa's home in East Flatbush. DeMeo was supposed to be picking up money due him—one of his favorite pastimes. When he arrived, Joey Testa and Anthony Senter were there. Roy sat at the kitchen table—wary. Something seemed off-kilter.

"Want some coffee?" Patty offered.

"Sure," Roy said.

As Patty poured Roy coffee, Joey and Anthony suddenly pulled out guns with the lethal quickness of a pair of rattlesnakes. Roy just had time to raise his right hand before they shot him. The first bullet was actually stopped by Roy's unusually thick and muscular hand. The rest of the shots, seven all told, reached their target—Roy DeMeo's deranged head. He hit the ground with a loud, meaty thump. The last image his brain recorded was the people he was closest to in the world firing guns at him . . . killing him.

Old towels at the ready were used to wipe up the blood. They all knew the bleeding would stop soon; they were experts at murder. Patty backed up Roy's Caddie into the driveway. They wrapped him in a blanket. He was too heavy for the three of them to pick up, so they ended up taping him to one of the kitchen chairs and carrying him like that to his car, where they put him in the trunk—an LCN tomb. A lamp that was to be fixed had been in the trunk and they placed it on top of DeMeo's body. The trunk was slammed shut. Anthony Senter drove it to the Varras Boat Club on Sheepshead Bay, as Joey Testa followed in a Porsche. They abandoned the Cadillac there in the parking lot. Soon, the freezing winds ripping off the Atlantic froze the body of DeMeo solid, his hands still defensively in front of his destroyed face.

Anthony Casso soon received the news. He was pleased. All went well. He sent word to John Gotti and Frankie DeCicco. They were overjoyed—the wicked witch was dead. Drinks were poured. Toasts were made. Hugs and kisses were exchanged.

"Good," Castellano said . . . "good," and smiled a rare smile, having no idea that John Gotti and Frankie DeCicco were already plotting to kill him; he had just sacrificed his ace in the hole, for "Gotti would not have moved on Paul with DeMeo around," Casso said.

Later that January night, Gotti and Casso and DeCicco had a celebratory dinner at Tomasso's on Eighty-sixth Street in Brooklyn. Gotti never thanked Casso. What he did say was, "You ever need something done, let me know," and they parted as friends, conspirators in an underworld society. But it wouldn't be long before Casso was stalking John Gotti and Frankie DeCicco . . . intent upon killing them . . . and sanctioned by the full Mafia Commission.

DeMeo's body wasn't discovered for a full week. The corpse had frozen solid and no odor came from the car. The people who killed him called the cops and told them about a "suspicious car" in that parking lot, and Roy DeMeo was found.

CHAPTER 33

DOUBLE, DOUBLE, TOIL AND TROUBLE

Racketeering and La Cosa Nostra go together as harmoniously as basil and tomato. Racketeering is one of the engines that drove LCN from its very inception. Even now, in Sicily, Naples, and all across the Calabria region, organized crime families run the unions—and new construction jobs—deciding what new municipal projects will get done and which families will get a piece of the action . . . everyone feeds like vultures, jackals, and hyenas on carrion.

Another industry LCN had a stranglehold on, on the East Coast of the United States was private sanitation; that is, the taking away of the tons of garbage all businesses and residences generate daily without fail.

Garbage, like the changing of the seasons, was guaranteed—a bountiful constant—another cash cow to be gleefully cut up by the families involved.

However, two heroic men in the far reaches of Long Island decided to defy the Mafia; decided to fight back; decided to work with police. Their names were Robert Kubecka and his friend, brother-in-law, and business partner, Donald Barstow; they would inadvertently cause one of the most successful cases to be brought against Mafia bosses—a first. It would become known as the landmark "Commission Case" and would result in the arrest of the heads of all five families—Genovese boss Fat Tony

Salerno, Big Paul Castellano (Gambino), Tony Ducks Corallo (Lucchese), Philip Rastelli (Bonanno), Carmine Persico (Colombo), and Christie Tick Furnari (Lucchese).

At the center of all these high-profile arrests—and convictions—was Robert Kubecka, a strong-willed, physically powerful man in his midthirties who had inherited a small private sanitation company from his father, Jerry Kubecka, on Long Island. He and his brother-in-law, Don Barstow, ran a carting business out of a nondescript office on Brightside Avenue in East Northport. They worked long hours and offered their customers better prices than the competition. They refused to rig bids or cooperate with Lucchese capo Sal Avellino. For long, tenuous years they defied the Mob threats and ongoing damage to their trucks and equipment.

Unlike his father, Jerry, Robert Kubecka refused to be bullied or frightened. He and his partner continued looking for new business to expand their operation, more than happy to undercut their competitors, who, unfortunately for Kubecka and Barstow, were connected to the Lucchese family. Fed up with the Mob's intimidation tactics, Kubecka decided to go to the police and seek their help. The Suffolk County Police Department's Criminal Intelligence Bureau was only too happy to use this willing though naive businessman. Robert and Don were assured protection and surveillance and that the cops would be their "guardian angels," but in the end they did little. Indeed, ultimately the police helped with shutting down Robert and Don—forever. Kubecka family attorney George Locks explained the situation thus: "They didn't know how much organized crime was making or that the biggest players in the Mob were behind it."

Eventually, Robert began wearing a wire and secretly recorded meetings he had with other carters connected to LCN, meetings at which he was regularly threatened. He got in way over his head, threatening the highest echelons of LCN, and he would end up becoming the linchpin in the Commission Case . . . a role he would pay dearly for.

Robert Kubecka believed in law and order, in doing the right thing, in fighting for one's rights. He believed that the bad guys would all end up in jail as a result of his testimony and cooperation . . . his courage. His wife, Nina, his family, and his sister Cathy—Don's wife—didn't want Robert going through with this. But he was stubborn and he was sure that justice would prevail . . . that right made might, and not the other way around. A fatal mistake.

A strange set of circumstances caused the Commission Case. It began with Lucchese capo Sal Avellino, who controlled the monopoly on the private sanitation business on Long Island. Avellino was also the personal driver and confidant of Tony Ducks Corallo, the head of the Lucchese family. When the Organized Crime Control Bureau (OCCB) of the NYPD realized this in the spring of 1983, they managed to bug Corallo's black Jaguar. Not only did law enforcement hear detailed accounts of an illegal monopoly in private sanitation on Long Island, but a long list of crimes the Lucchese family was deeply involved in, implicating the other families as well.

With this information, the feds got a court order to bug Paul Castellano's home on Todt Hill, and a treasure trove of still more valuable information was memorialized by the FBI for federal prosecutor Rudolph Giuliani of the South District of New York. Giuliani then masterfully used the RICO statute to indict the entire upper echelon of the New York Mafia, who were eventually sent away with one-hundred-year prison sentences.

Back on Long Island, however, the punishment for those causing all of Robert Kubecka and his brother-in-law's troubles initially amounted to little more than a hill of beans: fifteen people were indicted, most of whom got off light . . . 840 hours of community service for Sal Avellino and fines and probation for the rest. It was joke.

But, still, Robert and Don's assistance did, inadvertently, cause the arrest and sentences of all the heads of the families except for Paul Castellano, who was murdered before sentencing. It would take six long years for the boomerang that was Lucchese revenge to come full circle.

CHAPTER 34

GREAT USURPER

"What John Gotti did," Anthony Casso recently explained, "was the beginning of the end of *our thing.*"

John Gotti believed himself to be invincible. A brash, intelligent man, he was respected on the street because he always kept his word. In the end, Gotti made several fatal errors, which not only caused his own undoing but hijacked La Cosa Nostra of what little order and protocol it had left. He decided to kill the head of a Mafia family—the *capo di tutti capi*—without the hit being sanctioned by the full Mafia Commission—a cardinal sin. This reckless cowboy act was a by-product of Gotti's inflated ego, his hubris. Before pulling off his plan to kill Paul Castellano, Gotti carefully questioned each of the twenty-six Gambino captains, wanting to make sure they'd all line up behind him after Castellano's murder. Most of them backed Gotti, except Neil Dellacroce (underboss of the Gambino crime family), and the Sicilian faction of the family.

Gotti's right-hand man, Frankie DeCicco, was all for the coup, but even he had reservations. He knew the other families might come after John and those responsible. The Gambino family was, by far, the most powerful—it had the most soldiers, the most guns, and the most money—but if any two or three families formed an alliance and came after Gotti and company, they could very well all end up quite dead.

Frankie DeCicco managed to overcome his reservations. Gotti promised him he'd be made the Gambino underboss after Castellano's death, and with such a title DeCicco would become a very wealthy man indeed; DeCicco would also be the second-most-powerful man in the American Mafia.

There were few people in the world of organized crime that DeCicco trusted more than Anthony Casso. DeCicco had come to view Casso as one of the brightest stars in LCN's constellation. By now Casso had garnered a reputation as a diplomatic statesman whose wisdom far exceeded his years. He was also one of the sharpest knives in the drawer, a bona fide stiletto.

These two, DeCicco and Casso, had come from the same neighborhood and had known each other all their lives. They both knew the rhyme and the rhythm of the street, having come up the hard way—through violence and guile. They had balls the size of grapefruits.

They were friends.

Now, as John Gotti put together the pieces that would amount to the most audacious murder in Mafia history, Frankie DeCicco sought out his friend and confidant—Gaspipe. It was late 1985. They met at the 19th Hole, which Casso now owned.

Casso, perhaps more than anyone else in the American Mafia, was superparanoid about FBI surveillance, eavesdropping—snooping. His boss, Tony Corallo, had been bugged by the FBI. Paul Castellano had been bugged by the FBI. Casso well knew this and he vowed, quite literally, to never be recorded; he always spoke in whispers and made sure music was playing, and now he was having his home and car swept for electronic surveillance. He was paranoid in the extreme, and his paranoia prevented anyone in law enforcement from memorializing any of his words.

When DeCicco came to see Casso early that December, they went for a walk-and-talk on the sidewalk that ran along the cyclone fence surrounding Dyker Park. Here was where Casso had his meetings; here was where Casso plotted robberies and planned backstabbing and esoteric murders; here was where Casso discussed in detail plundering and racketeering. He knew the natural rhythm of this Brooklyn street as well as the palm of his hand, as well as Lillian's smile. He knew who belonged and who did not. A van that seemed out of place, he'd spot it in a second. Agents sitting in a car—he'd surely make them before they made him; here, the vast, empty expanse of Dyker Park would immediately give up any person or vehicle out of place. Off to the right Casso saw the Veteran's Hospital and the grand expanse of the Verrazano Bridge. The wind blew hard. It carried with it the smell of the sea. Gay Christmas lights adorned most all the homes, as well as smiling Santa Clauses and reindeer in a hurry.

Here, now, were Frankie DeCicco and Anthony Casso, both wearing ridiculously expensive cashmere coats, Brioni silk scarves adorning their thick necks, slowly walking along the Dyker Park fence.

"Anthony," DeCicco began, "I trust you as much as a brother. Something's up I gotta discuss with you. What I'm about to tell you has gotta stay here, between us; it's life and death."

"Of course," said Casso.

DeCicco took a long, deep breath. Casso could see he was weighed down by something very serious. DeCicco continued.

"John's intent on killing Paul—"

This caught Anthony off guard. He could barely believe his ears. The audacity of what DeCicco just said was a hard thing for his mind to wrap around. He knew the killing of a boss flew against the very foundation of the citadel that had become the American Mafia. This was anarchy; this was chaos . . . this, Casso knew, could be the beginning of the end.

Gaspipe said, "Fuckin' John's crazy. This is gonna do nothing but make trouble for everybody. The Chin and Vic won't sit down for this. We're gonna have to—all of us—come after John . . . not only John, but everyone involved in this, including you . . . Listen to me, listen to me carefully. There is no way John could pull this off and get away with it. You . . . you gotta stay neutral. If he's gotta do it, he's gotta do it. But, Frank, you've gotta be seen on the sidelines. I love you like a brother . . . you tie your wagon to this, you'll be dead within a year."

His words were quickly pulled into the flat expanse of Dyker Park by strong winds whipping off the nearby Atlantic Ocean. The wind caused their eyes to tear. By now, they had reached Benson Avenue. Here they stopped and turned and headed back toward the 19th Hole. They walked silently in their $400 shoes. Casso said, "You know, it really doesn't surprise me that Gotti would look to pull this off. I like John. He's one of the few guys whose word you could take to the bank. But this . . . it's a bad fucking idea."

"Problem is, John genuinely hates Paul. He thinks he's a greedy stupid fuck. The old man (Gambino) shoulda never made him the head of the family. You know it—we all do. For just allowing the feds to bug his kitchen is reason enough to kill him . . . let alone that he's a greedy cocksucker. He wants the lion share of everything . . . the guy's never happy."

"You know," Casso said, "if Roy DeMeo were still alive, John wouldn't even think of moving on Paul like this. Frankie, I'm not gonna repeat any of this—about anything, to anybody. But try to talk him out of it. He trusts you—you got his ear—sound him. He does this, the shit's gonna hit the fan. Big time."

DeCicco said nothing.

They walked on in a silence, punctuated by the mean Brooklyn winds.

CHAPTER 35

SPARKS STEAKHOUSE

B rash.
Stupid.
Audacious.
Ballsy.
Reckless.
Cunning.

These were all words used by people in the life and the media to describe John Gotti having Paul Castellano killed—murdered in front of scores of civilians. It was the kind of killing that gave the Mafia a bad reputation—caused the press and the police to turn up the heat, caused lawmakers in both Albany and Washington to allocate more money, more resources, more manpower to taking apart, indeed, destroying La Cosa Nostra.

Overtime would gladly be paid to scores of FBI agents in the field. Money for rats—informants—would be made available. Both federal and state prosecutors were only too happy to make sweetheart deals with bottom-feeding scumbags to get bigger fish with bigger teeth . . . the bosses.

At face value, Gotti killing Paul Castellano was a bold chess move that would, in a matter of days, catapult Gotti from the brash skipper of a Brooklyn drug-dealing crew to the vaulted position of boss of all bosses—the *capo di tutti capi*. Mafia royalty . . . a Mafia king.

———

The murder of Paul Castellano happened on December 16, 1985, in front of Sparks Steak House on East Forty-sixth Street between Second and Third avenues. Castellano arrived on time for dinner at 5:30 P.M., having no idea of the carefully laid plan for his murder or the bloodthirsty assassins who patiently lay in wait for him.

Like a pride of hungry lions cleverly surrounding the unsuspecting prey, with John Gotti and Sammy Gravano acting as puppet masters, an eleven-man hit team, all dressed in long white coats and Russian-type hats, converged on Paul Castellano and his confidant, driver, and bodyguard, Tommy Bilotti. As Castellano's car pulled up in front of the restaurant, a fusillade of rapidly fired bullets killed both Castellano and Billotti before they even knew what hit them. They went down as though they were struck by lightning bolts—lying on the street, bleeding.

It was, as it turned out, a flawlessly planned and executed double murder. After the killing, Gotti and Gravano, on their way back to Brooklyn, heard on 1010 WINS that Paul Castellano and Tommy Bilotti were dead. There was a sedate, quiet celebration in a closed Brooklyn restaurant, solemn hugs and toasts, kissing on the cheek by men who killed well for the new king.

The king is dead. Long live the king!

———

Within days—as is mandated LCN protocol—an acting head of the family must be voted on. All twenty-six captains showed up at Caesar's East Restaurant in Manhattan (owned by Sammy Gravano) and here John Gotti, not surprisingly, was nominated to be the new boss. Twenty-five-year-old capo Joseph Gallo announced that the killers of Paul were being "hunted" and that word would go out to the other families to show that the Gambino family was united and strong, intact and ready to deal with any kind of encroachment or aggression against it.

They were all truly good actors, because everyone there knew John had killed Paul Castellano, and that there might very well be a full-blown war because of it, yet they smiled and toasted their new king.

———

There were and still are those on the street who think John Gotti was a bold, assertive leader. They say that the way he killed Paul Castellano was how it had to be done. They say that Castellano's execution had to be loud—something everybody in LCN would see and know. They say, too, that when Albert Anastasia was assassinated it was loud and in the public forum (a barbershop), and they point to Carmine Galante, whose murder was also loud and in public. Who could ever forget the front-page photo of a very dead Galante with a still-smoldering cigar sticking out of his lifeless mouth? It is the way of the Mafia.

CHAPTER 36

JUSTICE, MAFIA STYLE

Gaspipe knew there would be trouble. It was in the air. The war drums carried the news of impending violence. The question was not if, but when and where. Casso hadn't believed that Gotti actually would kill Castellano. The plan was just too audacious and would draw too much heat to not only Gotti but all La Cosa Nostra.

Ultimately, though, Gaspipe accepted the murder as a daily part of the life he had come to embrace. For him, murder was standard operating procedure, as normal an undertaking as eating, breathing, and sleeping. Murder and LCN were an intricate part of each other; murder and LCN were synonymous.

Still, Gaspipe knew Gotti would have to pay, and pay dearly, for what he'd done. No one—not Jesus Christ himself—could get away unscathed after having killed a boss. Castellano was not just a boss, he was the boss of bosses, and he'd been shot down in the street like some errant punk, a mangy, rabid dog.

Where's the respect; where's the honor; where's the Mafia tradition that separated the Italians from other crime groups?

Four months to the day after the murder of Paul Castellano, the word went out that would bring the families together for the purpose of killing John Gotti. That day Casso was ordered by his boss, Christie

Tick, to meet Chin Gigante and his brother Ralph in front of the Victory Memorial Hospital on Seventh Avenue in Dyker Heights. Before Casso went near Victory Memorial Hospital, he made sure he wasn't being followed. When Casso arrived, Ralph and Chin Gigante were sitting in Ralph's car. They saw Gaspipe, and he led them to Christie Tick's house in Staten Island.

This was a highly secretive meeting—just the Genovese and Lucchese bosses would be attending. This is what John Gotti feared the most—the Genovese and Lucchese families becoming one in a common cause, and that common cause placing a bull's-eye on John Gotti's well-coiffed head.

Inside the house were Christie Tick and Tony Ducks, the bosses of the Lucchese family. After pleasantries were exchanged, Tony, Christie, and Chin went, mute and formal, into another room to talk. Ralphie and Casso had known each other for many years and were comfortable in each other's company. They made small talk, discussed the good old days and sports, but they said nothing about why they were all there. After an hour, the meeting broke up. John Gotti's fate was sealed. He was to be murdered forthwith in retribution for the killing of Paul Castellano. When Casso heard this, he was not surprised. He had expected it. It was the correct thing to do. It would put everything right.

Justice, Mafia style, would be served.

It was decided that Genovese soldiers from the New Jersey faction of the family would kill Gotti. It would be a sudden, violent attack. According to Casso, Chin Gigante was using his Jersey people because he felt they could be trusted more than any of his New York people.

Chin Gigante well knew that people in his own family were making money from drugs, off the record, because of John Gotti and his brother Gene. Greed, the Chin knew, might very well prevent the successful carrying out of this contract, but far worse could happen—the Gambinos could get wind of the plot and turn on Gigante and Tony Ducks.

This was a very dangerous business. The subtleties and subliminal nature of murder could be as delicate as the fluttering of a butterfly's wings; murder, for these Italians, was art, a blank canvas to be filled in with the bold color of blood. Murder, for these Italians, was not a simple black-and-white operation. There were family marriages and bonds to consider, politics—there was economics, there were the public and police reactions.

Murder like this, of such a larger-than-life person, had to be done just so . . . the right way.

Soon, lethal hit teams from New Jersey began to stalk John Gotti.

The killing of Gotti, however, proved to be far more difficult than initially thought. He was constantly surrounded by press. He was frequently at the Ravenite Social Club, and the traffic in Little Italy made any kind of getaway impossible. Traffic jams, parking problems, the press, and the FBI all conspired to make killing Gotti "very difficult," Casso explained.

CHAPTER 37

TOYS "R" US

In April 1986, the skies above Bensonhurst, Brooklyn, were ominously dark and foreboding. Trouble was in the air. With the promise of spring came the promise of sudden violence, retribution—revenge.

To successfully avenge the murder of Paul Castellano, not only would John Gotti have to die, but his right- and left-hand men would have to go as well. Thus, Frankie DeCicco had a contract put on his head, as did Sammy Gravano and half a dozen higher-ups in the Gambino family, one of whom was Gambino war capo Eddie Lino.

Here is where, for want of a better way to put it, La Cosa Nostra showcased its flexible killing prowess. Everyone in organized crime knew that Paul Castellano was backed and supported by the Sicilian faction of the family. Paul himself was Sicilian. Carlo Gambino, his brother-in-law, was also Sicilian. The Sicilian faction of the Gambino family, headed by Dominic Marino, hung out on Brooklyn's Eighteenth Avenue and made its restaurants and coffee shops their offices and meeting places—home base. Paul Castellano had his butcher shop, Castellano Meats, on Eighteenth Avenue, some fifty feet south of Eighty-sixth Street, a main shopping thoroughfare.

A zip got wind of the meeting John Gotti and the new upper echelon of the Gambino family would be having early Sunday afternoon, April 16, 1986, at Jimmy Brown Failla's Club on Eighty-sixth Street.

This was an invaluable piece of information; this is what everyone was hoping for . . . this was the time to act, to move swiftly and decisively—with the speed of a scorpion sting.

Because the Genovese hit team wasn't able to kill Gotti, the job was passed on to Gaspipe. Casso knew that the Sicilians, as a matter of course, used explosives to kill off their enemies, blowing them to pieces as they started their cars, as they ate in their favorite restaurants, as they sped along Sicily's autostradas. Casso decided if they killed Gotti at the restaurant—blew him up—all would think that Paul's Sicilian relatives had had their revenge, and it could all be put to rest. With the Chin's nod of approval, Gaspipe was given the go-ahead to blow John Gotti to kingdom come.

The Chin loaned Gaspipe a Genovese bomb expert by the name of Herbie Pate, an associate of the Chin's borgata. This was a colorful, interesting, very dangerous man. Once a police officer, Pate was now as crooked as any of the Mob guys in LCN. He was one of the people responsible for the famous French Connection's heroin being stolen from the NYPD's evidence office. An innovative, clever person, Pate lived in a fancy fortresslike house in Mill Basin, with a boat out back. He was one of those rare individuals who thrived on beating the system, on setting his own rules, on moving to the sound of his own beat. He was your basic black sheep sociopath.

Casso had a contact for acquiring the plastic explosive known as C4, which had the consistency of firm clay, but was much more stable than dynamite and could be set off with an electronic charge. He had C4 brought up from Florida to a motel he now owned, the Surfside Motel in Howard Beach, Queens. Several days before Gotti was supposed to show up at Failla's Club, Casso and Pate were plotting to plant an explosion that would be heard around the Mafia world. They went upstate to test the bomb Pate put together, to make sure the right amount of C4 was used. They tested the explosive on an old car, which was completely destroyed. Pate assured Gaspipe that C4 was very powerful stuff, "This is just the right amount—not too much, not too little . . . we don't wanna hurt any civilians."

"Absolutely," Casso responded, and they were soon on their way back to Brooklyn.

Pate wanted to use a remote-control device to set off the bomb. Both he and Casso had difficulty securing a remote, so Pate suggested they use a remote control from a toy car, which they could buy at a Toys "R" Us store. When Gaspipe heard this, he looked at Pate incredulously.

"Are you sure that'll work?" Casso asked.

"Absolutely. It's a simple electrical impulse. It'll work. No problemo."

Gaspipe and Pate were soon in the Toys "R" Us on Flatbush Avenue. It was a surreal sight, a *Saturday Night Live* skit, seeing these two in the toy car section, knowing the havoc they were really up to.

"Are you *sure* this is going to work?" Casso said, pointing at the remote-control car.

"It'll work—I've done it many times."

"You've used kids' toys to blow things up, that what you saying?"

"I'm telling you, it works!"

"My concern is that this stuff is made in Taiwan," Anthony said.

"It's just simple electronics. Don't worry about it," Pate said.

They bought three high-end electronic toy cars. When Pate tested them back at his home, they flawlessly sent a signal to the bomb trigger mechanism. They put together the bomb. Pate, a former U.S. Army munitions expert, hooked up the trigger mechanism to the C4. They would use a powerful magnet to affix it to the bottom of Gotti's car. Pate had engineered the bomb so its force would move up into the interior of the car.

The Gambino capo who had betrayed Gotti's whereabouts was Danny Marino, who had been loyal to Paul Castellano and who now wanted Gotti dead. This little bit of information was invaluable to the assassins.

Now John Gotti would get his. He would learn that the rules and regulations of LCN applied to him as well as everybody else—at least in the split second before he died.

Gotti, all the bosses believed, was the worst thing that had happened to LCN since Rudolph Giuliani. He was loud and brash—he flaunted his power. With his death, things would go back to normal; with his death, things would be made right, the assassins believed.

April 16, 1986, was a cloudy day. The sky was overcast and low. There was little wind. Stoves on every block held huge pots of tomato sauce filled with spices and gravy meats—sweet and hot sausage, spareribs, braciola, and succulent meatballs—slowly simmering. For Italians this was a day to sit with the family and share a great meal, catch up on one another's lives.

Yet La Cosa Nostra would use this day for murder.

John Gotti had called this meeting to help sort out the problems with the Sicilian faction of the family. They'd have coffee and Italian pastries and discuss business in low, barely audible voices. They'd then go home and enjoy the beginning of the baseball season on television, eat like kings, feeling whole and good and accomplished—knowing they had the American dream by the balls.

At one o'clock, the Gambino capos began showing up. They all arrived separately, parked their cars, and, unconcerned and unchallenged, walked into Jimmy Brown Failla's Club, where they hugged and kissed one another on each cheek. For these men, John Gotti was a star, their leader; all of these men were willing to fight to the death for Gotti.

Gaspipe, Herbie Pate, Vic Amuso, and his brother Bobby were in position. Anthony Casso was in his own car, parked a block and a half away from Failla's, wanting to see John Gotti's death.

Frankie DeCicco parked his black Buick Electra on Eighty-sixth Street. He got out of the car, crossed the street, and entered the place. He walked inside with a man who looked like John Gotti.

Showtime.

Pate then put the operation into action. He had two bags filled with groceries. He walked toward DeCicco's car, carrying the bags, just another innocuous shopper. Near the car he dropped one of the bags. Groceries spilled all over the street. As he was picking them up, he quickly stuck the bomb on the bottom of the car using a magnet. He put the groceries back in the bag and went on his way; the trap was set, the gun cocked—all was ready.

This peaceful, tranquil, Brooklyn Sunday would soon be shattered.

When DeCicco exited Jimmy Brown Failla's Club, Herbie Pate calmly drove toward DeCicco's car. DeCicco was with the man who looked like John Gotti—his name was Frankie "Heart" Bellino. He was a Lucchese soldier, a friend of DeCicco's who was in the wrong place at the wrong time. They crossed the street and got into the car. The doors slammed. Without hesitation, Herbie Pate pushed the button.

Immediately, the bomb exploded—*kaboom!*—its sound quaking the ground, trembling and shaking shop windows for blocks in all directions. The explosion literally tore Frankie DeCicco apart. His body was strewn all over Eighty-sixth Street. Frankie Heart survived the attack, although his left shoe had been blown completely off and his foot was broken.

The elation of successfully carrying off a complicated, esoteric, important murder like this was soon dampened, when all those involved, all those wanting John Gotti dead, realized that they had gotten the wrong man. The killing of DeCicco, though, was a reasonable consolation prize.

Gotti quickly figured out exactly what was afoot. For him it was just a matter of finding out who ordered the murder. The fact that an explosive was used immediately turned his mind toward the Sicilian faction of the Gambino borgata, just as Gaspipe had planned.

Still, John Gotti prepared for all-out war.

CHAPTER 38

A CURSE FROM THE GRAVE

I t was an unusually warm November evening in 1987 when it began to unravel. A combined federal and city narcotics task force headed by FBI agent Lew Schiliro was going to make a late-night bust. Bobby Farenga had fucked up—he'd sold a pound of coke to an undercover cop and now, at 3:00 A.M., the police were coming to arrest him as he lay in bed with his girlfriend. The door suddenly burst open.

Farenga, they all knew, was a nobody, but he might lead them to a somebody to get himself out of trouble. For selling a pound of coke, Bobby was facing twenty to twenty-five years in jail—basically a life sentence. This is exactly why wise Mob bosses Carlo Gambino, Chin Gigante, and Paul Castellano—the old regime—didn't want their people dealing in drugs. The punishment was too severe. Men would be tempted to turn on their own.

Though Bobby Farenga was only a wannabe—lacking fortitude, talent, and toughness—he knew things. He had aces up his sleeve in the form of Shorty Spero and Richard Scarcetta. He had helped Gerard Pappa dispose of the bodies. He immediately played his aces, saying to Agent Schiliro, "I got something for you—something big. Cut her loose [his girlfriend] and promise me you will help me if I help you, and I'll give you two Mob-related hits."

Schiliro, slightly built with a mustache and glasses, didn't appear like the jaded street guy he was, but he well knew that people will promise all kinds of things and in the end deliver little. He told Farenga that if he was pulling his chain, he'd pay dearly.

Conversely, if he was sincere, it would "surely benefit you," he said.

With that, Farenga was soon in an unmarked government car filled with gruff, heavily armed FBI agents, speeding over to the Williamsburg building that housed Arista Windows, which had been the tomb of Shorty Spero and Richie Scarcetta—who'd been pissed and crapped on now for nine years.

———

Federal prosecutor Charlie Rose was contacted. He sped to Brooklyn in the middle of the night. When he heard what Farenga had to say, how Pappa had killed these two men, how Farenga had helped bury them, he saw the possibility for something larger than just two murders. Within twenty-four hours, Charlie Rose was staring at Peter Savino, Gerard Pappa's former partner. Savino was not a hard man. He was not made. He was a businessman who got caught up with Mafia characters, rather than being a mafioso himself. He was married; he had children. When Charlie Rose offered him a deal to become an informer for his freedom, Peter Savino grabbed it. With the coaxing of Charlie Rose and FBI handlers, Peter Savino was soon hanging out in the Chin's West Village club, wearing a wire. For some unfathomable reason, the Chin dropped his guard with Savino, and on several occasions, Savino heard the Chin walking and talking and acting like a normal man. In reality, the Chin, though, did not talk; he always whispered. You had to get close enough to him to smell him to hear what he had to say. Thus, the federal government found the Achilles tendon of the Genovese crime family.

CHAPTER 39

MEAN STREETS

Because Gaspipe and Russian mobster Marat Balagula hit it off so well, Casso was soon partners with Balagula in a diamond mine located in Sierra Leone, Africa. They opened a business office in Freetown.

Casso also arranged for an Orthodox Jewish friend of his named Simon Stein, a diamond expert and a member of the DeBeers Club, to travel from the Forty-seventh Street diamond district to Africa to smuggle—in the lining and collars of great overcoats and in secret compartments of very expensive leather luggage—particularly brilliant diamonds back into the country. Casso loved diamonds and they loved him right back.

Lillian, who loved the diamonds Anthony was always surprising her with, had a breathtaking collection of diamonds earrings, bracelets, necklaces, and rings. She knew they had great resale value and would always be there for a rainy day; she had no idea about the perfect storm slowly, methodically heading toward her and her husband. Lillian did not question Anthony or ask where these diamonds came from. She turned a blind eye to their origins.

———

It didn't take long for word on the street to reach the Russian underworld: Marat Balagula was paying off the Italians; Balagula was a punk; Balagula had no balls. Balagula's days were numbered.

This, of course, was the beginning of serious trouble. Balagula did in fact have balls—he was a ruthless killer when necessary—but he also was a smart, diplomatic administrator and he knew that the combined, concerted force of the Italian crime families would quickly wipe the newly arrived Russian competition off the proverbial map.

Make no mistake—this wasn't because the Russians didn't have the stomach or will to kill decisively. Just the opposite. They came from an overtly corrupt society, in which brutal murder was the norm, not the exception, a place where the rule of law is regularly perverted and only applies to those with money and connections. They were all Russian Jews, tough and smart and very adept at finding new sources of income.

They, the Russians, not only killed their enemies but also entire families—excluding children—just to get to an enemy, settle a business dispute, or a slight of some sort, or to take over a racket.

It didn't take long for an infamous Russian, an accomplished hit man, to step up to the plate. His name was Vladimir Reznikov, and he was a full-fledged psychopath, one bad dude. He had been a paid killer in Russia, emigrated to Brooklyn via Israel, and quickly set up his business—the taking of lives. He killed whole families, coldly and methodically mutilated children, and eviscerated women from the pubic hairline right up to the throat—he was one badass motherfucker. Even Marat Balagula feared him. Reznikov, a strong man with a hard face as inanimate as a piece of ice, broad shoulders, and powerful arms, first moved on Marat's operation. He went to Marat's office on Avenue U in the Midwood section of Brooklyn. Without hesitation he took aim with an AK–47 and let loose a fusillade of .39-caliber bullets, which made Swiss cheese out of Marat's office, killing a close friend and associate of Barat's and wounding several female secretaries. He then calmly drove away. He was not afraid of the Italians. Reznikov often said he thought that they, the Italians, had grown fat and weak.

Reznikov next boldly went to Marat's popular Odessa nightclub. He brazenly parked his burgundy four-door Nissan Maxima right out front, ignoring the burly bouncers who tried to stop him—halfheartedly—as he made his way into the club, the scent of premiere vodka and expensive perfume greeting him as he entered. The bouncers knew him and wanted nothing to do with him. He had a very well-deserved reputation as a stone-cold killer, a sadistic butcher, a Rasputin-like madman. He soon found Balagula. They went to the club's office.

Suddenly, without preamble, Vladimir put a cocked 9mm Beretta to Balagula's head and demanded, through thick, nasty, tight lips and clenched teeth, six hundred thousand dollars.

Marat knew this was no idle threat. In seconds he was covered in sweat; his heart raced, his hands shook, his life ran before his panic-stricken eyes.

"And," Reznikov said, "I want in—I want a piece of the action."

"No problem, come tomorrow and you'll have the money," Marat assured.

"Fuck with me and you're dead—you and your whole fucking family; I swear I'll fuck and kill your wife as you watch—you understand?"

"I understand," Balagula whimpered, eyes cast down.

"Tomorrow," Reznikov said, and was suddenly gone, only the fetid, threatening stink of him remaining, like that of a large rabid dog.

The first thing Marat Balagula did was call Anthony Casso.

The second thing he did was have a massive heart attack.

By the time Casso caught up with Marat Balagula, he was home, surrounded by his personal physicians, the best heart specialists on the East Coast. Money was no object. He also had two full-time nurses scurrying around. His family hovered nearby. Marat, the head of the baddest Russian gang in America, the man who had developed the very brilliant tax skimming from gasoline, looked up at Gaspipe as he entered his room and saw his savior. Marat had come to view Gaspipe as the quintessential mafioso. He believed, correctly so, that Casso was cunning, honorable, and deadly. He was, Marat thought, the kind of man you wanted on your side—the kind of man you wanted to be in the foxhole with. Marat asked to be left alone with Casso. He explained what had happened, what was said, and how he felt. He had come to view Gaspipe as a friend. Casso listened with a solemn, stoic face, his funereal countenance. As far as he was concerned Vladimir Reznikov had done this to *him*. He took it as a personal affront. Casso believed that Reznikov was directly challenging him, defiantly spitting in his face, and daring all of La Cosa Nostra. He had known this day would come—and he knew exactly how to handle it. He said, "Send word to Vladimir that you have his money, that he should come to the club tomorrow. We'll take care of the rest."

"You're sure? This is an animal. It was him that used a machine gun in the office."

"Don't concern yourself. I promise we'll take care of him . . . okay?" Casso said.

"Okay," Marat said, sensing and feeling Gaspipe's steely-eyed confidence, knowing that this was what Casso excelled at—that he was a killer of killers.

"You have a photo of him?" Casso asked. "And what kind of car does he drive?"

———

It was now June 13, 1986, a warm summer day. The sidewalks were thick with people on the way to the beach. It was a particularly hot day, and the sun shone relentlessly. The Mets were in first place and on their way to winning the World Series. Times were good. Wall Street was booming.

At 1:00 P.M., big badass Vladimir Reznikov pulled up in front of the Odessa nightclub in the same four-door Maxima. Overconfident and petulant, swaggering, he left the car and went inside looking for Marat. He soon learned that Marat was not there.

Angry, cursing, threatening, he left the club and made for his car. There was a 9mm in his waistband. He knew where Marat lived and was, in his mind, heading there. Bathers were on their way to Brighton Beach. The smells of suntan lotion and the sea were in the air. Waves of rubbery heat issued from sidewalks and streets.

Gaspipe had chosen Joey Testa and Anthony Senter to kill Vladimir. Here, for the first time, is what occurred.

Joey and Anthony, two star players from Roy DeMeo's infamous crew and the killers of Roy DeMeo, each with scores of murders under his belt—two of the most psychotic killers ever produced by LCN—were in Anthony Senter's car, keyed up, waiting, cocked and exceedingly dangerous.

They had watched Reznikov pull up and, with the plates and photo they had, confirmed that it was him. They waited. Joey was going to be the triggerman, Anthony the wheelman—he'd pick up Joey and make sure they got away unscathed. A second car would act as the blocker behind Anthony and Joey and stop any kind of pursuit. Their escape was already carefully mapped out. They'd take the first right, go to the Belt Parkway a few blocks away, then head east, quickly disappearing in the fast-flowing traffic toward Canarsie, where they both grew up and knew the streets as well as their bloodstained hands.

As though in a well-choreographed ballet of death, when Vladimir Reznikov opened the door to his car, Joey Testa, tall and thin and muscular, full-lipped and angry-eyed—as focused as a hungry lion spotting prey—stepped from Anthony Senter's car and made his way toward Reznikov, approaching him from behind, taking fast, silent steps.

Before Reznikov even knew he was there, Joey raised a 9mm Beretta, took aim, and began firing, hitting Vladimir in the head, neck, and upper torso with numerous shots, killing him instantly. Anthony Senter pulled up. Joey quickly got in the car. They went right on Coney Island Avenue and were soon speeding east on the Belt.

Anthony Casso was soon called at the 19th Hole. Word that the deed was done, that all had gone well, was passed on to him. He smiled. It was an unpleasant smile to see—if you can imagine a white shark smiling, then you know what it must have looked like.

CHAPTER 40

HSSSSSSST

As Gotti moved the Gambinos to a war footing, tried to figure out who had attempted to blow him up, and who killed his right-hand man, Casso went about business as usual.

Of all the people Gaspipe dealt with in the underworld—all the thieves, muggers, murderers, rapists, larcenists, drug dealers, liars, and degenerate gamblers—he liked Burton Kaplan least of all. True, Casso did business with him, a lot of business. They made great amounts of money together. Kaplan had contacts Casso used and exploited; Kaplan moved enormous amounts of drugs for Casso. Casso felt Kaplan feared him so much, and so well understood the consequences of fucking with Casso, that he would never betray Casso or try to backstab him in any way. It was as if Anthony could almost trust Kaplan.

This would be one of Gaspipe's great mistakes, he would later confide. It was, after all, Burton Kaplan who had brought crooked NYPD detectives Stephen Caracappa and Louis Eppolito to Casso's attention. They had been a valuable source of information—and were paid assassins for Casso. When Kaplan called Casso in the summer of 1986 and asked for a meeting, Casso willingly met him. They usually rendezvoused at a luncheonette on Bay Parkway, next to the Marlboro Theater. Always wary of Kaplan, Casso sat down to listen to what Kaplan had to say.

"Anthony," Kaplan began, "I'm having a problem with a drug dealer. He owes me money, don't wanna pay. I'd like to take care of him." Kaplan stopped. "Me, Ray Fontain, and Frankie Santora. I'll do it."

"Are you asking me for permission?" Casso said.

"No, no, not at all," Kaplan said. "What I need, what I was hoping you had, was some .22s with silencers."

Casso remembered a while back that he had mentioned to Kaplan that he had gotten a case of these weapons, stolen from Kennedy Airport. Guns—Kennedy Airport was a virtual bonanza of guns: AK–47s came from Russia, Uzis from Israel, Berettas from Italy, and Walther PPKs from Germany. In a very real sense, the Lucchese family provided the entire La Cosa Nostra community with weapons stolen from Kennedy Airport. Gaspipe turned to Kaplan and promised he'd get him two of these weapons. A .22 auto with a silencer is an assassin's gun. It is, quite literally, the perfect killing tool. With a silencer on the weapon it made a sound that was little more than a belch, and the small-caliber slug had a tendency to bounce around inside the skull causing massive damage to the brain.

Casso again mentioned wanting to transfer the Seventy-second Street house back to Lillian's name. "Sure, sure, any time you want, just let me know," Kaplan replied.

"Okay, good," Casso said, and they parted and went their separate ways.

That Thursday Kaplan showed up at Casso's house. Casso handed him a paper bag with the two .22s and the silencers. These were particularly difficult to come by—automatics with manufacturers' silencers—and Kaplan thanked Casso for them. They made plans to meet the following week.

CHAPTER 41

THE GOLDEN OX INCIDENT: GOTTI'S REVENGE?

On September 14, 1986, the now forty-four-year-old Anthony Casso very nearly lost his life.

A hit team led by a Brooklyn killer named James Hydell was given a contract to murder Anthony Casso. Hydell knew this was a particularly dangerous business, and there would only be one shot at killing him. Hydell also knew the contract was coming from the Gambino crime family. Hydell, a psychopathic Mafia wannabe, was chosen for this job because he didn't have the good sense not to try to kill Gaspipe and he was just ballsy enough to pull it off. He was given the contract by Gambino capo Angelo "Quack Quack" Ruggiero. Ruggiero would later say that he did this without John Gotti's blessing, that Gaspipe was taking a larger piece of the heroin pie the Gambino and Lucchese families shared, and that he felt Casso was an imminent threat to the well-being of the Gambino family. Ruggiero's days were numbered.

September 14 was a quiet, lazy Sunday, a balmy day. Anthony had dinner at home with his family—his wife, Lillian; his son, Anthony Junior, age thirteen; and his daughter, Jolene, age sixteen.

———

James Hydell had been trying to murder Gaspipe for several weeks now. He knew if he didn't pull it off soon, Gaspipe might very well learn of the contract and strike first. Casso had numerous plants and contacts in all of the families, and the FBI and NYPD as well; time was definitely on his side. Hydell knew he was playing a deadly game here and he was intent upon winning it. This murder, he was sure, would immediately raise his stature in the underworld and would ensure that his earning capacity would increase exponentially. He would be respected; he would be rich; he could walk with his head higher. People would point at him and stare in awe.

Hydell had tried, without luck, to find out where Gaspipe lived. He had, however, learned on Friday, September 12, that Casso would be meeting Fat Vinny, a Gambino thief who had access to stolen bearer bonds he regularly sold to Casso, at the Golden Ox on Sunday, the fourteenth.

The Golden Ox was a restaurant at East Seventy-second Street and Veterans Avenue, a mile as the crow flies from Casso's home at East Seventy-second Street.

Casso, himself a consummate professional assassin, knew intimately the rhythm of murder—efficiently taking a human life when and where and how the job called for. As a matter of course, he constantly checked the rearview mirror, people's body English and their eyes, and made sure he knew all that was going on around him. All this he did automatically, unconsciously . . .

When Anthony got up to leave ten minutes before eight that balmy Sunday evening, Lillian asked him to pick up some Carvel ice cream. He said he would and left, having no idea that four tense men with very bad intentions, guns cocked and ready, were waiting to kill him.

Casso slowly approached the Golden Ox Restaurant. It was in a small triangular shopping center. He passed it and made sure all was clear, his dark eyes automatically reading and analyzing what he saw. He made a U-turn a block away, just in front of Hydell's car at Seventy-first Street. Hydell knew Casso was driving a tan Lincoln Town Car; he now saw Casso, and he and his cohorts quickly ducked down in time and Casso did not make them. Hydell had a pump shotgun clutched in his hands loaded with double-ought buckshot; it was a weapon that could blow a cantaloupe-sized hole in a man and readily tear off an arm or a leg. Casso made his way west along Veterans Avenue. He eased the Town Car into a bus stop, parked, and turned off the engine. This was an unusually wide two-way street and was virtually abandoned on this mid-September night. Stars glimmered in a cloudless black velvet sky. The weather was balmy and pleasant.

Now Casso made the dark-windowed car slowly creeping up alongside his car, the ominous barrel of a pump-action shotgun suddenly and insidiously protruding from the open window. Before he could reach for his gun under the seat, the car pulled up alongside and a thunderous fusillade tore into Casso's car.

Luck was with Casso: by his leaning back, the wide window post protected his head. Bullets and buckshot ripped through the doors, shattered windows. Gaspipe was hit. He got low and rolled catlike to the passenger side and opened the door. The driver had come too close to Gaspipe's car and the shooters could not open the doors. They were boxed in—an error in judgment that no doubt saved Casso's life. Casso got out of the car and, staying low, swiftly running in a zigzag pattern, took off like a bat out of hell. The shooter's car moved several feet. Hydell and Nicky Guido jumped from the car, firing recklessly at Gaspipe. He was hit several times more but continued to run with amazing speed.

He ran through the parking lot and ducked into the Golden Ox Restaurant. Bullets and buckshot shattered the glass of the front door. Like a madman, covered in blood, Casso tore through the restaurant, scaring to no end the wide-eyed patrons. He pulled a tablecloth from a table and used it to slow the bleeding. The restaurant had a rear entrance that opened onto Avenue U. Just near this rear door, Casso ducked into a flight of steep stairs that led to the basement. Having no idea of how seriously he was shot, Casso hid in the restaurant's freezer. He knew the cops would soon be there and wanted nothing to do with them. At this point he had no idea who had tried to kill him but if he lived, if he made it through this, he'd find them and make them pay dearly—profoundly.

Tough as rusted barbed wire, Gaspipe stoically sat on a barrel, seething, waiting for the hurly-burly above him to die down. The cold inhibited the bleeding somewhat, but he could feel himself growing weaker; rage and anger and adrenaline—pure hatred—kept him awake and alert.

Who? he wondered. *Who would order this?* His mind played over the possibilities—John Gotti, Gigante, someone in his own family—who? His mind reeled with questions.

When Casso was sure the police had gone—they had assumed he'd gone out the back door—he hurried from the freezer and made his way to Avenue U. He walked one block, found a pay phone, and called Vic Amuso, the head of the family, who hurried right over.

"Jesus H. Christ, what happened?" Vic asked, shocked at Casso's condition. He quickly drove him to Kings Hospital.

At the hospital, Casso explained that he'd been shot in a robbery attempt, still not knowing he'd actually been hit six times. The wounds were cleaned and dressed. Casso refused to let the doctors x-ray him or remove the slugs. He didn't want the slugs to be able to be used as evidence. Casso spent the night there. In the morning he left and went back home, the bullets still lodged in him, to his wife and children. Lillian had been worried sick and was appalled by his wounds, but as always she was helpful and supportive—she did not recriminate or condemn him. She was his helpmate and support no matter what, through thick and thin, till death do them part. The following day, Casso went to his own doctor, who arranged for a surgeon friend of his to come to the office and remove the six slugs.

Now it was Casso's turn to become the hunter, and everyone in LCN knew it—knew that Gaspipe had been shot numerous times, knew that he had survived, knew that heads would roll . . . literally. Casso immediately put the word out that he wanted to know who was behind the assassination attempt. The drums of the Mafia jungle resonated with that question.

More than anyone else in organized crime, Casso had law enforcement contacts, stoolies, plants everywhere. He reached out to them.

———

Greg Scarpa, the fierce, two-fisted war captain on the Persico side of the Colombo crime family (Vic Orena headed the Orena faction), was six feet, two inches and broad-shouldered and had a fierce countenance, dark eyes, and thinning black hair. Little if anything scared this man. He had, from the early 1960s on, unbeknownst to LCN, secretly worked with the FBI when it was convenient. He was a registered FBI informant, though he was very careful about what he told his "handlers."

More important, Scarpa had up-to-date information from various FBI agents.

As mentioned earlier, Casso and Scarpa were close. It was Scarpa who first told Casso that a Brooklyn tough named James Hydell was responsible for the attempt on Gaspipe's life. Casso knew Hydell in passing and didn't like anything about him; he knew, for instance, that Hydell had abducted a young woman, a neighborhood girl, from a bus stop near the 19th Hole when she was on her way to work, raped her, and shot her to death.

Hydell hung out, Casso also knew, at a candy store on Eighty-sixth Street, Josie's, a stone's throw away from the 19th Hole.

Why, Casso wondered, *would someone with his head on his shoulders give an important contract like his killing to a lowly tough like James Hydell?*

It made little sense. The only reason, he decided, was because Hydell was to be killed after he, Casso, was dead, thus ending any connection to the people who ordered the hit. It was *them, their* identity Casso was after. Hydell, Casso knew, was a mere cog in the wheel that had tried to crush him. He would, he vowed, find out who was behind the hit. Rather than just murder Hydell, Casso planned to abduct him and get him to a safe house, where he could properly exact revenge and, more important, find out who was really behind the contract.

Gaspipe first turned to FBI agent Doug McCane, who had been on the Lucchese payroll for ten years. He met McCane at an out-of-the-way diner in Flatbush and told him what he knew. Agent McCane promised to get back to Casso soon, knowing how important this was, because both he and Casso knew Hydell would more than likely make a second attempt on Casso's life.

For Hydell, the clock was ticking; it was just a matter of time.

Gaspipe soon found out that James Hydell lived with his mother on Staten Island, that he was always heavily armed, and that he had an uncle, Donny Marino, who was connected to the Gambino family. Hmm . . .

———

Gaspipe now turned to one of his secret weapons, the two crooked NYPD detectives he had on his payroll, Louis Eppolito and Stephen Caracappa. Casso ordered James Hydell to be picked up and brought to him.

"Make sure he's alive," he said through clenched teeth.

CHAPTER 42

HONOR THY FATHER

Surely, one of the finest books ever written about the American Mafia is Gay Talese's *Honor Thy Father.* This not only was an in-depth study of the Mafia's violence, but also explored in great detail how the Mafia came to be—why it was successful. It portrayed the life of crime of Joe Bonanno, the head of the Bonanno crime family.

Many people in La Cosa Nostra felt the book was too specific, and it created unnecessary heat because it spoke in detail about the Mafia as an enterprise—an ongoing criminal entity. It took a writer of Talese's talent to forge an understanding of the Mafia, focusing more on its traditions and mind-set rather than how the modern Mafia is really nothing more than a violent, bloodsucking underground society.

Honor Thy Father had been a runaway bestseller. People from all walks of life read it with great interest. It's a wonder it was never made into a feature film. More than likely that was because Gay Talese did not portray a sympathetic hero character anywhere in the book, but rather told the truth about a criminal society that was complicated—shaded and nuanced and filled with never-known-before details.

One of the more interested readers of this book was aspiring, hard-working, and career-oriented Rudolph Giuliani. There are two ways people think about Giuliani. Some love him and think of him as a hero, but many others see him as a dictatorial "my way or the highway" self-serving politician. Giuliani immediately saw that LCN was indeed an ongoing criminal enterprise and that laws passed as a result of Robert F. Kennedy's hearings on the Mafia could be used to go after the Mafia bosses with conspiracy charges. Eventually these laws would become known as the RICO statutes.

The first thing Rudy Giuliani did was steal the famous Commission Case away from the Eastern District Court of New York. For all intents and purposes, the Commission Case should have been tried in the Eastern District because the crimes were played out there, and most all the participants actually lived under its jurisdiction. Giuliani, however, saw the Commission Case as a publicity bonanza, as a way up the ladder of politics.

The Commission Case was named thus because Giuliani would go after the full Mafia Commission—the actual heads of the families themselves—and he would successfully forge a new way to fight organized crime that would result in the convictions of Paul Castellano, Anthony Salerno, Carmine Persico, Anthony Corallo, Aniello Dellacroce, Philip Tastelli, Gennaro Langella, Salvatore Santoro, Chris Furnari, Ralphie Scopo, and Anthony Indelicato.

Tony Ducks Corallo saw the handwriting on the wall. He and his co-defendants hated Giuliani with a fervent passion, but they had to admire him because he was a no-holds-barred, tenuous prosecutor who would do anything to win a case. Corallo knew that a long sentence for him would be a death sentence and he accepted that. Corallo was old-world Mafia; he knew that jail went with the territory. Corallo knew, too, that before his conviction the Lucchese family would need new bosses. He was willing to take off his crown; he was willing to put down his governing scepter. He just wanted to be sure that the hands he put the scepter in were able hands, callused hands, hands that could be gentle—but hands that could be brutal, too. As far as Corallo was concerned, there was nobody in the Lucchese family more deserving, or more capable, than Anthony Gaspipe Casso, Christie Tick's right-hand man.

Gaspipe was the biggest moneymaker in the family, and he understood the inner workings of LCN like very few. If the Mafia could have a prince in the latter part of 1986, surely that prince was Casso. Both Casso and Vic Amuso were ordered to a meeting at the home of Christie Tick.

When they arrived, Tony Corallo was sitting there as wise and strong as a stone Buddha.

Briefly, Corallo explained why he was sure he would lose the Commission Case. He cursed Giuliani. He talked about America not being a good place to live anymore. He said in his soft voice: "This fucking RICO law's un-American. They're looking to put us away for just talking. Anthony, I wanna give you the number one slot, but I gotta know you want it—I gotta believe I'm putting the family in the right hands. You want the number one position, Anthony?"

This, for Anthony Casso, was like having ice-cold water poured on his head. Gaspipe did not want to be the head of the family. He did *not* want the responsibility of dealing with all the Lucchese captains and soldiers and their egos or the task of resolving the squabbles and the problems between not only the different captains and soldiers, but also their wives. Casso dreaded having to administer, like a mayor over a city, the wide expanse of the Lucchese family.

Anthony wanted to do one thing—and that one thing was make money, plan and execute robberies, infiltrate unions, and create new and original ways to turn drugs into piles of cash. He didn't give a flying fuck about power. Since he was a young man he'd been Christie Tick's confidant. It was like he had his own crew—but in truth what he had was, in a sense, carte blanche over all LCN.

In a very real sense, Gaspipe was an envoy with diplomatic immunity that enabled him to travel throughout the realm of LCN, to make deals and friends, to generate money for everybody, to kill people.

But everyone knew Gaspipe was a "secret sweeper." Casso killed those within LCN's community who needed killing. He was a killer of killers.

Now, Casso looked back at Tony Corallo, a man he had as much respect for as the pope, and he was going to deny him. He took a long, deep breath as he said, "Give the position to Vic. I'd rather stay right where I am."

Corallo blinked several times, but he understood. He had half-expected it. His eyes moved from Casso to Vic Amuso. Corallo did not like Amuso; more important, he did not respect him. Amuso did not have the diplomatic savvy Casso had; Amuso did not have the political connections within LCN's world that Gaspipe had. But as Corallo sat there and stared at these two men, he realized Casso would make himself available to Amuso, that these two men, Amuso and Casso, might be a good working team. He didn't see Amuso being able to be a *capo di tutti* without Gaspipe there to advise him. By Casso proposing Amuso for the number one spot, he was telling Corallo and everyone in the room that he would support him, that he would advise him, that he would make all his resources Amuso's.

This was a given.

Nothing else had to be said.

Thus, Amuso became the head of the Lucchese borgata, and so began a new regime.

Tony Ducks now told Gaspipe that he wanted Lucchese Bronx capo Anthony "Buddy" Luongo killed. Tony Ducks had heard rumors that Luongo was planning a takeover of the family. As a ruse to get Luongo to Brooklyn, he was told there was going to be a sit-down over the Gambinos trying to kill Casso. Luongo showed up at the 19th Hole, got into Amuso's car, and was brought to a nearby house, where Casso, Bobby Amuso, and Little Dom Carbucci were waiting, having black coffee. Unsuspecting Buddy Luongo sat down for coffee and was shot dead by Bobby Amuso with a .22 auto equipped with a silencer.

CHAPTER 43

"YOU'RE UNDER ARREST"

Stone-faced and deadly serious, playing both sides of the fence, thinking they were invincible, above the law, Detectives Louis Eppolito and Stephen Carracapa were cruising Brooklyn and Staten Island streets looking for James Hydell. They had staked out his hangouts, his mother's home. At one point Hydell's mother actually walked up to them and questioned the two detectives. They were so obvious, bold . . . and outright arrogant.

Eppolito was a large, heavyset man. He had a huge round head, three double chins, and large, bulbous fish eyes. In his younger days he had been a muscular weight lifter; now he was an aging, overweight NYPD detective. He had written a book, *Mafia Cop*, and told how he had relatives who were La Cosa Nostra. Stephen Caracappa, tall and thin, was attached to the organized crime unit. He had a gaunt face, a long, straight nose, and dark circles under his eyes. Both of them had a sour sneer about their faces.

The two cops finally located Hydell in a Brooklyn Laundromat, washing his clothes. They showed their badges and placed him under arrest. He went along with them quietly, having no idea of the living hell that awaited him. He was cuffed and placed in the back of the unmarked police car . . . business as usual.

"What's this about?" Hydell asked.

"You'll find out," Eppolito menacingly assured him.

The two crooked detectives drove to a desolate Brooklyn garage. There they demanded Hydell get out of the car. Now Hydell knew that something wasn't right, that he was in serious trouble. His worries were compounded a hundredfold when he was roughly placed in the trunk of the car.

"Keep quiet!" Caracappa threatened him in little more than a whispered growl.

On the evening of October 18, 1986, the two NYPD detectives pulled into the parking lot of Toys "R" Us in Mill Basin. Casso was sitting in a car there waiting for him, anxious to get his hands on Hydell.

While this was about revenge in a big way, this was also about learning all there was to know about who exactly ordered the hit.

Hydell, he knew, was a mere triggerman. Casso still was not sure just who had tried to kill him, if it was Gotti, Gigante, someone in his own family . . . perhaps a relative of one of the many he had personally killed or had put to death, but he would find out, of this he was certain.

Gaspipe took the car Hydell was in and drove it to the safe house in Mill Basin. The quiet streets of Mill Basin were lined with trees filled with bright yellow leaves. As strong winds blew, the leaves took flight. In the garage of the safe house, Gaspipe opened the trunk, his face set in a pockmarked granite mask. Anger turned him red. Adrenaline shot through his system. When Hydell saw Casso sneering at him, reaching for him, his worst nightmare was realized; he was looking at the devil himself, he knew. Casso effortlessly pulled Hydell from the trunk by his thick, long hair, beat him with fists, then dragged him to a finished basement where he had laid out a plastic tarp.

"Who," Gaspipe demanded, "put you up to it?"

Hydell immediately spilled the beans, saying that a capo in the Gambino family, Angelo Quack Quack Ruggiero, had given Michael Paradiso and him the contract. Ruggiero was nicknamed Quack Quack because he had an amazing way of ducking indictments. Hydell also said that Nicky Guido and Robert Bering—a retired cop—were in the car. Bering was driving. There was a fourth man, Sammy Russo, driving a second car that would assist in the getaway.

This confirmed what Casso had suspected all along—that John Gotti was behind the attempt on his life.

As Hydell moaned, Gaspipe paced back and forth, thinking this out, looking at it from different perspectives. Contrary to what was commonly believed about Casso—that he was a ruthless psychopath, an out-of-control killing machine—he was in fact a judicious, particularly cunning, pensive man . . . a wily mafioso who kept his cards close to his thickly muscled chest.

He would not run into this headfirst; he would be careful. He decided to send for John Gotti and his new underboss, Sammy the Bull Gravano, to hear what they had to say after they heard Hydell, who didn't quite look human anymore. Hydell was so beaten and battered, his eyes were swollen shut and he had few teeth left in his mouth . . . a pitiful sight. Casso would later explain that he even felt sorry for him. Casso next dispatched Vic D'Arco, a trusted Lucchese soldier, to invite Gotti and Gravano to come hear what Hydell was laying down.

Gotti, not surprisingly, flat-out refused to come see Gaspipe and listen to Hydell. However, he was not about to ignore Casso because he knew that could spark a full-scale war among the Gambino, Lucchese, and Genovese families. Gotti was sure he'd win a war with any one family, but not with two families at one time.

Instead, he sent two of his most trusted, loyal captains, Joseph "Joe Butch" Corrao and "Good Looking" Jack Giordano. By now nearly forty-eight hours had gone by. Hydell's head had ballooned to obscene proportions. His face was a mass of black and blues, and the whites of his eyes were filled with crimson blood. Even Corrao and Giordano, two seasoned street guys, genuinely tough men, groaned at the shocking sight of Hydell when they saw him.

"Tell them what you told me," Casso ordered, still seething with anger, and Hydell dutifully told the two Gambino capos the story he'd told Casso. Wary, on guard, they listened. When Hydell finished, Gaspipe pulled a 9mm Beretta from his waistband and shot Hydell fifteen more times, finally killing him. Both Corrao and Giordano assured Casso that Gotti would immediately learn about this, that John had nothing to do with any of it, and that they'd make certain Ruggiero was dealt with properly—severely. "I want his head," Gaspipe said in a calm, chilled voice.

"It's yours," Giardano said. They left. Gaspipe turned Hydell's body over to Anthony and Joey Senter. They cut him up and left pieces of him in a Brooklyn landfill.

Thus, the stage was set for an epic underworld drama of Shakespearean proportions, the likes of which the world had never seen.

Mug shot of Anthony Casso,
Brooklyn, July 1972.
(New York Daily News)

Fifth Avenue and Union Street as it appeared in 1949, the place where
Anthony Casso was born. *(Brian Merlis, BrooklynPix.com)*

The Mob-controlled Brooklyn docks where Anthony's father, Michael, and later Anthony worked. *(Brian Merlis, BrooklynPix.com)*

The dreaded Albert Anastasia, CEO of Murder, Incorporated. *(The Associated Press)*

Union Street between Fourth and Fifth avenues as it is today. The young Casso spent much of his youth there. Casso's boyhood home is in the foreground, right. *(Courtesy of the author)*

The famous Mangano Social Club was several doors from the Casso home. *(Courtesy of the author)*

Mr. and Mrs. Michael Casso, Anthony's parents. *(Courtesy of Anthony Casso)*

Genovese capo Sally Callinbrano's club on the Flatbush Avenue Extension was a stone's throw from the Manhattan Bridge. It is here that the young Anthony Casso was first exposed to La Cosa Nostra society. The author is pictured here. *(Courtesy of the author)*

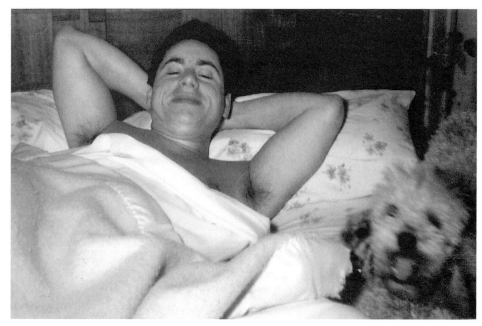

A relaxed Anthony Casso waking up in his Brooklyn home.
(Courtesy of the Carlo family)

Anthony and Lillian Casso posing at the Carlo home circa 1974. *(Courtesy of the Carlo family)*

Anthony and Lillian Casso relaxing in the Carlo kitchen circa 1977. *(Courtesy of the Carlo family)*

The attached home of the Carlos and the Cassos. The Cassos lived on the ground floor of the house to the left. The Carlos lived on the second level of the house to the right. *(Courtesy of the Carlo family)*

Next-door neighbor Dante Carlo was Casso's only friend in the legit world. *(Courtesy of the Carlo family)*

(LEFT TO RIGHT) Anthony Casso, Doreen Carlo (the author's sister), Lillian Casso, Nina Carlo (the author's mother), and Dante Carlo (the author's father) dining at Gurney's Inn at Montauk, Long Island, 1982. *(Courtesy of the Carlo family)*

Tommy Lucchese
(New York Daily News)

"Tony Ducks" Corallo
(New York Daily News)

Christie Tick Furnari
(Courtesy of the FBI)

Vic Amuso
(Courtesy of the FBI)

Vincent
"The Chin" Gigante
(AP Photo/Karl DeBlaker)

John Gotti
(AP Photo/Richard Drew)

Sammy
"The Bull" Gravano
(New York Daily News)

Amuso and Casso leaving a
restaurant.
(Courtesy of the FBI)

Police surveillance photo of John Gotti, Sammy "The Bull" Gravano, Anthony Casso, and Vic Amuso leaving a restaurant after lunch. *(Courtesy of the FBI)*

Casso attempted to kill John Gotti but blew up Frank DeCicco and his Buick on Eighty-sixth Street in Bensonhurst by mistake. *(Anthony Pescatore, New York Daily News)*

Anthony Casso shortly after his January 1993 arrest. *(Newark Star Ledger)*

NYPD Detective Lou Eppolito and his partner, Stephen Caracappa—also known as the "Mafia Cops." Both Eppolito and Caracappa were accused of killing eight individuals on Casso's orders. *(AP Photo/Louis Lanzano)*

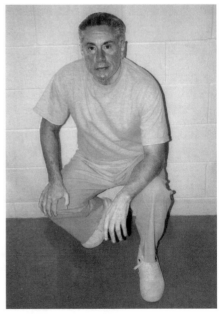

Criminal attorney Joshua Dratel is presently working on getting the federal government to honor the deal they made with Casso in 1994. *(Courtesy of Josh Dratel)*

Anthony Casso at ADX Florence Maximum Security Prison in Florence, Colorado, 2005. *(Courtesy of Anthony Casso)*

CHAPTER 44

THE BULL

From the day John Gotti killed Paul Castellano, the Mafia was in upheaval. That fateful day, Sammy the Bull Gravano had been sitting in the car with Gotti, giving orders, controlling the shooters. After Castellano's killing, Gotti made Frankie DeCicco his underboss. Since DeCicco had been blown to pieces on Eighty-sixth Street, Gravano quickly insinuated himself into the number two spot. He was now Gotti's second in command—second in command of the Gambino family. This was a high position. After all, the Gambino family was the largest Mafia family in the world . . . it had twenty-six captains, some twenty-five hundred made men, and thousands of associates.

Gravano would end up playing a pivotal role in Anthony Casso's life. They had known each other now nearly twenty years and had been making money together in scores of different rackets, the least of which was the dealing of drugs: tons of marijuana, cocaine, heroin, and Quaaludes. One example of the Casso-Gravano affiliation involves when the old West Side Highway had to be disbanded and taken apart. Casso and Gravano managed to get that job because of the Lucchese family's control of the Ornamental Iron Workers Union, Local 580, and they wound up being paid by the State of New York—splitting $2 million. They were also partners in the Russian gasoline tax business.

Gravano was born in Bensonhurst on March 12, 1945. Like Casso, all his life he wanted to be a gangster. Unlike Gaspipe, he did not have a college education in organized crime. He did not care about history or have the affinity for La Cosa Nostra's rules and regulations, or its mandated protocols.

As mentioned earlier, when he was a teenager, Sammy Gravano was a member of a notorious street gang known as the Rampers. The head of this gang was Gerard Pappa.

Now Pappa was dead.

Now Gravano was Gotti's right-hand man.

Regardless of how Gaspipe felt about Gravano, the fact that they had made millions of dollars together, and never had problems as such, did not mean for one instant that Casso trusted Gravano. Casso trusted nobody, least of all the underboss of the Gambino crime family. Trust, in the world of LCN, was a rare thing. The killing of one's best friend, the killing of one's son or father, was the norm—not the exception. Because of this, the men of LCN developed, deep within their beings, an invincible armor to live within the confines of the treachery inherent in that world. Innumerable victims of LCN were murdered and never even knew it; they were shot in the back of the head without so much as a how-do-you-do.

Every morning when Casso woke up, he felt the pains of his shooting; he saw in his mind's eye the assassins repeatedly firing at him. He knew that there were three bullets still lodged in his body. He'd lie in bed staring at the ceiling, becoming angrier and angrier, wanting revenge, needing revenge. Until Gaspipe had revenge, he would remain a victim. The whole LCN community knew that Casso had very nearly been killed. Not having gotten revenge was an embarrassment.

As hard a pill as it was for Casso to swallow, the realization that John Gotti might have been responsible for putting out a contract on his life infuriated him and kept him awake at night. Casso knew that Gambino capo Angelo Ruggiero had given James Hydell the contract to kill him while the both of them were housed at the Brooklyn House of Detention, and for a while Casso believed that Ruggiero had issued the contract without Gotti's knowledge. Now, Casso wasn't sure.

Since the meeting at Christie Tick's house between Chin Gigante and Tony Ducks Corallo, since the day that the order to murder John Gotti had been issued, Gotti had proved to be a very difficult man to kill. There's an old Mafia adage, "Keep your friends close and your enemies closer," and toward that end Casso reached out and set up a sit-down between himself, Vic Amuso, John Gotti, and Sammy the Bull Gravano.

Gotti, always wary, always paranoid, also seemed to possess an innate sense for a setup, and it was very hard to get this man into the sights of a gun.

Still, Casso knew, it would just be a matter of time. Meanwhile he'd break bread with him.

In reality, it was no secret that a contract had been issued to kill Gotti. The FBI came to John Gotti's club, the Bergen Hunt and Fish Club in Ozone Park, Queens, and as he was leaving they came up to him and flat-out told him there was contract out to kill him.

"Yeah, what else is new," Gotti replied dryly, smiling and showing off his pearly white teeth.

Nevertheless, in both camps, guns were loaded, cocked, ready.

The meeting between the Lucchese and Gambino upper echelons took place at La Tavola on Fort Hamilton Parkway in Bay Ridge. While Casso, Gotti, Gravano, and Vic Amuso dined like kings, the restaurant closed up tight. The windows were darkened. No one knew what was going on inside.

John Gotti actually liked Casso. He respected him, knew he kept his word, believed him to be a "man of respect." Still, with these men, personal feelings were irrelevant—they didn't matter; all that mattered was the making of money. All that mattered was being treated with reverence and respect.

Initially, the meeting between these four men was stiff and formal. Behind the warm greetings, the shaking of hands, the kissing on the cheek, and the hugs, there was animosity. There was the threat of sudden, instant murder.

Gaspipe, always a diplomat, now told Gravano and Gotti of a stool pigeon—Vincente Sly—in the Gambino borgata. He had gotten the name from Doug McCane. FBI agent McCane would be indirectly responsible for another murder, for the mark would be dead within two weeks. Agent McCane's giving Anthony Casso the name of different informants was commensurate to a death sentence.

Heroin was another reason why this meeting was happening that day. There was just too much money in the selling of heroin for LCN to look the other way. Casso and Gotti had been dealing in heroin for many years, and now from the vaunted positions they held, they could quite literally control the entire U.S. heroin trade. They were all readily in agreement that they collectively work together; they would import, distribute, and dominate the heroin trade in the United States. All "off the record," of course.

John Gotti's younger brother Gene had been given a stiff fifty-year sentence for trafficking in heroin, but that was not about to dissuade the Dapper Don, as Gotti had become known, a moniker he had come to grow fond of.

By the end of their three-hour meal, they were all friends . . . telling jokes, remembering old times, talking about different women they knew intimately. If you looked at them, they appeared like the heads of successful American corporations. In a way, they were successful American CEOs; their corporations just happened to be named the Gambino and Lucchese crime families, and their business was the business of crime.

"Anthony," Gotti said, "I'm glad we finally managed to sit down and break some bread. Let's do it more often."

"I'd like that," Casso said.

"Problem is, there's all these . . . rumors out there, about you, about me, and it's easy for misunderstandings to be created—this is something we need to avoid."

"I couldn't have put it better myself," Casso said.

Casso actually liked John Gotti. He felt he was an "old-world mafioso" who he kept his word. There were so many people in LCN whose word was worthless. John Gotti was not one of those people. However, John Gotti did have issues. One was his monumental ego. Casso felt that Gotti more often thought with his ego than with the very clever brain he had. Neither Amuso nor Gravano had much to say. Both Gaspipe and Gotti were in charge. When they were ready to go, Casso called for the check.

"Let me get it," Gotti said, and insisted on paying.

When they stood up, they each kissed each other on the left and right cheeks and embraced, as is LCN custom. To an outsider, they looked like friends—they looked like they enjoyed each other's company. In fact, both Casso and Gotti were positioning themselves to take the first and fatal shot at the other. When the right time presented itself, when the moment was right, Gotti would kill Casso or Gaspipe would surely kill Gotti. Because

John Gotti killed Paul Castellano without the murder being sanctioned, it was just a matter of time before he went the way of Paul Castellano: shot down in the street like a mad dog.

Years later, Gravano would take the stand in open court and swear on Bible after Bible that he never sold drugs, that he never sold heroin. This was not only a bold-faced lie, this would eventually come back and cause the entire Justice Department tremendous embarrassment . . . make a laughingstock of Attorney General Dick Thornburgh and all his underlings—Andrew Maloney, J. Bruce Mouw, and John Gleeson, prosecutor.

Not only would Gravano brazenly deny having anything to do with the heroin trade, he would deny that the meeting at the restaurant between Casso, Amuso, Gravano, and Gotti ever took place. However, the FBI would prove that this meeting did in fact take place, for they were staked out opposite La Tavola, and through the tinted windows of a blue van, they took pictures of Amuso, Casso, Gravano, and Gotti exiting the restaurant that day together.

Soon, the four men parted and went their separate ways. In Casso's mind, he knew it was just a matter of time before either he killed Gotti, or Gotti killed him.

CHAPTER 45

HOUSEKEEPING

asso, using NYPD detectives Caracappa and Eppolito, methodically went about killing all those involved in the attempt on his life. He first murdered Fat Vinny, shooting him to death and leaving him in the trunk of his car. Fat Vinny, Casso had come to believe, had set up Casso the night Hydell tried to kill him. Nicky Guido was the second shooter; his life was saved by his being arrested on cocaine charges and sent to prison. However, a second Nicky Guido incorrectly identified by Gaspipe's crooked cops was mistakenly murdered in front of his home in Brooklyn. Thus, Caracappa and Eppolito caused the death of a perfectly innocent man. The driver of the car, retired cop Bob Bering, died of a heart attack in mid-November. Sammy Russo was the fourth man involved. Russo had been driving a backup car. Casso discovered he had not known anything about the hit. Word on the street had it that Russo thought it was about a robbery, and this is what Anthony came to believe. Casso also found out that he lived with his mother. When he found this out, he decided to give him a pass, let him live.

Gaspipe was still unsure about who, in reality, ordered the hit. The question was, of course, did Quack Quack Ruggiero do this on his own, or did he get the order from Gotti? Either way, Casso wanted Ruggiero dead. But cancer beat him to it on December 5, 1989.

As Gaspipe had thought, with the mantle of power that Tony Corallo bestowed on Vic Amuso and, by default, on him, came a whole new world of responsibilities. A whole new world of troubles.

Between 1986 and 1990, a blood purge would take place within the confines of the Lucchese family, costing the lives of many Lucchese associates and innocents. Most observers of these violent killings would attribute them—some thirty-eight murders—to Anthony Casso's paranoia, as well as to his and Amuso's avarice and greed.

However, Casso was being fed a constant stream of information from crooked FBI agents and New York City and Nassau and Suffolk county detectives. Casso was killing informers.

There is truth in both motives. When Tony Ducks Corallo appointed Casso underboss and Amuso boss, he went off to prison for one hundred years thinking he had left the family in "good hands."

Relatively speaking, the Lucchese family had been so successful because they all seemed to work and play well together. Its previous bosses were wise, introspective individuals who ran the family applying the old-world methods.

But this was something else entirely; here now were two young brash Brooklyn upstarts—Casso and Amuso—suddenly controlling one of the biggest, most successful crime enterprises in the history of La Cosa Nostra, indeed in the history of the world. Relatively speaking, Casso and Amuso were very young to be in such vaunted positions.

The Lucchese borgata consisted of four different factions—the Bronx, Manhattan, New Jersey, and Brooklyn crews. All together it had 130 made men with more than a thousand associates. It had control over numerous unions and JFK Airport and had infiltrated just about every service industry in the New York tristate area, including restaurants, hotels, and private sanitation for all commercial businesses.

Many of the other Lucchese capos angrily resented Amuso and Casso being made heads of the family, and vocally said so.

This was not a smooth transition of power; here a bloody civil war was brewing.

Gaspipe felt the resentment. It was like static electricity in the air. That, combined with the fact that an attempt had just been made on his life, made him a very dangerous man.

Kill or be killed—one of the first lessons Casso had learned on the street—echoed inside his head.

It was no secret that Michael Pappadio—a Bronx Lucchese made man whom Tony Corallo had seriously considered for the number one spot—was resentful of Amuso and Casso. A dark-haired, broad-shouldered man in his late fifties who walked with a distinct limping gait, Pappadio saw Casso and Amuso as two upstarts. Corallo had put Pappadio in charge of an exceedingly profitable trucking company that operated in the garment district, and Casso believed he was skimming, stealing millions from the Lucchese family. Casso and Amuso abruptly replaced Pappadio with their own man, Sidney Lieberman, a move they felt would further ensure their control over the garment trucking industry; furthermore, they believed that because Lieberman was a Jew, the Jews of the garment industry would more readily do business with him. Pappadio was resentful. He began to publicly slander Amuso and Casso, complaining that they had put a "Jew bastard" in charge of a business that he had worked hard to nurture (the trucking company had an annual income of $20 million).

This was a fatal mistake; this would cause the handwriting to be written in blood on walls in the Bronx, New Jersey, and Brooklyn.

Gaspipe dispatched a hit team one Sunday morning to the Crown Bagel Shop on Rockaway Boulevard in Queens. Pappadio showed up there thinking he was going to a meeting with Frankie "the Bug" Sciortino, but he ended up being beaten severely and shot to death. His body was taken to the Woodhaven Cemetery on Woodhaven Boulevard in Queens by Frankie the Bug and, thanks to Casso's associate George Zappola, Michael Pappadio was unceremoniously cremated. Michael Pappadio would be the first of many condemned to the crematorium by Casso—the new regime of the Lucchese family.

Soon, a second Bronx capo, one Michael Salerno, ended up dead toward the end of 1989 because he vocally complained about Amuso and Casso being given the number one and two spots. He was found with bullet holes in his head and his throat slit from ear to ear several blocks away from his home. Casso and Amuso took over his shylocking book, which was worth some $7.4 million.

"He was a rat," Casso said of Salerno.

Next, on February 4, 1990, the crooked NYPD detectives Caracappa and Eppolito helped Gaspipe kill a Bronx soldier named Tony Dilapi, Tom Mix Santoro's nephew. Dilapi had been a business agent for the Teamsters union, which the Luccheses had held sway over since the early 1950s. Seeing the bloody handwriting on the wall, Dilapi, who was a wealthy man, hightailed it out of town, settling in sunny California. Fat and Skinny located him, and Gaspipe dispatched a lethal four-man hit team to murder him.

These killings were not lost on law enforcement officials—and among them Casso became known as "King Lear."

"Amuso," federal prosecutor Greg O'Connell observed, "has the title of boss but the real brains and driving force behind the family is Gaspipe."

Next it was John Petrucelli's turn. He was a Lucchese soldier and had made the fatal error of hiding fellow mafioso Gus Farace. Farace, a Bonanno associate, had stupidly murdered a federal agent and the feds' hair was on fire. They would not rest until Agent Everett Hutchen's killer was delivered to them either alive or dead. The Luccheses, like the other families, were suffering because of the intense heat, and Casso decided to put an end to it.

"You don't kill cops" was a cardinal LCN rule that was cut in stone and Gus Farace broke it. There was no forgiveness—no reprieve. He had to go. When Petrocelli refused to kill Farace, Casso had him shot to death, then found Gus Farace and he, too, was killed.

And Bobby Boriello, another Lucchese soldier, was also fingered by the crooked cops and murdered in front of his Bensonhurst home.

Bruno Facciola made the fatal error of *not* visiting Casso as he recuperated from the September attempt on his life. Caracappa and Eppolito, now on Gaspipe's regular payroll, four thousand a month apiece, also told Casso that Facciola was an FBI informer, that he had named the Dilapi killers.

Gaspipe hated rats.

He was the exterminator of rats.

Bruno sinned further by hanging out with some Gambino soldiers. Ruggiero had not yet been delivered to Casso by Gotti and—had not yet died of cancer—so Casso was still very much on fire. He still wanted revenge.

———

Anthony Casso had drastically changed. He stopped cracking jokes and was much more serious and introspective. He often just stared malevolently at empty space. He'd become a stoic, angry man with an army of dedicated assassins at his disposal. His reputation grew to monumental proportions. He was respected. He was feared. He was loathed.

Casso did not like the name Gaspipe. No one ever called him Gaspipe to his face. However, he knew he was known as Gaspipe and reluctantly accepted this sobriquet. It was almost like Casso had become two people—the Anthony that his wife and immediate family knew . . . and the dreaded Gaspipe.

Bruno Facciola was set up by being lured to a Canarsie auto body shop. As he entered he realized he was being set up and tried to flee. He was grabbed and dragged back into the garage, stabbed, and shot to death. A canary was stuffed into his mouth. His body was found in the trunk of his Buick, which was parked on a Bensonhurst street . . . a classic LCN hit.

As often happens, Bruno's death sparked two more killings to prevent friends of Bruno from retaliating. Next, Lucchese associates Al Visconti and Larry Taylor—B&E men—were killed by Casso's assassins. Visconti, believed to be gay, was repeatedly shot in the groin area.

LCN does not like "fags."

CHAPTER 46

THE CHIN

The Windows Case inevitably began to haunt Casso and many La Cosa Nostra players. Through the crooked FBI agent Doug McCane, Casso learned that Peter Savino—the man who began Arista Windows with Gerry Pappa—was regularly wearing a wire, that he was a dedicated government rat. Gaspipe immediately requested a sit-down with Chin Gigante.

Vincent "the Chin" Gigante was by far one of the most wily, creative, shockingly brazen Mafia godfathers. To put it mildly, he was "some piece of work," as a former FBI agent put it. For more than fifteen long years he was able to evade investigations in a most brilliant way: he acted crazy. He walked around his Greenwich Village neighborhood wearing tattered pajamas and a bathrobe, talking to himself, sometimes serious, sometimes laughing—always seemingly way out of touch with reality. The press ultimately dubbed him "the Oddfather," when in fact his ruse was a brilliant disguise. Sir Laurence Olivier, Robert De Niro, or Marlon Brando could never duplicate the Chin's outstanding performances. However, little by little, like peeling away the leaves of a stuffed artichoke, his ruse was slowly uncovered.

Whenever the Chin wanted to give orders to anyone in his borgata, he only met with the top boss. If he had to attend a sit-down involving other families, he would only do so with the head of the families and their underbosses. He trained everyone in his borgata to only point if they wanted to make reference to him. Nobody was allowed to make use of his name.

Gaspipe was liked by the Chin. Gigante thought of Casso as a star; he knew Casso to be trustworthy. It was because of one of Casso's crooked FBI agents that a sit-down was arranged at the Chin's mother's home on Thompson Street. When the Chin had a sit-down, it was often in his mother's home. She never left the house and it was pretty much impossible for the FBI to get a bug in her apartment.

The Chin had Casso and Amuso come at three in the morning. The Chin was convinced FBI agents did not work in the wee hours, and he held all his meetings then, "when the squares are sleeping," as he said. He had devised a clever though comical way for LCN visitors to come see him.

Casso and Vic Amuso were met several blocks away in the Village by Benny "Eggs" Mangano, the Chin's underboss, who took them up and down desolate downtown streets to make sure they weren't being tailed by cops or agents. Satisfied they were unobserved, Benny Eggs directed them to an elevator garage on Fourth Street. They parked their car, went into a tenement on Sullivan Street, and then made their way through a serpentine maze of basement cellars, passing sweating pipes, scurrying rats, and large water bugs; the smell of raw sewage was strong.

"It's like *Wild Kingdom* down here," Casso observed.

They finally reached the Sullivan Street tenement where Mrs. Gigante resided. They went up a rickety set of wooden steps and entered her apartment on the ground floor.

A larger-than-life character, a genuine legend in his own time, Gigante was calmly sitting at a simple wooden table. Everything about him was tranquil and relaxed except his eyes. They were dark and deep and shined like black oil.

Clearly, they were the eyes of a predator at the top of the food chain. He had been the head of the Genovese crime family now since 1981. He had, without second thought or remorse, ordered scores of murders. He could be as cold as dry ice, but he was obsessively dedicated to his mother, his siblings, and his children. He was the quintessential doting dad and concerned, loving grandfather, the ultimate dichotomy.

Yet the Chin was an ice-cold killer; even dressed in his frumpy bathrobe, he emanated power. He now warmly greeted Casso and Amuso as his peers, though in reality he was a seasoned statesman and they were fledgling journeymen. There was a very good bottle of cognac on the table. The Chin offered them a drink. Casso, of course, declined; he knew one does not ever drink alcohol at a sit-down. These were very serious meetings that often involved life-and-death decisions. Decisions had to be crystal clear, sober ones. Drinking was not only inappropriate, but a sign of bad character.

Amuso, however, said yes. The Chin poured him a glass. Amuso downed it too quickly and took still another. This pissed Casso off in a large way. He was becoming more and more disenchanted with Amuso. He felt he was lazy, greedy, and "stupid."

"My picking Amuso for the number one spot was . . . a mistake, in plain English," Casso recently said.

The purpose of this sit-down was twofold. The first issue was to re-solve the half-million-dollar loan that Casso and Amuso had given Peter Savino and Gerry Pappa to invest in Arista Windows. The second concern was Peter Savino.

The money, as usual, came first. The Chin listened to Casso explain how his and Amuso's investment had not been repaid and that since the Chin had ordered Gerry Pappa killed, he was responsible. Technically, Casso was right, but it took balls to demand the money from the Chin.

At first, the Chin disagreed with Casso. Immediately, foolishly, Amuso raised his voice, even banged the table for emphasis. Casso wanted to slap him.

"Vic, calm down!" Casso ordered, giving Amuso a look as sharp as an ice pick. "All we're looking for is what's rightfully ours."

They talked back and forth. Ultimately, the Chin agreed with Casso's position because what Casso said was just and reasonable. They had loaned Pappa and Savino a half a million dollars. The Chin had ordered Pappa killed. Therefore, theoretically, the Chin owed Casso and Amuso the money.

Pleased, Casso then told the Chin that he'd heard that Peter Savino had gone bad. Casso said, "We have a very reliable source—an FBI agent; he guarantees that Savino turned bad, that he's cooperating with the feds, that he's wearing a wire."

When Casso said this, the Chin showed no emotion. He had the ultimate poker face. This was an insult, for Casso was implying that the Chin could not keep his own house clean—or be trusted.

"I'll take care of it," the Chin said in his customary gruff voice. "What about Gotti?" he asked Casso after a few beats.

"Very difficult. He's all the time being watched by the government, and the news media. John Miller's feet are sticking out of his ass half the time." (John Miller was a dogged reporter who made a career out of constantly pursuing Gotti.)

"He loves the attention," the Chin said, shaking his head.

"Yeah, seems so," Casso agreed.

"He thinks he's in show business."

"I know."

"What I wouldn't do for a little privacy," said the Chin.

"Yeah," Casso said, nodding in agreement.

Relatively speaking, Casso had been lucky. He was not a focal point of attention by the FBI like the Chin was. The FBI has known for years that the Chin was, in reality, the consummate actor, that he had been making fools of them and they could do little about it. The Chin's very able attorneys had argued successfully numerous times that he was genuinely out of touch with reality—"crazy, as loony as a loon"— and that his mental problems stemmed from the years he'd spent as a heavyweight, then light-heavyweight prizefighter. Regardless of who believed what, the Chin's public insanity performances were a thing to behold.

Casso both liked and respected the Chin, though he thought of him as the most dangerous man in LCN. He was, Casso knew, cunning and wily in the extreme . . . a poker-faced killer.

The sit-down soon ended. Weary, Casso shook the Chin's hand, the two men hugged and kissed on the cheek, and Anthony and Vic soon parted the way they'd come.

As Amuso and Casso made their way back to Brooklyn, Casso turned on the radio to WINS with the volume up loud. While the station's customary rapid New York news reports—"You give us twenty-two minutes, we'll give you the world"—filled the interior of the fast-moving car on the Belt Parkway, the calm flat expanse of the Narrows on their right, the majesty of the Verrazano Bridge just ahead, Casso whispered to Amuso, "We gotta be careful; I'm thinking before he coughs up that kind of money, he'll make a move on us."

Amuso said nothing. He did not have the street savvy or the foresight Casso possessed in abundance; he didn't have the innate ability to decipher and understand the reality of his adversaries. Casso, however, possessed a gift. He could not only see way beyond his nose, around the next turn, but he had a sixth sense.

"We'll see," he said, his words drowned out by the news report. They got off the Belt Parkway at the Bay Eighth Street exit—the very heart of Brooklyn's Mafiadom—Bensonhurst. Casso parked in his usual spot in front of the 19th Hole. He and Amuso got out of the car and entered their home base.

The 19th Hole had become a popular watering hole for both Mafia elite and Mafia wannabes—guidos and guidettes. The jukebox in the back was hot. There was dancing, drinking, flirting. On any given night, you could find a dozen capos from different families, bosses and underbosses. The 19th Hole was neutral territory. Here it was safe for them to let down their hair.

Of late, young attractive Russian women with long legs and hungry eyes had begun hanging out at the 19th Hole, knowing there were very wealthy, oversexed, powerful men there looking to have a good time.

"How ya doin'?" Casso greeted a tall, voluptuous blonde at the bar.

It was all about unspoken gestures, eye contact, and body English.

———

Anthony's wife, Lillian, deeply loved Anthony. She was dedicated to him. He was her sunrise and sunset. She suspected that he had affairs, perhaps a mistress, but that was something all wives of LCN had to live with. For Anthony, any extramarital activity he had was nothing more than a passing physical thing—"fun," as he put it. It never went deeper than that, or became emotional.

Anthony recently explained, "Most all men in my life, everyone I know, had girlfriends. It goes with the territory. Women are drawn to us, the power, the money, and we're drawn to them. But only in passing. Some guys treated their mistresses better than their wife, but that's a fuckin' outrage. No class. Only a *cafone* does that. I never loved any woman but Lillian. She and my family always, always came first."

In the course of living the life Casso was ordained for, he was now spending, on the average, $30,000 a week on clothes, women, food, wine—the best restaurants in New York. Just pissing it away.

———

As promised, the Chin gave Casso and Amuso the $500,000.

CHAPTER 47

THE COMMISSION

This was a momentous occasion—the first Mafia Commission meeting since the Apalachin Conference of 1957. It took place in the apartment of Frankie Dap's brother, Louie, in the same building where Chin Gigante's mother lived. The attendees were John Gotti, Sammy the Bull Gravano, Chin Gigante, his underboss Benny Eggs Mangano, Anthony Casso, and Vic Amuso. It had taken many weeks of careful planning to pull this off. It was a hot August night in 1988.

Since the murder of Paul Castellano and the attempted murder of Casso in September 1986, all the chiefs of La Cosa Nostra were understandably skittish. They all knew it was just a matter of time before bullets flew and the upper echelon of LCN was shot full of holes. The Bonanno family was not invited—they were still persona non grata for openly dealing in drugs against the full Commission's mandate and because they allowed FBI agent Donnie Brasco, aka Joe Pistone, to infiltrate, and do much damage, to the Bonanno family. No one from the Colombo family was invited, either, because of the ongoing civil war between the Persico loyalists and the Vic Orena faction.

For these six men, Gotti, Gravano, Gigante, Mangano, Casso, and Amuso, having such a meeting was a near-impossible event, not only because of constant FBI surveillance, but because, in plain English, they were scared of and did not trust one another. In a very real sense, this meeting represented the world of the American Mafia . . . the United Nations of Crime.

To get to the meeting, Casso and Vic Amuso were driven to a nearby garage while lying under blankets in the back of a van. They were then escorted to the meeting place by Benny Eggs Mangano, again through a clandestine route that involved going through the basements of a half-dozen buildings. When Casso and Amuso arrived, Gotti and Gravano were already there. Casso had planned it that way; he purposely came late to make an entrance. Stiff hugs and kisses were exchanged, as is the way of these men.

Looking at these larger-than-life characters, all in the same room, all at the same time, was—surreal.

Brash and aggressive, always overconfident, pugnacious John Gotti began the business of weaving a tapestry of blatant falsehoods that would seem as truthful as the day is long.

"We've been doing the best we could to find out who took out Paul," he said. "We got a couple of leads. I got a few people in Italy tracking down some sources. With a little luck, we'll have their heads soon."

Casso and the Chin looked at each other incredulously. Everyone there knew for sure that Gotti had killed Big Paul, yet he had the temerity to look in their faces, boldly and without hesitation, and lie through his teeth.

This was a colorful charade, Gotti knew, they all knew, that had to be played out; this was a Shakespearean drama that would end with the letting of much blood, betrayal—the very fuel that drove LCN. John Gotti's performance was astounding and he would soon be rewarded for it.

"Well, good . . . that's good to hear," the Chin said, shaking his enormous head.

Casso remained speechless. He admired Gotti's moxie; it was hard not to.

Now that Gotti had openly denied having anything to do with the Castellano killing, here before his peers, the Commission could move on to one of the other reasons the meeting had been convened. In order for Gotti to become head of the Gambino family, he would have to have the official backing and support of all the men in this room. An actual vote was taken now and everyone in the room nominated John Gotti to be the head of the Gambino family, and thus Gotti was the official head of the largest Mafia family in America—a Mafia milestone.

Later, Casso would relate, "Of course everyone at that meeting knew Gotti did it. We were all plotting to kill Gotti since Paul's murder. Making Gotti the official boss would mean nothing once we killed him. It was all a mind game."

There were no congratulations or salutations. Interestingly, though, the Chin said, "Someone's going to have to answer for Paul's murder down the line," his words ominous.

They next voted on whether or not to allow the Bonanno crime family back into the Commission. This was voted down—they would not be allowed into the fold. Joe Massimo, though, was allowed to remain the Bonanno boss.

Now, finally, who would end up as the acting boss of the Colombo family was on the table. The Commission voted "Little" Vic Orena acting boss, not Persico.

A kind of pressure seemed to lift from the room now. The main order of business had been discussed and resolved without rancor or discontent. Everything was in place as it should be. The nuts and bolts that held LCN together were tightened and fastened. The machine that drove organized crime in America was well oiled and running smoothly, all these men knew as they walked away from the meeting—their heads high, their shoulders back, their step sure and steady.

And they all carefully looked over their shoulders as they went their separate ways that night, tight lipped and stiff, walking softly.

CHAPTER 48

SANITATION

Anthony Casso's obsession with rats, informers, those who would undermine the workings of the underworld, was at a boiling point. He had little patience for such people . . . in Anthony Casso's mind the only lower form of life than an informer was a rapist. Casso had come to view Donald Barstow and Robert Kubecka—the Long Island private sanitation entrepreneurs—as little more than rapists. It took six long years for revenge to come knocking on the doors of Barstow and Kubecka.

Because of his fumbling machinations, Lucchese capo Sal Avellino helped send away all the heads of the families, very much like dominos falling in a line. Avellino had been Lucchese boss Tony Corallo's driver. After Avellino left Corallo's Jaguar unguarded at an event in 1983, the NYPD Organized Crime Control Bureau managed to install a bug inside the car. Consequently, the NYPD was able to hear about all the goings-on of the Lucchese family, as Avellino drove Corallo all over the tristate area. Although Avellino managed to slip through the gilded net he had inadvertently handed the feds, the information garnered from the bug became the foundation for the so-called Commission Case and helped the government prove an ongoing conspiracy by all five families to commit crimes.

Now time was finally running out for Avellino so he turned to the greatest power he knew, and that was Anthony Casso. They met at the Surf Side Motel on Crossbay Boulevard, and Avellino made a formal request for the murders of Robert Kubecka and Kubecka's brother-in-law, Don. According to Casso, "These guys were informers. In this life there's only one way you deal with informers—you kill them. They were going from the state to the FBI. We had no other option."

By 1989, after being made underboss of the Lucchese family, Gaspipe rarely ever got blood on his hands . . . he pointed, nodded, somebody died.

Casso assigned two Lucchese killers, Rocco Vitulli and Frank Frederico, to do the job. For several days the Lucchese hit men stalked the Kubecka family. The job of trailing is intense—every hour that goes by on such an enterprise, the chance of exposure grows. Both Kubecka's and Barstow's homes and business were in quiet residential areas where strangers in strange cars stood out. As the hit men's anxiety slowly grew, so did the possibility for mistakes—and exposure. When, on August 10, 1989, the two assassins finally moved, they found Don Barstow and Robert Kubecka in the simple office of their private refuse-carting company in East Northport.

The two killers barged in and started firing guns. Don was killed quickly, dying at his desk with a look of surprise upon his youthful face.

Robert was another story. For years now Robert had been expecting this moment. Now, as he saw his partner and brother-in-law murdered, Robert exploded with years of pent-up anger and adrenaline fueling him. With the ferocity of a Bengal tiger he attacked the attackers, with fists and feet of fury, but ultimately, he was shot dead. So fierce was his attack that he caused Rocco Vitulli to bleed—and to leave traces of his blood behind. Not only that but Barstow also forced the assassins to leave a duffel bag behind containing a second pistol—evidence. In the world of professional murder, this was a major blunder. To leave behind one's blood and a tool of the trade—a gun—were mortal sins.

From a publicity point of view, the murder of two upstanding businessmen, hardworking little guys trying to make ends meet, was a major blow to La Cosa Nostra. On the other hand, however, such low-level murders sent a warning—shock waves, really—to those who would defy LCN. *You'll pay with your life.* It was a loud, resounding message that few could ignore. Both these men, two brothers-in-law looking for a little slice of the American pie, were laid out in coffins for all to see and know, brought down before their time, leaving behind loving parents, wives, children, friends, and neighbors.

This kind of killing—murder outside those within the world of LCN—would prove to be a major fuckup. The day that Robert and Don were killed, they were forty and thirty-five years old, respectively; they left behind five children.

In reality, it was not only the Lucchese crime family that was responsible for the deaths of Don and Robert. All along, from the very beginning, they had been promised protection by different police departments. They had been assured twenty-four-hour police protection and security cameras. They had been assured that a vast network of informers would know, would give warning way before violence actually occurred. All this turned out to be painfully untrue. Whether it was malicious behavior or incompetence or, more than likely, a fusion of the two, the fact remains that Robert and Don were as easy to hit as the side of a barn. These were not street-savvy individuals who knew the irrationally violent rhythm of LCN. They were hardworking men who found themselves in a competitive business dominated by the Mafia.

Later, in a lawsuit brought by the widows of Robert and Don, a federal judge found that the authorities were "grossly negligent" in protecting the lives of Kubecka and Barstow, and in an out-of-court settlement, the families were awarded $9.6 million.

These killings were surely among the worst ever of LCN.

CHAPTER 49

SAUSAGE FINGERS

Lucchese war capo Fat Pete Chiodo was six feet, six inches and weighed 410 pounds, a hulking monster. He had black hair and a huge, oddly good-looking face with big round eyes that seemed to match the roundness of his head. He was a fierce war captain in the Lucchese family, a trusted ally of Gaspipe's—a natural-born killer. Since he was a little boy he'd been known as Fat Pete. He was always bigger and stronger than any of his classmates, and he learned to turn his disability, being excessively heavy, into an asset. When he was a young boy, he was a strong and fearless fighter. Raised in Bensonhurst, Chiodo was born into the Mafia culture. Since he was a child his dream was to be made—a man of respect, a man who was feared not for what he said, but for what he did. Early on in his career of crime he was a strong-arm man, collecting bad bets and money owed to La Cosa Nostra shylocks, and so on. The thing about Fat Pete Chiodo was that he seemed to enjoy it when people didn't have the money due. He relished beating them up, breaking arms, making sure they never forgot their run-in with him. Peter Chiodo liked to leave an impression on people, and that impression was, "Don't fuck with me!"

Many times over the years, Casso had seen Fat Pete brutalize people, breaking bones and tearing flesh—leaving people so beaten and battered they could not move for many hours on end and would never be the same after. Peter also was an efficient killer. Before being made captain, he personally murdered over a dozen people.

It was a funny sight watching Peter Chiodo and Anthony Casso walk down a Brooklyn street, for Chiodo dwarfed Casso like an adult a child. But in the world of LCN, it was Casso who dwarfed Chiodo. It was Gaspipe who was the giant, and Chiodo who was the smaller of the two.

For the most part, Peter Chiodo was one of the few people in LCN whom Casso trusted. He thought of Fat Pete more like a brother. Like Casso, Fat Pete loved good things (wine and beautiful women and expensive clothes). He had a diamond pinkie ring as large as a walnut on his enormous right hand. He also had scars and bruises from pummeling people with his huge right fist.

Chiodo ran his own crew and was a very good moneymaker. He moved awfully fast for such a big man, and he was one of those rare individuals who had an inherent abundance of street savvy.

One of the many enterprises Chiodo was involved in was a landfill in New Jersey. He allowed all kinds of illegal refuse to be dumped while gleefully collecting exorbitant amounts of money. The FBI somehow managed to bug his office near the landfill, and even installed a camera at the top of a nearby telephone pole to document who was coming and going. Gaspipe's contact in the FBI, Doug McCane, advised Fat Pete of the camera and said that he should be very careful. But instead Chiodo got a black employee of his to climb up the pole to take a look. The very next day McCane told Casso about this event, which took place only twenty-four hours after McCane initially told Chiodo about the camera. Thus the feds already knew that Chiodo had been tipped off by one of their own.

The FBI did not take kindly to this. During the many years of J. Edgar Hoover's stewardship, the FBI prided itself on always being above reproach. The bureau's PR let the world know there was no such thing as an FBI agent on the take, as was the regular case with city and state municipalities across the country. It was only after J. Edgar Hoover's death, and a certain lowering of standards on the FBI's part, that crooked agents were being discovered. Because the camera had been found out so quickly, the FBI knew one of its own was a traitor, that one of its own was not just working with the enemy in the 24/7 struggle between LCN and the FBI but was immediately feeding them information.

Suddenly, agents' lives were at risk; suddenly, agents working on building a case against the Lucchese family started looking over their shoulders. This was far more than a matter of a bad apple; this, the agency knew, could be a typhoid fever that infected the very foundations of the FBI's war against organized crime.

Agents began to scrutinize one another, wondering if their partners were traitors . . . if their partners were sleeping with the enemy.

When Casso found out what Fat Pete had done, he was surprised and angered, and he called Fat Pete on the carpet for it. This infraction would just be the beginning of a literal, all-out war between Gaspipe, Vic Amuso, and Fat Pete Chiodo.

———

Fat Pete was one of the Lucchese people drawn into the Windows Case. As close as Fat Pete and Casso were over the years—like brothers—Fat Pete knew Gaspipe would kill him in heartbeat if he had to. Nothing personal, just business. Still, he would be dead as a doornail.

The fact that Casso was killing Lucchese soldiers all over the place was not lost on Fat Pete. But Fat Pete felt close to Casso, and he did not yet think in terms of trying to kill Casso before Casso tried to kill him. He would be respectful; he would make sure that he kept Casso as close to him as possible—a friend.

When Fat Pete was drawn into the Windows Case, his life was radically altered—it caused him to flee into the Witness Protection Program, caused him to become an informer against the people he had been closest to his entire life—caused him to be shot twelve times.

CHAPTER 50

STARTER

Beginning in the 1950s, the Lucchese clan began infiltrating unions thanks to Tommy Lucchese. This proved to be one of the most lucrative of all La Cosa Nostra schemes. The Mob was able to rig bids and control plum jobs, making millions of dollars every year. The Mafia also had free access to union pension funds and regularly made sweetheart deals—borrowing money at no interest rate, which the families turned around and shylocked on the street for outrageous rates.

In the late 1980s, union boss James Bishop—Gaspipe learned through his crooked detectives Caracappa and Eppolito—was talking to the Manhattan D.A.'s office. His fate was sealed. Casso dispatched two Lucchese hit men, and Bishop was shot in the head with automatics with silencers.

Tough-as-steel John "Sonny" Morrissey was a shop steward in the ironworkers' local, repping window installers. Their union had been controlled by the Luccheses since the early 1950s. Mistakenly, Casso came to believe that Morrissey, a bagman for LCN, was a rat, and he ordered Morrissey killed—though he didn't want it to look like a murder. "Just make him disappear," he said. "I want it to look like he took it on the lam."

Casso had Morrissey's remains buried in a Canarsie landfill. They were never found.

There was a growing discontent—uneasiness—in the Lucchese family. No one knew who might be next. Fear and paranoia were creating discontent, the rumblings of rebellion.

Casso, of course, sensed this, which only heightened his sense of isolation.

For him, it all added up to that old adage, "He who fires first, fires last."

———

With Gaspipe's new role of underboss came a whole host of entanglements and involvements. He no longer had time for the hands-on approach to new crimes, scores, and schemes. In addition, his many new responsibilities stole him away from his kids—Anthony and Jolene—and from Lillian. He was home less and less. Most of the time when he went out with Lillian now, it was to some kind of LCN event—a wedding, christening, birthday party, or funeral. Lillian was blindly dedicated to Anthony and loved him dearly. Anthony told her very little about his business, his high rank in LCN, but Lillian knew that her husband wielded a great deal of power. She saw the respect he was given, how people bowed to him and treated him with absolute reverence; she also saw the abject fear he caused in people.

Casso made sure anything his wife or children needed was quickly provided. Nothing was too good for them. He spent millions on their new home in Mill Basin. He hired a well-known architect, Anthony Fava, a handsome, snappy dresser, to plan the design and oversee construction. Fava had also done work on Lucchese capo Peter Chiodo's home.

Then, Anthony came to believe that Fava was a threat. "He knew too much," he recently explained.

There were rumors that Fava had insulted Anthony by prematurely presenting an exorbitantly high bill, that he had been disrespectful to Lillian, that he had made a pass at her, that he was reporting to the FBI the large sums of money Anthony was spending on the home, and that he was having an affair with Lillian.

"All nonsense," Casso says. "He was close to Fat Pete and we knew Fat Pete went bad. He knew too much. Period."

Fava, however, was not only murdered, he was severely tortured before he was killed. There were numerous bullet and knife wounds all over his body, plus he'd been tortured with fire—his face, arms, legs, chest, and genitals had been scorched. He was found in the trunk of a stolen car on Thursday, September 19, 1991, a tattered shell of who he'd been. Casso says that Fava should not have been tortured, that he had just ordered him "hit."

"They got carried away," says Casso. "I gave Richie Pagliarulo, a Lucchese soldier, the job. Richie was a little demented, I would say."

CHAPTER 51

THE KILLING OF VINNIE ALBANO

Crooked cop Vinnie Albano was one of the arresting officers in the French Connection Case. When recently queried about this infamous case, Anthony Casso had a lot to say, because he knew intimately what happened—how seventy-two kilos of heroin had been stolen from the evidence office of the NYPD. Albano had arranged with Lucchese associate Herbie Pate to steal the heroin. This was a bold, audacious, amazingly ballsy scheme that involved Herbie Pate posing as a uniformed cop, walking up to the clerk, and presenting the right forged papers as he smiled and cracked jokes and said all the right things the right ways; amazingly, he was given the heroin.

Albano and Pate then partnered up in the selling of the dope, and without difficulty they sold it all within several weeks, making millions of dollars, a percentage of which was kicked up to Casso.

Pate and Albano became tight like brothers. They bought homes close to each other on the waterfront in Bergen Beach, Brooklyn. For years they sold heroin for Casso, everyone making stacks of money. After a time, Albano began accusing Pate of taking money behind his back, of lying about the amounts of money that the heroin sold for, and the two men quickly became enemies. Vinnie Albano was a physically tough man. He had a bad temper. Alarmed by his aggression, Pate went to Casso and complained about him, and he asked Casso for a gun. Casso provided him with a five-shot Smith and Wesson. At this time, Herbie was employed as an oiler with the engineers' union and was working at a job at the Owls Head water plant located right off the Belt Parkway, near Sixty-ninth Street. One evening, in an irrational fit of anger, Albano tried to run Herbie over with his car when he showed up for work. Pate jumped out of the way just in time . . . Albano leapt from the car and began to pummel Pate. He got Pate on the floor and kicked him and punched him in the head and the face. Pate managed to pull out the gun Casso had given him and emptied it into Albano's chest. Albano was dead before he knew it, the reports of the gunshots ringing in his dying brain.

Pate, remaining cool, put Albano in the trunk of his own car, drove to a nearby telephone booth, and called Gaspipe. He told Casso to meet him at the Bay Parkway exit off the Belt . . . that it was "important." Casso, who had come to trust and like Pate and to know that he was not an alarmist, agreed to meet him. The ride from Casso's home to the Bay Parkway exit was a mere ten minutes. Pate explained what happened and showed him Vinnie Albano's body.

"Okay, follow me. I know exactly what to do with him," Casso said, always cool, always in control.

Casso led Pate over the Verrazano Bridge to Staten Island and parked Albano's car across the street from a doctor's parking spot at University Hospital and left it there, where Casso believed the body would be found quickly. Casso then drove Pate back to his job, feeling bad for Vinnie Albano. He had a nice family, a lovely wife, great kids, and he had once helped Casso's bypass gang destroy evidence in Brooklyn's Supreme Court building: in that instance, Albano had taken a briefcase containing incriminating tapes, which were to be used as evidence, from the D.A.'s office on the seventh floor up to the courtroom; while in the elevator Albano used large magnets hidden in a briefcase to erase the data on the tapes. He had used his gold detective shield to smuggle the magnets into the building. The case, of course, was thrown out of court, the assistant D.A. scratching his head, wondering what the hell had happened to the audio on the tape.

But murder was part and parcel of La Cosa Nostra's world. Casso had grown callous deep inside and whatever empathy he had for Albano was summarily forgotten.

Casso continued to feel bad, however, for Albano's family, his wife and children. This was one of the more intriguing dichotomies of Anthony Casso, how on the one hand he could be so cold, then on the other hand such a dedicated family man. When Albano's body was finally discovered after a week or so, Casso made sure to leave an excessively large amount of money—ten thousand dollars—with Albano's wife.

After dropping Pate off at the Owls Head, Casso drove back home that night. Lillian was up watching television. She loved classic movies and often stayed up late at night to watch them. She was glad Anthony was home, as she dreaded his being out of the house. Lillian well knew that every time he stepped outside, he could be shot down—or just disappear. She had no illusions about the life her husband was so deeply enmeshed in, yet she never complained to him; she never did anything to distract him from the serious business that he was in. Lillian understood that Anthony was involved in a secret society with all kinds of strange rules and regulations, the violation of which could cause sudden, irrational death.

Anthony would literally do anything for Lillian. Whatever she wanted was hers. She didn't even have to ask—if he just saw her look at something, it was hers. Anthony often brought Lillian huge bunches of red roses.

When he arrived home that night, he looked in on his children, how they slept like little angels, and he was reminded of his vulnerability. If he was killed, he knew his children would suffer . . . they'd be without a father, through no fault of their own. As he kissed his sleeping son, then kissed his sleeping daughter, he wished he had another life, but that was not in the cards for him and he quickly buried the emotions that made him have second thoughts about who he was and what he did.

In reality, Casso loved his life and had come to view himself as the CEO of a large corporation. He knew most every great fortune in America had been based upon crime one way or another: the Kennedys had been bootleggers, the Rockefellers had been racketeers, the Carnegies treated their workers unfairly, the Hearsts were prone to blatant libel, and the duPonts regularly fixed prices.

Later, when Anthony finally got to bed, he and Lillian made love. He slept deep and well.

There were no nightmares, no bad dreams for Anthony Casso.

CHAPTER 52

RACKETEERING

The Gambino, Lucchese, and Genovese families controlled Local 813, the union that represented garbage truck workers, headed then by Bernard Edelstein. Edelstein also controlled the airport workers' union for the Lucchese family for many years. As were most union bosses, Edelstein was in the back pocket of the Mafia.

Throughout the mid-1970s and 1980s, Chris Furnari had solely dominated and controlled New York District Council 9, which represented the more than six thousand workers who did the painting and decorating for all the finest hotels, city bridges, subway stations, and so on. Christie Tick managed this through the union's secretary and treasurer, James Bishop, and his associate, Frank Arnold. They would pick up cash payments from the contractors, who would charge a 10 to 15 percent "tax" on all major commercial painting jobs in the New York metropolitan area. This so-called tax went directly into Mafia coffers.

In the late 1980s, Jim Bishop and the union came under fire by state investigators looking into Mob ties. At this point, Amuso and Casso assumed responsibility for the union workers. Casso felt that Bishop would become a liability because of this investigation. He sent war capo Fat Pete Chiodo to lean a little on Frank Arnold, to explain the facts of life to Arnold—that it was time for Bishop to retire.

Arnold was an exceedingly wealthy man who lived with his three daughters and wife in exclusive Sands Point, Long Island. He was short in stature and regularly wore shoes with high heels—like a flamenco dancer's.

Fat Pete Chiodo grabbed Frank Arnold as he left his office and took him, against his will, to a factory building on Staten Island. There he took a loaded double-barrel shotgun and rammed it in Arnold's mouth, cocking the two hammers. Arnold was so utterly frightened that he literally shat in his pants and stunk the place up. He got the message loud and clear.

The next day, unannounced and uninvited, Frank Arnold came by Casso's house in Bergen Beach and handed him a brown paper bag containing seven hundred thousand dollars . . . "this is just for starters," Arnold promised Casso.

Still, even with the prodding of Arnold, Bishop was not about to retire. He was an independent tough Irishman who had come up through the ranks the hard way. He was not about to be told what to do, how to do it, or when to do it. He was from the same mold as colorful union boss Jimmy Hoffa. He would end up walking the path in life that Jimmy Hoffa walked.

Toward the end of 1989, rumors reached Casso that he and Amuso were about to be indicted and drawn into the so-called Windows Case. Under normal circumstances, if he had the time, Casso might have shown Bishop more patience, but in lieu of an upcoming indictment, and considering what was at stake, Casso was not about to waste a minute.

One last time Casso suggested a new head to District Council 9, a fellow he knew by the name of Eddie Capalado.

"No way!" Bishop said . . . sealing his own fate.

Gaspipe now did what he had become expert at; he choreographed, with the keen eye of Balanchine, the murder of Jim Bishop. As was Casso's way, he went to a person close to the victim—in this case, Frank Arnold, who was so utterly, totally, completely terrified of Gaspipe that he would have done anything Casso asked.

"I know you are our friend," Casso told Arnold. "We don't want to hurt anybody. We're just lookin' to do business here. It's nothing personal, but Bishop's hardheaded and unreasonable. We've given him every chance to move on his merry way, take whatever money he made, and we'll all part as friends. But he's being unreasonable. He's writing his own ticket, and it's a one-way trip. We want you to help do what has to be done."

"Anything," Arnold said. "Whatever you need, Anthony. Please, just ask."

"I want you to set up Bishop for us."

"No problem," Arnold said.

"I understand he's got a girlfriend."

"Yeah, for sure. She lives in Whitestone, Queens, in a condominium complex there. The Cryder Point Condominium Complex. The fact is he's going to be there tonight, I know that for sure."

"Okay perfect," Casso said. "When he's there, he'll be relaxed; he'll have his guard dropped. What I need you to do is call him and tell him you want to see him—you gotta see him. You're sure he's going to be there?"

"He said he would," Arnold said.

"Okay, you call him and tell him you gotta meet him around nine o'clock. Got it?"

"Got it."

True to his word, Frank Arnold set up Jim Bishop that night. As per Casso's instructions, he called Jim Bishop and with just the right amount of urgency, said he had to see him, and set up a quick meeting.

Bishop had been in flagrante delicto. In a huff and a puff, he got dressed and went to meet Arnold, sure this had something to do with those wop pains in the asses. Jim Bishop had come to hate the Italians. He viewed them as bloodsucking vampires; yet he had been robbing and stealing from Local District Council 9 for many years now. Somehow he never equated what he was doing with what the Italians were doing.

Bishop, like most Irish gangsters, apparently thought he had a God-given right to steal at will, whenever the chance presented itself. Jim Bishop swaggered from his girlfriend's apartment complex that night, unaware that the Italians he hated so much were circling him.

Richie Pagliarulo was given the assignment of killing Jim Bishop. Richie was with Fat Pete's crew. He was unflappable. Sitting in the driver's seat of his car, his eyes dark and steady, he watched Jim Bishop moving toward his car. As Bishop reached his car and opened the door, Pagliarulo calmly got out of his car. With a practiced, easy gait, he reached Bishop's car, raised an automatic fitted with a silencer, and shot Bishop through the driver's window eight times . . . killing him.

Eddie Capalado got the job as the head of Local District Council 9. This was a classic example of how the Mafia took control of and ran just about every union in America. First they asked for what they wanted; then they told what they wanted. If neither of those things worked, they started breaking bones. If that didn't work, they killed. They did this to Jimmy Hoffa. They did it to Jim Bishop.

Business as usual.

BOOK IV

GONE WITH THE WIND

CHAPTER 53

GASPIPE'S CRYSTAL BALL

Trouble was in the wind, serious trouble that could not only cause Casso to spend the rest of his life in jail but also cause his death. It was all an outgrowth of the Windows Case—the interminable, endless, all-consuming Windows Case. From the government's point of view, the Windows Case was like a map, which clearly delineated the working connections between the different Mafia families. Here, in a sense for the very first time, the government was able to prove that the Mafia was a well-oiled criminal enterprise whose sole function was committing crime.

This particular case had taken on a life of its own. It had become an insatiable monster that the government had on a leash, chewing up mafioso after mafioso after mafioso with the ease of hyena crushing bone and gristle and flesh. Through Gaspipe's contact in the FBI, whom he had dubbed his "crystal ball," he had learned that both he and Vic Amuso would soon be indicted and arrested—and presented with a long list of racketeering charges.

After meeting with his crack criminal attorney Mike Rosen, Casso decided it would be better for him to take it on the lam and wait and see what happened. In other words, let the other defendants go on trial and see what evidence the government had exactly—let the government play out their hand—then Casso and Amuso would give themselves up and allow themselves to be brought to trial, knowing the idiosyncrasies and finer points of the government's case. Thus, he believed—according to his lawyers—he would most definitely beat the case.

Casso did not like the idea of going on the lam. It seemed a punk thing to do—like he was running away. Plus, he was very reticent about leaving the family's business in charge of anyone but himself. Casso trusted few people. He had seen in his life of crime, over and over, people's avarice and greed and incompetence do them in. He had seen men make fatal mistakes because of women, gambling, and drugs.

Men, Casso had come to believe, were eminently fallible.

His intention was to continue running the family while on the lam. This would be no easy task for he would be a fugitive on the FBI's most wanted list, no doubt, with his face plastered on post office bulletin boards across the country. His disappearance would become big news, he knew. He carefully set up a means of communication that involved taking down the phone numbers of dozens of public phones in Brooklyn, Long Island, and the Bronx. Not only did he record their phone numbers, he also wrote down their exact addresses. Like this he created for himself a systematic way to reach out to his underlings without any connection to him. It was a simple though brilliant way for him to run the family from afar.

Anthony lay awake at night, Lillian soundly sleeping next to him, wondering who he could put in charge, who would blindly do as he was told, never stealing a dime and precisely following orders. The answer kept coming down to one person . . . "Little" Al D'Arco.

D'Arco had been a wannabe mafioso for most of his adult life. He was thin and frail and wore granny glasses. He appeared more like a complacent accountant who wouldn't hurt a fly. He'd been brought up in Mafiadom's principal locales—Bensonhurst and Canarsie. D'Arco knew the walk, knew the talk, but that was it. As a criminal, he was a failure. He had already done ten years in jail for dealing drugs and bookmaking. Casso did not like his nickname, Little Al. He didn't think it fit the image of a Lucchese soldier, so he renamed him "the Professor." Anthony loved nicknames, and he still had a wry, nutty sense of humor.

As unassuming and as innocuous as the Professor appeared, though, he had helped Casso with the logistics in the murder of over fifteen people. He made sure the details were carried out as Casso mandated, that the victim, killers, and guns were all where they were supposed to be—and that the bodies went where they were supposed to go . . . and were in the condition Casso wanted them. Sometimes mutilation was required. Sometimes it was a single bullet in the head. Casso had come to trust D'Arco the way you grow to trust an obedient Labrador retriever.

Yes, the Professor would be the mere surrogate head of the family while Casso and Amuso were gone. As the clock slowly ticked away, Anthony prepared to be incognito for as long as it took. The first order of business was his family—his blood family. He went to his wife, Lillian, and told her he needed to talk to her. That night, he took her to one of the finest restaurants in Manhattan, Da Noi on the Upper East Side. Lillian didn't think that anything particular was in the wind. Anthony often took her to sumptuous restaurants.

Sitting opposite his wife in the restaurant, Anthony took her hands and said, "Lil, I have to take off for a while. Indictments are coming down soon and if I stick around, I'm going to get arrested. Both me and Vic are taking off."

Her face all grave, Lillian said, "When . . . for how long?"

"It's hard to say at this point. A lot of guys are getting arrested on conspiracy charges. The lawyers tell me, 'Stay away until the trials run their course and then we'll know exactly what they have.'"

"Will I be able to see you? What about the kids? Will the kids be able to see you?"

He drew a long, exasperated breath. His daughter, Jolene, was now eighteen, his son, Anthony Junior, fifteen. He stared at her for a long time. He didn't quite seem to be there now. Lillian knew Anthony very well, better than anyone else in the world, but still she had no idea what was going on behind his dark Mediterranean eyes.

"The problem with that," he said, "is that the government knows that all they have to do is watch the family and you'll lead them directly to me; you know that—I know you know that."

Lillian knew that what Anthony said was true—it was an actual, literal war between the FBI and men like her husband. She had decided long ago where her loyalty lay and that, of course, was on the side of her husband. Lillian knew it truly was a matter of life and death. She read the newspapers. She socialized with the wives of other mafiosi. She knew the death toll. This was not a game. This was deadly serious.

"Anthony," she said, "I'll do anything for you. You know that. If we can't see each other, I'll understand. It's the kids . . . the children I'm concerned with."

"Yeah. Of course, I know," he said. "As soon as I can get this cleared up, I will. You know that. I know you know that."

"I do," she said, a steady sadness growing in her large, saucer-shaped eyes.

Anthony leaned over and kissed his wife gently on the lips. They hugged. As he sat back, he was seething inside. All this, he believed, did not have to come to pass. It was happening because Chin Gigante had consistently refused to kill Peter Savino; this even after multiple warnings that Savino was a rat, that he was wearing a wire, that he was going to testify at the trial, all of which turned out to be true. Had Gigante killed Savino, the case would have fallen by the wayside.

All he could do was shake his head in dismay and wonder why the Chin had not only exposed all the upper echelons of the East Coast La Cosa Nostra but, in sum, had allowed himself to be arrested as part of the Windows Case; Chin, too, was going to trial.

Was it stupidity?

Was it obstinacy?

Was it arrogance?

Those questions would never be answered. Later that night, Anthony made love to Lillian in a way that was different . . . softer, gentler—more meaningful.

Afterward, he did not sleep. He lay awake and stared at the ceiling, his burning anger at Chin keeping him awake. This anger would grow and grow still more, would become like a cancerous malignancy that would cause Casso to betray his oath of *omerta*.

Why? he wondered. *What is really at the bottom of this?*

CHAPTER 54

UNDERGROUND

Six days after Anthony's forty-eighth birthday, he went on the lam. It was a bright, cloudless, sunny day. When he said good-bye to Lillian and his children, there was a tangible, choking sadness in the air. For all they knew, this could be the last time that they saw one another.

———

Vic Amuso, being cautious, had taken off two weeks earlier and had sequestered himself in the Scranton, Pennsylvania, house he had bought months earlier. One of the last things Casso did before he left his home was call Al D'Arco and say, "Meet me by the cannon."

The cannon was a regular meeting place for the Lucchese borgata. It was located in Fort Hamilton Park at Fourth Avenue and 100th Street. The cannon was a huge, thousand-pound, twenty-inch Rodman gun that was cast after the War of 1812 and once dominated the Brooklyn Narrows. It could blow apart any ship that passed in front of it. Casso and D'Arco sat on a dark green park bench near the cannon, a stone's throw away from the Verrazano Bridge, and Casso laid it out for D'Arco. He gave him the list of telephone booths and their addresses and told him he was in charge, that he would run the family until further notice. He said, too, that Al was to work in unison with the other Lucchese capos—Anthony Bowat, Sally Avellino, Frank Alstorono.

This was all somewhat overwhelming to D'Arco. All his life he had been nobody. All his life he had wanted this, but what he was now being given on a silver platter was not due to any brilliance on his part, but by default. Casso was making him the boss, in a sense, because he was the least suitable for the job. Casso believed he was obedient—D'Arco would sit, stay, lie down, roll over, or fetch at Casso's will.

So much of being a successful La Cosa Nostra boss had to do with being a good judge of character. Casso, to a large degree, had that trait, unlike John Gotti, for example. Gotti made Sammy the Bull the underboss—a major blunder—and Gotti appointed his son head of the family only out of nepotism, not because Junior was best for the job. Casso would never do such a thing, though his choosing D'Arco would prove to be a bad move. They sat by the cannon for two hours that day, and Casso told the Professor what was expected of him.

D'Arco, who was deathly afraid of Gaspipe, would never do anything to betray him or to undermine him or to steal from him. He well knew that to steal from Gaspipe was a one-way ticket to the graveyard. By the same token, D'Arco recognized that Casso was generous. He made sure all his people not only made money but that they did very well, rewarding loyalty with abundance. Sitting there, staring at the fast-moving water under the bridge, D'Arco knew he'd be making real money—millions per year—for the first time in his life. He would no longer be a nobody.

D'Arco slowly walked Casso to his car, unobserved by the FBI. Casso got in the car, stepped on the gas, headed toward New Jersey, and never looked back. Believing he was speeding to a bright new future, he was in fact speeding toward hell on earth.

CHAPTER 55

THE FBI COMES KNOCKING

Just as Casso had been told by his mole in the FBI, federal agents rang his doorbell on East Seventy-second Street at 9:00 A.M. that Monday morning, May 28, 1990. There were half a dozen agents. They knocked. They had a warrant for his arrest. Lillian told them honestly that he wasn't there, that she had no idea where he'd gone. They gave her the warrant and searched the premises thoroughly. Lillian stared at them with hostility. They stared right back at her with equal hostility. Certain hurtful remarks were made to Lillian about girlfriends Anthony had, which she paid no attention to.

Lillian, in her own way, was as tough as Anthony.

It didn't take long for the FBI to learn that Casso hadn't been seen recently in any of his normal haunts. They staked out the 19th Hole; they staked out all the places he was known to frequent. They soon realized that Casso had been tipped off, that he had taken it on the lam. They put Casso on the FBI's Ten Most Wanted List. The story of his disappearance was featured in all the major New York papers. *America's Most Wanted* did two feature pieces on the disappearance of Casso and Amuso. Mug shots of Casso's stoic face appeared in post offices across the country. As the citizenry stared at that face in those mug shots they wondered, collectively, where he got the name "Gaspipe."

Casso, always ahead of the curve, had planned for many months exactly what he'd do when he had to go into hiding. In preparation, he had bought a home in Mount Olive in northern New Jersey about forty miles west of Newark. It was rural country, quiet and pristine, near Budd Lake. Knowing he would need female companionship, somebody he could trust, Casso had arranged for his old flame Rosemarie Billotti to stay with him. She and Casso had been lovers since they were kids together back on Union Street. Casso felt close to her, though he didn't hold her in the high esteem in which he held his wife. He viewed Rosemarie more as a loose woman who just happened to be fond of him rather than a woman who had dedicated her life to him. Casso believed that because she was from the same neighborhood as he was, that because she knew the rules and regulations governing the street, she'd keep her mouth shut and never give him up.

As the FBI continued to search high and low for Gaspipe, he quietly went about the business of running the Lucchese family from afar. He grew a beard and sported baseball caps pulled down low over his eyes; using the list of telephone booths he had given the Professor, he managed to oversee the operation of the Lucchese crime family surprisingly well.

Days quickly slipped into weeks, which turned into months. Anthony did not try to contact Lillian; he didn't meet with her; he didn't speak with his children. Every other week, he sent messages to her stating that he was okay, that she shouldn't worry. He also sent her paper bags filled with hundred-dollar bills. Anthony trusted Lillian and he knew she would stash the money in the appropriate places at the appropriate times.

Now, at a time like this, when he was so far apart from his wife, Anthony knew he had made the right choice marrying Lillian. He felt sure that not only was she loyal to him but also that she was taking excellent care of their two children. Lillian was so much a part of the Mafia culture that she was actually proud that Anthony would rather fight the government than acquiesce to its strong-arm tactics. Most of Lillian's best friends were the wives of made men. Among this close-knit sorority, Anthony was a hero. Lillian had lunch with her cronies. They went on frequent shopping trips. She kept herself busy. She bided her time. She had every confidence that Anthony would prevail.

As had always been Casso's way, he woke up late every day, between ten and twelve o'clock. He went for long walks with Rosemarie. He went fishing in a nearby lake. He was an avid reader of newspapers, and he made sure he stayed abreast of current events, especially those pertaining to the Mob and John Gotti.

In reality, it was surprisingly easy for Gaspipe to direct the workings of the Lucchese family. As time passed he became more and more confident in the way he had set things up. Once a week, he'd meet the Professor at nearby shopping centers, restaurants, or malls; over lunch or dinner, Casso would listen to all the workings of the Lucchese family, and the other families as well.

As Casso had hoped, the Professor turned out to be the perfect puppet. Still, Casso was wary of giving any one person so much control; he felt that sooner or later D'Arco would betray him.

Staying up late at night, walking back and forth, thinking things out, Casso devised a series of methods by which he would be able to know for certain if D'Arco was carrying out his orders as mandated. He began giving him "curved directives." That is, he gave him chores to do that would allow Casso to independently ascertain if they were done as per his dictates—amounts of money to be distributed among captains, who would get what percentage from different robberies and scores, amounts of money paid for different murders, who won and lost betting on sports games. For the most part, the Professor came through with flying colors.

Also, as was Casso's way, he was constantly scheming about new ways for the family to make money. At one point, he suggested to D'Arco that he, D'Arco, go to Vic Orena and the Persico faction and see if they'd be willing to become part of the Lucchese family. Casso saw this as a way to end the civil strife—war—between the factions and also as a way to make the Lucchese family become the most powerful family in America.

D'Arco, unlike his usual self, openly disagreed with Casso. He told Casso that they would view it as a power play; that they would believe that the Lucchese family wanted to take over the Colombo family; and that, inevitably, their answer would be not only to kill D'Arco but also to go after the whole Lucchese family.

At first Casso was put off by D'Arco's disagreement with him, but then Casso saw the wisdom in what D'Arco was saying—such a proposal could very well spark a war between the Luccheses and the Colombos. Sitting there and staring at D'Arco, Casso realized that he had changed, that he was not the round-shouldered, unassuming wannabe he had once been.

On the one hand, Casso was glad about this because, after all, D'Arco was effectively running the family; on the other hand, this new D'Arco kind of caught Casso off guard. Casso made a mental note to be all the more careful.

Casso also began meeting with the other capos of the Lucchese family: Anthony Bowat, Sally Avellino, Frank Alstorono, and Fat Pete Chiodo. Casso came into New York and met his capos in out-of-the-way hotels and restaurants. He took to having a mobile office. Using a blue van with tinted windows, he had himself driven by George Zappola Jr. to different Brooklyn neighborhoods. He had impromptu meetings in the van, giving him a more hands-on approach to running the family . . . divvying up different robberies, deciding who would receive what percentage of money, overseeing the many different criminal enterprises the family was immersed in.

Now Casso began hearing complaints about the Professor. Once he began meeting with his capos directly, he realized that D'Arco was demanding and receiving money from the different capos that Casso knew nothing about. This was what he had been concerned with all the while. By now, Casso knew D'Arco had become a wealthy man. He'd opened a successful restaurant in Little Italy, called La Rosa, and then bought a building near it. Rather than being angry about and upset by what he learned, Casso was more let down—disappointed. Greed, he knew, sooner or later would undermine D'Arco's credibility.

Instead of calling D'Arco on the carpet now, Casso figured he'd give him enough rope to hang himself. Casso was still on the lam and he needed D'Arco.

———

In January 1991, Casso called a meeting at the home of Frankie Socks in Staten Island and invited all the capos and D'Arco. This was when Casso finally accused D'Arco of extorting from the other captains. Of course, D'Arco denied this seven ways from Sunday. He pulled out papers on which he had written long lists of neat numbers proving what he got, when he got it, and where he'd gotten it from. He was so convincing that he made it look as though it was more of a misunderstanding than actual pilfering. Casso took him in another room and D'Arco cried and said, "Anthony, how could you think this of me? I'd never steal a penny from you." He pleaded, holding Casso, looking him in the eyes, "Every single cent I've gotten, I've given to you. Straight up. I've never stolen anything from you." Under normal circumstances, D'Arco would have already been dead. Be that as it may, Casso told D'Arco he believed him, that it was just a miscalculation of numbers, not any avarice on his part. They hugged, kissed on the cheek. For the moment, it seemed okay, D'Arco thought.

However, when D'Arco drove home that night, he felt a cold stone in his stomach, a coldness that spread from his stomach to his limbs. He knew Gaspipe well. He had helped him murder many people. He couldn't imagine Casso just taking his word. He would now be very careful; he would look over his shoulder; he wouldn't go anywhere without people he trusted who were heavily armed.

From afar, with the help of a battery of top-notch criminal attorneys, Casso watched the proceedings in the Windows Case. He didn't like what he saw. The government had a very strong case: Peter Savino proved to be an amazingly good rat. It seemed he had a natural gift for getting people to drop their guard, including the Chin's brother Mario and Benny Eggs. He had been able to get people to talk even after Casso had warned the Chin several times that Savino was an informer. Savino had an outgoing, beguiling personality; he could charm the stripes off a zebra and was a great story and joke teller. Savino was so personable, likable, that it was hard for people—the Chin and those in his immediate circle—to believe he was an informer. But because the Chin did not kill Savino—because he thought it would draw heat directly to himself—Savino had managed to undermine the very foundation of the New York Mafia.

Casso saw this . . . and stewed.

He began assigning hit teams to find Peter Savino and kill him. Casso still managed to freely communicate with his mole inside the FBI, Doug McCane, and he emphasized how imperative finding Savino was.

Word quickly came back to Casso that Savino was being kept at an army base in Hawaii and would be nearly impossible to get close to.

Shaking his head in disgust, Gaspipe cursed Chin Gigante. It was all his fault. Savino should have been dead.

Still, Casso had come to believe that his going on the lam was a good move because, little by little, the government's case was being exposed and he would ultimately, he was sure, be better prepared to fight it.

CHAPTER 56

FAT AND SKINNY

The cold winds of war had been blowing north, south, east, and west across Brooklyn since the murder of Paul Castellano in 1985. From a strategic point of view, Casso knew that one of the Gambino capos had to be taken out. His name was Eddie Lino. He was a fierce war captain, blindly loyal to John Gotti, his personal attack dog, without a doubt the most badass capo the Gambinos had. A large, austere man, Lino had broad shoulders and a thick, strong jawline—and a mouth that didn't seem capable of mirth. If the Gambino family had a Luca Brasi, it was Eddie Lino.

Lino had also been born and bred in Bensonhurst. He, like Casso, was destined to be part of La Cosa Nostra since his early teen years. As well as being extremely efficient at murder and mayhem, Eddie Lino was a moneymaker—he was an exceedingly wealthy man, a snappy dresser, always well groomed and well coiffed. When Eddie Lino walked into a room, people noticed him and showed him reverence and respect.

In that Eddie Lino was an assassin's assassin, he was a hard man to kill. Both Genovese and Lucchese hit men had been looking for an opportunity for months now to no avail. He always seemed a step or two ahead of those who would kill him.

In the spring of 1990, Gaspipe, always willing to think out of the box, turned to crooked cops Stephen Caracappa and Louis Eppolito—the "Mafia cops."

While on the lam, Casso brazenly met with the two cops in the parking lot of Toys "R" Us on Flatbush Avenue and gave them the contract to kill Lino for $75,000.

Casso agreed to provide the two detectives with the kind of car that NYPD detectives drive, in this case a blue Plymouth with blackwall tires. He left the car for them in the Flatlands section of Brooklyn, and the two cops began to stalk Eddie Lino. Casso had also provided the two detectives handguns to carry out the deed. The two cops realized this was a very important hit; they knew that Lino was a capo and that killing him would be a major feather in their cap.

Deadly, wolflike, the two stoic detectives stalked a stalker.

As it happened, it took more than six months for Caracappa and Eppolito to finally make a move. It happened in late fall of 1990—on the evening of November 6. The trees that lined Brooklyn's streets were filled with dying leaves, yellows and bold reds, sad browns and bright oranges. November 6 was a particularly windy day and the blowing leaves filled the air and hurried across Brooklyn sidewalks and mean streets.

Eddie Lino was on his way that fateful day to an induction ceremony. New made men would soon be part of the Gambino borgata—already the largest crime family in the world. The two cops followed Lino onto the Belt Parkway.

Audaciously, they pulled up alongside his black Mercedes-Benz near Lincoln High School and put a speeding red light on the dashboard of the bullshit detective car; Eppolito flashed his gold badge in the direction of Eddie Lino.

Suddenly the clock was ticking for Eddie Lino; now, seemingly out of nowhere, like errant leaves falling from the dark November night, the grim reapers had caught up to him.

Eddie Lino recognized these two cops; he knew Caracappa was part of the organized crime division of the NYPD.

What do these two scumbags want? he thought.

Cars on the Belt Parkway sped by. They were in the Brighton Beach section near Ocean Parkway. Windblown hedges and trees shielded what was about to happen from the service road that ran parallel to the Belt.

Stephen Caracappa was an excellent marksman—a crack shot. He got out of the car and slowly approached Lino.

"Yeah, what's up?" Lino asked.

And the answer he received was a hail of bullets, which tore into his flesh, breaking bones, piercing vital arteries, creating searing dime-sized holes in his brain.

The last image that Eddie Lino had in his life was of a New York City detective with icy eyes killing him.

Caracappa had been careful not to extend his arm as he fired. He kept the gun low and close to his body as he shot, lest it be seen by a passing motorist or a civilian out walking a dog.

Thus, the most feared war capo the Gambino family had was no more.

And the grim reaper was a few steps closer to John Gotti.

Casso sent the balance of the money due for the Lino hit to Caracappa and Eppolito by way of Burton Kaplan. Later, when Casso met with Caracappa and Eppolito in an Avenue U luncheonette, he learned the details.

CHAPTER 57

LIGHT ON HIS FEET PETE

It was spring of 1991. The Lucchese family's Mighty Joe Young, Fat Pete Chiodo, had also been indicted on RICO charges stemming from the Windows Case.

In that Fat Pete already had been indicted on other racketeering charges, he saw little benefit in going to trial. His lawyers advised him that if he lost the case at trial, he would surely spend the rest of his life in prison, a fate he wanted to avoid at all costs.

Going against Mafia protocol, Fat Pete decided to plead guilty to the two indictments, hoping he could get a ten-year sentence . . . something he could live with. He was forty-five years old. If he was out in ten years, he figured he still had a life worth living before him.

In the minds of Casso and Amuso, this was a cardinal sin. By Fat Pete pleading guilty, he was inadvertently acknowledging the guilt of Casso and Amuso. This was an unpardonable error. Casso called D'Arco at a pay phone near Kennedy Airport and told him, "I want Pete taken out."

This particular order bowled D'Arco over for he knew how close Casso and Fat Pete had been, that they were more like brothers than the friends they had been since childhood, and that Casso had trusted Fat Pete with numerous sensitive jobs. Yet here he was, ordering D'Arco to kill Fat Pete.

D'Arco's mind swirled with this order. He knew if Casso could kill Fat Pete, he could kill anyone—including him.

D'Arco had, in fact, been stealing from Casso. First it was a little here, a little there . . . then the amounts grew. He became more confident. He figured he'd never get caught. But now, with Casso's ordering this murder, D'Arco believed Casso would kill his own mother. As he walked back to his car, low-flying planes roaring overhead, he felt a kind of vertigo take control of him and make him dizzy.

How, he wondered, *could Anthony kill Fat Pete so easily?*

By instinct, Fat Pete knew what was in the air, that it was just a matter of time before the killing machine that was the Lucchese family slowly rotated and came to stop on him. He became triply cautious. He rarely left his house. He was very anxious for the sentencing day to come so he could go off to jail and do his time in peace.

Unfortunately, Casso had come to believe that Fat Pete was a rat—that he had pled guilty and would be treated leniently because he had "turned." The truth was, Fat Pete had not become an informant at all. Fat Pete refused to cooperate with the authorities. He was just trying to plead guilty, do his time, and enjoy the years he had left.

Because Fat Pete was a professional assassin, he was also a difficult man to kill. By way of a Mob associate who was an employee of the phone company, D'Arco actually managed to have his phones tapped, trying to get a jump on where he'd be at any given time. This was how the family learned that he was planning to "disappear" until the sentencing date. This made them all the more desperate to take him out. Fat Pete planned to depart for his hideaway on May 8. Rather than take a plane, which would leave a paper trail, he decided to drive to a safe house in upstate New York. Before he left, he took his Cadillac into a Staten Island service station for a tune-up and an oil change.

A Lucchese hit team composed of three men, including D'Arco's son Joe, was waiting at the Gulf station when Fat Pete pulled in with his big-ass white Cadillac.

Fat Pete was bending over, looking at the engine of his car, its hood up, when he spotted the three assassins quickly approaching him with that unnatural, stiff gait. He'd figured this would happen; he'd been waiting for it to happen—and without hesitation, Fat Pete pulled out a Browning 9 millimeter and began firing, moving with surprising speed for such a big man. He actually managed to get off six shots before they even had their guns drawn. Unfortunately, his accuracy wasn't as good as his hand speed and he missed his assailants, and with the three of them firing nonstop, Fat Pete was hit twelve times and he collapsed in a heap of thick, fat flesh and bones. Surely, the assassins thought, he could not survive the bullets they had put in his body. Confident Fat Pete was dead, they got in their car and pulled away.

Thanks to excellent medical care Fat Pete received that day from a team of surgeons and on-the-ball nurses at University Hospital on Staten Island, he didn't die. By all rights he certainly should not have lived. There were multiple gunshot wounds to his stomach, and a bullet pierced the artery of his right arm, but, miraculously, the thing that Fat Pete had been ashamed of all his life—the excessive fat on his body—was what saved his life. It acted, the surgeons told him later, like an impromptu bullet-proof vest. In reality, the bullets were not stopped by Fat Pete's fat, but it did slow their trajectories into his body and thus he avoided being shot in any vital body parts . . . his heart, brain, lungs. No matter how you cut it, however, Fat Pete was a very, very lucky man. There are few men who could take twelve bullets and live to tell about it.

But not only did Fat Pete live to tell about it, Fat Pete would become the government's star witness against Casso, Amuso, and others in the Lucchese crime family. He would become a four-hundred-pound canary. By trying to kill Fat Pete that clear May day, they created what they feared the most—a highly motivated, highly intelligent witness who would glee-fully point the finger, naming names, dates, times, and places crimes had occurred.

Unwittingly, Casso and Amuso had created a Fat Frankenstein.

When the Luccheses learned that Fat Pete had survived, they were in a panic—something had to be done. In desperation, they sent hit man John Fortuna dressed as a doctor to the hospital where he lay recovering. With the help of an actual nurse who worked at the hospital, and with her guidance and knowledge of hospital routine, the assassin got to within feet of where the enormous Chiodo lay. But the FBI knew such a thing was not only possible but more than probable and they descended upon the would-be killer and arrested him.

Federal prosecutor Charlie Rose would later explain, "We [origi-nally] offered Fat Pete leniency if he would testify against Casso and

Amuso, and he flat-out turned us down. I remember well what he said. He said, 'I appreciate what you guys are trying to do here but no thanks—good-bye and good luck.'"

But, now, spurred on by twelve bullet holes, Fat Pete was ready not only to talk, but to sing an opera, whose final act would be Anthony Casso dying in jail.

———

Of all the things in the world that Casso dreaded the most, he dreaded dying in jail. For him, it was a form of castration and mummification. He would be taken away not only from the life he loved but also from the only people he loved: his wife and children.

He would go from being a respected man to whom people said, "Yes sir, Mr. Casso!" to being a mere number, a nameless, faceless animal kept behind bars, fed when his zookeepers wanted to feed him, told when he could wash, told when he could eat, told what to think, told what to do.

For a man like Gaspipe, this was hell on earth—a fate he would avoid at all costs.

Soon, Charlie Rose and his partner, Greg O'Connell, the federal prosecutors handling the Windows Case, were sitting in comfortable chairs at Fat Pete's bedside as he outlined in detail numerous murders he was involved in. Repeatedly, he named Casso as the man who had given him the order.

———

Casso's hair was on fire. He was like a madman. He could lose all he had. He had to stop Fat Pete.

What exactly happened next is, to a degree, up for debate. Casso says Amuso gave the orders. Amuso said Casso gave the orders. The point is that for the first time in the history of the American Mafia, guns were turned on the family member of a mafioso. Word was sent to Fat Pete that if he testified against Amuso and Casso, his elderly parents would be killed.

Such a thing, such a dictate, was an unspeakable cardinal sin. Family members were off-limits. This had been cut in stone since the very beginning of the modern American Mafia. It had been agreed upon by Luciano, Costello, Genovese, Gambino, and the others. It was the law.

The killing of an innocent was an outrage; a man of respect did not do such a thing. This was the action of a jackal, a scavenger, not a predator, not a mafioso. Yet here were Amuso and Casso, all ready, willing, and eminently able not only to go against this commandment of the Mafia but also to do it openly, not surreptitiously. This would be a public execution.

Fat Pete Chiodo took the threat seriously. Rather than be cowed by it, however, he was incensed by it. His parents, his wife, and his children were quickly whisked away and placed in the Witness Protection Program. They seemed to disappear from the face of the earth.

Now, believing that his family was out of harm's way, Fat Pete went about the business of preparing for trial. In desperation, the Luccheses struck at the only target they could find—a beloved uncle of Fat Pete's. His name was Frank Signorino. He was shot to death multiple times and found stuffed in the trunk of his car. This did not dissuade Pete.

Then Lucchese assassins did the unthinkable: they went after a woman—Patricia Capozzalo, Fat Pete's sister. Patricia ran a small book-making business in Bensonhurst, Brooklyn. She had nothing to do, for the most part, with her brother or her brother's business, but Lucchese henchmen found her and shot her with silencer-equipped pistols after she dropped off her children at school. The shooters were Michael "Baldy" Spinelli and his brother Robert. Patricia survived. This "bungled" hit further enraged Fat Pete because he was close to his sister.

Now, no matter what, come hell or high water, Fat Pete was going to testify against Casso and Amuso. Nothing was going to stop him.

It had been the Professor who had been given the orders to kill Fat Pete, to kill his uncle, and to kill his sister; and he had fucked up every one of the hits. U.S. Attorney Liz Lesser said of this crime, "It was a terrible crime. It strikes at the very heart of the system of justice."

In a very real sense, the so-called Professor had taken shovel in hand and slowly dug his own grave. Now all that was left to do was for him to quietly get in the grave, lie down, and wait for dirt to cover him. When D'Arco looked up at the sky, it was dark and it was filled with storm clouds. In the distance he saw lightning and heard thunder. And slowly, inexorably, the lightning and thunder moved closer and closer and closer still, and as he watched lightning bolts rip open the sky, he knew one of those bolts was destined for him.

A man who would be king, suddenly he found himself at the lowest pecking order of the jungle. He was again the lowly mouse he once had been. Now he would have to find little holes he could crawl into; now he would look for the foul, stinking, shadowed places where no one ventured but vermin. Now, he believed, he was vermin again. He grew pale. He lost weight.

How did he get himself in such a predicament? Why, he wondered, had the gods turned on him so? Pacing back and forth, he thought, *Twelve times, twelve times we shot him but he survived!*

When D'Arco looked in the mirror, he saw a beaten man with dark circles under his eyes, a mere shell of the man he had almost become.

———

Back in Mount Olive, New Jersey, Anthony Casso was fit to be tied. He realized he had made a huge mistake in giving D'Arco such large responsibilities. He blamed himself. He grew angry at himself. He grew angry at the world. When Casso looked in the mirror now, he wanted to punch himself in the face.

But he knew crying over spilled milk wouldn't do any good for anybody, least of all himself.

In July of 1991, Casso called a meeting at the Staten Island home of Lucchese soldier Richie Pagliarulo. The meeting was attended by the other Lucchese capos, Anthony Bowat, Frank Lastorono, and Sally Avellino. Both Casso and Amuso showed up. Each of them was clean-shaven and didn't seem concerned with being recognized. They had taken great pains not to be followed from their respective hideaways. By the same token, they wanted to present a strong, we've-got-our-shit-together front to their capos. Gaspipe did most of the talking. He said, "Al's no longer captain of the ship. From now on, the responsibilities of running the family will be spread amongst the four of you." D'Arco felt this like a stinging slap across his face in front of the others.

Casso continued, "We realize this might have been too much for any one guy to handle, so from this day forth, we're splitting up what needs to be done between the four of you."

Casso went on to give a rundown of who would do what, when, where, and how.

For the most part, Amuso was silent. He looked everywhere but at

D'Arco. In fact, Vic hadn't said a word to D'Arco since he'd gotten there. This, D'Arco viewed as a bad omen; this, D'Arco saw as a blinking red traffic light signaling danger up ahead. Amuso had never had an affinity for D'Arco and D'Arco knew it. It was Casso who had taken him under his wing; it was Casso who had nurtured him; it was Casso who had ultimately put him in a position of trust and responsibility. The others were relieved to hear this news. They had all felt slighted; they had all felt that D'Arco had no right to hold the position of trust that Casso bestowed on him.

D'Arco, however, seemed to shrink within himself and, right before the eyes of the others, he grew smaller, more round-shouldered. His head seemed to droop farther forward. He appeared a beaten man.

Casso continued. "I want the four of you to meet once a week and go over the family's business. I want no problems between you four. I want you to get along. We aren't going to be on the lam much longer. Soon as the government shoots its load, we'll turn ourselves in and beat them in court. Does anybody have any questions?"

This, Casso knew, was a crucial question—for the one who questioned Casso and Amuso's dictate would inevitably be the one who caused problems down the road. This was not lost on the others. In a very real sense it was rudimentary—so rudimentary that they all remained mute and still. Funny, if you looked at them, you had to be reminded of the monkeys that speak no evil, hear no evil, see no evil—

"Good," Casso said. And they went on to discuss family business until the wee hours of the morning.

People, society at large and the police, don't realize that much of the business of organized crime—the agreements, the disputes, the divvying up of different rackets, the introduction of new rackets, the creation of new robberies and new scores—was done late at night when most people slept. These men were night owls. It was as though they had a midnight-to-eight job.

Skittish and weary, Al D'Arco made his way home early that morning. He felt that people were watching him. He felt hostile eyes boring into his back. He believed it was just a matter of time before he was struck down. He had killed over a dozen people on the orders of Anthony Casso because Gaspipe believed those people to be informants. Nobody knew better than D'Arco how violent and utterly ice cold Gaspipe could be.

If, D'Arco knew, Gaspipe got so much as a whiff of someone being an informant, he'd kill him.

Where, he wondered, *could he flee?* He had a loving wife, parents he was very close to, and a son. The FBI, certainly, was no place for him to turn. He believed in his heart of hearts that Casso had the FBI in his back pocket. He'd seen it himself. Over and over, Casso had foreseen the future. He knew when the FBI was going to come to try and arrest him and Amuso before it happened. As D'Arco got in his car, he was afraid it would blow up.

Fuck, he thought. *How did I get myself into this?*

CHAPTER 58

BACKFIRE

Mafia capo Anthony Accetturo ran all the criminal enterprises in New Jersey—and Florida—for the Lucchese family. Accetturo had been born and raised in Newark, New Jersey's, toughest slums. He was a particularly rough, two-fisted individual who had worked his way up the ranks of the Mafia the hard way... through cunning, violence, murder, mayhem. He was such a fierce street fighter that he was nicknamed "Tumac," after the ferocious caveman from the 1940 film *One Million B.C.* He was from the same mold as Greg Scarpa Sr. and Eddie Lino— "a naturally tough bastard."

Accetturo was an old-fashioned mafioso. He believed in the Mafia's code of honor; he believed in the Mafia's oath of loyalty. His being in the Mafia had made him an exceptionally wealthy man. He had beautiful homes in New Jersey and in Hollywood, Florida.

Tony Ducks Corallo loved Accetturo; the two men were more like brothers than colleagues. Their relationship of over thirty years was silk-smooth, unblemished by bumps or curves.

Accetturo took in several million dollars a year, though on his annual tax return he reported only $100,000. He was deeply involved in gambling, loan-sharking, narcotics, and extortion, and he was particularly adept at taking over legitimate businesses. He loaned strapped businessmen money; they wouldn't pay back the loan on time—suddenly they had a new partner, Anthony Accetturo. He also had investments in real estate, insurance, asphalt and concrete, and equipment leasing and garbage carting companies.

Accetturo had seen the burgeoning potential of south Florida very early on. In the early 1970s, he realized the amazing potential in south Florida's booming economy. Most south Florida police jurisdictions were as naturally crooked as a NASCAR racetrack. Taking money and looking the other way was part and parcel of how southern law enforcement worked. For the slick, quick-witted, fast-moving Anthony Accetturo, this was an ideal setting, a home away from home, an idyllic situation for La Cosa Nostra.

In reality, the very powerful, dangerous Santo Trafficante was the boss of all of Florida. Anthony Accetturo was careful to never step on Trafficante's toes. He showed him deference and respect—made sure to never offend him, to pay promptly any money due him, and to ensure that none of his people infringed upon Trafficante's operations. These two men were cut from the same mold, old-world mafiosi as tough as rusted nails. Rumors had been swirling around for years that Trafficante was, in fact, responsible for the murder of John F. Kennedy. Casso, who knew about this via LCN's grapevine, said, "It was really Robert they wanted. He was making heat for everyone all over. But they knew if Robert was killed, the brother would stop at nothing to get his killers, so they decided to kill John, believing that would get rid of Robert, too. Trafficante got the job."

Tony Ducks had pretty much let Anthony Accetturo run his business in Jersey and Florida the way he wanted to. But as the years went by, Accetturo gave less and less money to Corallo. Corallo, who, over the years, had become enormously wealthy, was really not that concerned about what the Jersey faction of his family was kicking up. More important than money, in Ducks's mind, was that Accetturo could be trusted, that he never caused problems and that he was blindly loyal to Ducks. The loyalty alone, Ducks knew, was worth its weight in pure gold.

All this, however, changed when Tony Ducks appointed Vic Amuso the head of the family and Anthony Casso its underboss. In reality, Ducks had seriously contemplated making Accetturo the head of the Lucchese family; he was just on the verge of doing it. But he knew that the Brooklyn and Bronx factions of the family—by far the most powerful, by far the most dangerous—would never stand for someone they perceived as a lowly Jersey capo running the family. And so, ultimately, Ducks ended up appointing Amuso and Casso.

Initially, everything continued to run smoothly. But when Casso and Amuso realized how little Accetturo was actually kicking up, they were outraged, and demanded a full 50 percent of everything the Jersey crew was taking in. Naturally, Accetturo refused. "How dare these fucking upstarts look to shoot me down!" he said. "I was made while they were still in diapers!"

But in his heart he knew that he couldn't win a civil war with Amuso and Casso, the New York faction of the family. In 1987, Accetturo was indicted on a long list of RICO charges. He refused to plead guilty or accept a plea, and so he went to trial. The trial lasted twenty-one months. While he was on trial Casso and Amuso left him alone. It was the longest criminal trial in New Jersey's history and it ended up with all twenty defendants being found not guilty. The New Jersey jury did not believe the government's witnesses or the government's case. Court observers thought the government's case was too convoluted, had too many witnesses, and that some of the witnesses' backgrounds were so tainted they were unbelievable.

This was a major embarrassment for New Jersey law enforcement. It was an amazing, joyful time for the New Jersey Mafia . . . for mafiosi everywhere. Casso and Amuso invited the New Jersey faction of the Lucchese family into Brooklyn for a celebratory dinner. Only half the Jersey crew showed up, weary and skittish, and like a gaggle of nervous hens, they gathered in front of the restaurant, smoked cigarettes, and debated whether or not to go in.

Ultimately, comically, they figured Gaspipe was luring them all to their deaths, and they hurriedly got back in their cars and sped away. Casso and Amuso took this as a big insult. They had reached out in friendship and respect and the New Jersey men had spit in their eyes. It looked like war was imminent within the Lucchese borgata. Casso sent more and more demands to New Jersey. He convinced half the Jersey crew to come over and join them, while the other half remained loyal to Accetturo.

Suddenly, there were rumors on the street that Anthony Accetturo was a rat. Another rumor was that his wife, Geraldine, was transmitting instructions to different mafiosi. If either one of these accusations were true, they were punishable by death. Under no circumstances were women allowed to be part of business. In terror, more and more of the Jersey crew came over to Casso's side.

Ultimately, only fourteen members of the New Jersey faction of the Lucchese family stayed loyal to Accetturo, and Casso ordered every one of them shot to death. He gave pictures, names, and addresses to Lucchese hit teams and sent them off into New Jersey. Gaspipe also dispatched killers to murder Accetturo and his son Anthony Junior.

Wisely, Senior and Junior took refuge in Florida. It was familiar turf for them but unfamiliar for the New York killers. In addition, the Accetturos had the Florida cops in their back pockets. When, at one point in time, they spotted the hit team, they called the cops and suddenly police cars surrounded the Lucchese squad.

As the feud between the Lucchese factions escalated, less and less attention was paid to protecting their interests from law enforcement observation, infiltration, and what the FBI calls memorialization—recordings.

Stunned by their failed first attempt at putting the senior Accetturo away, the New Jersey Police carefully built a second case against him. Accetturo was again put on trial. He beat a series of murder charges, but this time he was convicted of racketeering. Overweight and suffering from high blood pressure, Accetturo appeared a beaten man. He was facing up to thirty-five years in prison and he had no doubt that any judge he appeared before would dole out the harshest sentence—a death sentence.

Left alone in his Jersey jail cell, he brooded and walked back and forth. All his life he had been loyal to the oath of *omerta*. All his life he had been a dedicated mafioso. Yet here he was being hounded by both his mafiosi brothers and law enforcement. He became depressed and morose.

He began thinking of actually cooperating with the government and really exposing all he knew about, not only the workings of the Lucchese family but also of the Mafia at large. In a very real sense, Accetturo was like a senior dean of the Mafia, a long-tenured professor at a prestigious college.

The straw that ultimately broke the camel's back was when Accetturo learned that Anthony Casso gave photographs of not only him to hit men but of his *wife,* too. This made his blood boil. He loved his wife of forty-five years dearly; he thought it an infamy that because of disagreements he had had with Casso and Amuso, they'd kill his wife. It was unconscionable, unspeakable—unthinkable.

What kind of fucking people are these? he wondered. *Wanna play dirty? I'll show you what dirty is, you fucking scumbags.*

To mark Accetturo's wife for death, those in the know say, was a blunder on Casso and Amuso's part. They, in return, say that she knew too much about Lucchese business and she had to go. They said the moment Accetturo enrolled his wife in the business workings of the family, she was in a very real sense marked for death.

"He should have never done that," Casso explained.

Accetturo reached out to a childhood friend, Bobby Buccino. Buccino was connected to the State of New Jersey attorney general's staff. His job was supervising cases brought against New Jersey mafiosi. He, like Accetturo, was a tough, two-fisted individual who had worked his way up the ranks. His career in law enforcement began as a state trooper. While he'd been a state trooper, he'd quickly garnered a reputation as a tough straight shooter. Buccino had no hesitation about walking into a bar brawl all by himself and knocking out half the combatants; this man had no hesitation about getting into shoot-outs when he was outnumbered, and he always came out unscathed.

Bob Buccino was a cop's cop—admired and respected by all his colleagues. When Anthony Accetturo decided to turn, he reached out to this man. They sat down and began to talk. Slowly, little by little, like peeling away layer after layer of a large, stinking onion, Accetturo drew a comprehensive, three-dimensional, highly detailed account of not just how New Jersey organized crime worked but how the Mafia worked across America.

Ultimately, the detailed, esoteric information coming from Accetturo and the soldiers who'd remained loyal to him persuaded twelve other members of the Lucchese family to plead guilty to a long list of federal and state charges, including nine homicides.

Single-handedly, Accetturo shut down the Lucchese crime family in New Jersey, exposing the Mafia and its inner workings in ways never seen before.

Needless to say, this did not bode well for Anthony Casso. Some would say that Casso made a major blunder when he tried to strong-arm a mafioso with the experience and wherewithal of Anthony Accetturo. Casso counters that Accetturo was a rat, that he allowed his wife to become part of the inner workings of the family, that he had to die.

But it was Casso's heavy-handedness that forced Accetturo to resort to playing his hand to law enforcement; Casso had boxed him into such a tight corner that the only way the elder mafioso could get out was by fleeing through the back door. In this case the back door opened to Bobby Buccino—the police.

Now, effectively, Gaspipe would soon have three hostile Lucchese capos—Al D'Arco, Pete Chiodo, and Anthony Accetturo—gleefully pointing their fingers at him and telling all they knew.

CHAPTER 59

ET TU, BRUTE?

The Mafia, since its very inception, has brilliantly used subterfuge and betrayal—backstabbing and usurping. The Mafia made the court of Versailles seem like a jovial playpen filled with people who were brimming with love for one another. Duplicity was the fuel that drove the engine that was La Cosa Nostra.

On July 19, 1991, Vic Amuso was at a shopping mall in Scranton, Pennsylvania. As Amuso approached a phone booth, a crack team of FBI agents surrounded him, cuffed him, put him in a black Dodge with all black tires, and sped him away. According, however, to someone in the know, there was an anonymous phone call the day before stating, definitively, not only that Amuso would be at that particular mall but also the time he'd be there. It didn't take Sherlock Holmes to realize that Amuso had been betrayed by one of the people who knew about the telephone system they'd set up.

Amuso was quickly charged with RICO violations and locked away. There would be no bail. He had proven beyond a shadow of a doubt that he was a flight risk.

Thus, Anthony Casso became the head of the Lucchese family. More paranoid and weary than ever, he ran through his mind who could have given Vic up; for the life of him he couldn't figure it out. Casso sat down and wrote Vic a letter stating that if he wanted him to, Casso would be willing to give himself up and face the Windows Case with him. Casso decided he would fight the charges with Vic if that's what Vic wanted—if Vic's attorneys thought it would be advantageous. Not only did Casso write him this letter, but he put $250,000 in cash in a shoebox that was due Vic with the letter and sent it to Vic's wife, Susan.

For some unfathomable reason, Mrs. Amuso did not open the box, did not see the money or the letter, and so Amuso didn't know about Casso's gesture.

Casso was being exceedingly magnanimous by not putting himself first. He was trying to do was what was good for his family—the Lucchese family. But Amuso knew nothing of the letter and he moved through the system that is the federal courts, the United States Justice Department, alone.

———

Boldly, Casso went about his meetings; he collected money, he ran the Lucchese family the way Captain Bligh ran the *Bounty*. Everyone had to be shipshape and smart—no slackers allowed. As Mob bosses go, Casso wasn't overly greedy. He had hands-on knowledge of the inner workings of all the family schemes, but he'd never been an administrator. He'd always been in the field, with the troops, giving orders, making money, in contact with the street. Casso never wanted to be a boss. He was angry that here he was, head of the family, worrying about everybody else's problems with no time to put together new schemes—new robberies, new exciting ways to make money.

And he missed his own family terribly. He missed quiet times with Lillian, Sunday nights together. He missed waking up in the morning and finding her in their spotless kitchen, always with a joke, always with a smile, always there for him. He missed her sense of humor. He missed laughing with her, missed the banter of his children, teaching his son how to throw a ball. *What kind of father am I?* he often asked himself. He never had an answer.

He was now at the top of the food chain; D'Arco was at the bottom. Casso passed word to his captains that everything would move forward as before, that the arrest of Amuso meant nothing. Once a week, as Casso mandated, the four captains, Anthony Bowat, Al D'Arco, Sally Avellino, and Frank Alstorono continued to meet.

———

On Thursday, September 19, 1991, D'Arco showed up for a meeting at the Kimberly Hotel in midtown Manhattan, on East Thirty-eighth Street. In the middle of the meeting between the four capos, Lucchese soldier Mike DeSantis showed up unannounced and uninvited. DeSantis worked with another Lucchese capo, Frank Lastorino. DeSantis, a short, thick, stocky individual, was a Lucchese hit man; his specialty was murder. Casso frequently used him to "clean house."

At one point that day, D'Arco spotted a pistol in DeSantis's waistband, and he noticed he was wearing a bulletproof vest.

In D'Arco's mind, DeSantis was there for one reason and that reason was to kill him. As he sat there staring at DeSantis, he felt he was looking at the grim reaper himself. Nervously, like some jack-in-the-box, D'Arco popped up and said he had to go.

"Gotta go, I've gotta run," he said. "Something came up."

He headed for the door like his ass was on fire, over the innocent protesting of the others. But D'Arco was not marked to be hit that day.

Ninety-nine percent of what he felt in the Kimberly Hotel was his own paranoia—uncontrollable fear. When D'Arco got home later that night, he put loaded guns in strategic spots all over his house. He paced back and forth like a man condemned, like a man living out the last hours of his life, and he planned.

His "plan" involved going to the FBI, giving himself up and telling all he knew. But how, he wondered, could he give himself up to the FBI when he knew that Casso had FBI agents on his payroll, in his pocket?

Pacing, pacing, pacing. *How?* he wondered.

His wife, Dolores, had the answer.

"Go," she said, "to an FBI office outside of New York. No matter what you think, Anthony is not an octopus, he's not a ghost. He can't be everywhere at once. Get a grip, man."

Dolores's words rang true. D'Arco grabbed some money he had stashed in the house—$57,000—then took his wife, parents, and son and fled the city. When he stopped running, he was in front of the New

Rochelle FBI office. He knocked loudly. Smiling, they slowly opened the door and welcomed him in. Within hours after establishing who he was and what he knew and why he was there, federal prosecutors Charlie Rose and Greg O'Connell were speeding toward New Rochelle from their downtown New York offices.

This, they knew, could be the break they'd been waiting for all along, a corroboration of what Fat Pete had been saying. This could be the chink in the armor of the Lucchese family they'd been searching for. When the two bright, astute prosecutors showed up in the New Rochelle FBI office, they found D'Arco surrounded by agents. They also found D'Arco scared to the core of his being. He refused to talk in front of any of the agents; he refused to believe he was safe; he wouldn't say anything until the three of them went into the bathroom alone, away from the agents.

There, in the bathroom, his eyes moving back and forth furtively, he told them why he was frightened. He told them Gaspipe was every-where. He said, "You've gotta know how dangerous this guy really is. He has sources. He has agents. He knows what's going on. I've seen it with my own eyes. Don't trust those guys inside. Please, I'm begging you. I'll give you anything you want. I've got it all, I've got it written down, I've got it here in my head. And I'll give it to you on a silver platter. All I ask is that you listen to what I'm saying. The FBI cannot be trusted. Why do you think Anthony's on the lam? Why do you think Amuso was on the lam? He already knew they would be indicted. Four days before the feds came to arrest him, he told me they were coming. You get it? You get what I'm saying?"

"Yeah," Rose said. "We get it. We understand. Don't you think we know that he took off right before we came for him? Don't you think we know why he took off? Let me put it to you like this: you won't be dealing with anybody but myself, my partner here, and only people we would trust with our own lives, with the lives of the ones we love, the lives of our children. We weren't born yesterday. We're not stupid. You can trust us. You can take that to the bank if you're straight up with us. If you lie, you're tying an anchor around your foot and throwing yourself overboard."

Rose's big, fat puppy dog eyes did not leave D'Arco's mouselike face for a second. "You understand?" Rose asked, his voice firm and steady . . . eminently believable, sincere.

Rose gave D'Arco a feeling of confidence; he was the antidote that D'Arco was looking for. Charlie Rose, in the very real sense, was an Anthony Casso. He was a man's man. You could take what he said as gospel.

"Okay?" Rose asked.

"Okay," D'Arco said, and they shook hands. Charlie Rose's handshake was strong and firm and steady—and it was done.

Now there were two highly motivated, highly informed Lucchese capos willing to testify against Casso and Amuso—spill the beans maximum. The worst possible scenario had happened. Not only were D'Arco and Fat Pete willing to testify, they were anxious and in a hurry. And, more important than anything, they were now under the government's care, under the government's watchful eye. They, as well as their family members, were in the Witness Protection Program. The Witness Protection Program had been a big success. It had been formed to encourage and foster the turn of mafiosi away from their oath of silence, away from any family loyalties.

It didn't take long for Casso to hear that D'Arco had, in fact, turned; D'Arco was going to be a hostile government witness. This, Casso knew, was bad news. D'Arco knew more about the murders and the inner workings of the Lucchese family than anyone else outside of himself.

Somehow, Casso would have to find D'Arco and kill him. Casso still had tremendous faith in his moles in the FBI and in the NYPD. After all, Steven Caracappa was still in the NYPD. Louis Eppolito had retired, but Caracappa was still working in the organized crime division of the New York Police Department. It was possible that Caracappa could find out the locale of D'Arco and give Casso the opportunity to "toast" him.

Meanwhile, Casso continued to run the Lucchese family from Mount Olive, New Jersey. He again grew a beard. He took to having trusted Lucchese soldiers drive him around as he held court in the back of the van. He had a cooler for bottles of water and soda. He had an impromptu toilet made out of a five-gallon plastic container. He would bend, but he would not break. He was indestructible. He was Anthony Gaspipe Casso.

CHAPTER 60

ESCAPE

Angry and bitter, Vic Amuso sat in jail stewing, wondering who had betrayed him. He blamed everybody but himself for getting caught. But the truth was that he had dropped his guard, he had been lax, and the FBI had nailed him.

From jail, he accused Gaspipe of not giving him his end of the money that they had loaned to Anthony Bowat, a Lucchese captain. But Casso had already given Amuso his end—the $250,000 in the shoebox that his wife had never opened.

Casso did not like a lot of things about Amuso and was very regretful that he had put him in the number one spot, but he still felt a bond with him. They had known each other many years. It wasn't Vic's fault he came up short in the brains department, Casso reasoned.

Diplomatically, Casso sent for Vic's brother Bobby and Frank Lastorino to meet him at a Holiday Inn in New Jersey. There, Casso told Bobby about the money in the shoebox and the letter sent months ago.

"You find that shoebox," Casso said, "you'll find your brother's money. To tell you the truth, I'm baffled that he would even think I'm capable of taking money from him. In a way that's always been your brother's problem, everything's always about money, money, money. There's more to life than money. Tell him—tell him I said that."

Bobby promised he'd pass Gaspipe's words on to Vic, that he'd hurry back to Howard Beach and look for the shoebox. Early the very next morning, Bobby contacted Casso as per their agreement and Bobby did, in fact, find the shoebox with the money and with the letter. Bobby profusely apologized for his brother's mistrust and misguided words.

———

Again, Anthony Casso thought out of the box—went for long walks around pristine Budd Lake, enjoying the scenery and how when the lake was calm, it mirrored the slow-moving, silklike clouds perfectly. For the first time in his life he saw egrets—tall, elegant fishermen, as white as snow.

Casso began hatching a plan in which Amuso would escape from prison. Casso did not like Amuso in jail. For a host of reasons, he knew it would be better if Amuso was free, least of which was the fact that Casso was concerned that Amuso would turn on him.

In underworld crime, there are many interconnecting lines of communication. To an astute eye, the links that make up organized crime are very much like a spider's web.

Amuso was being kept at Danbury Federal Prison in Connecticut where, coincidentally, a member of Gaspipe's brilliant bypass gang was also doing time. His name was John McCarthy and, lo and behold, McCarthy had one of the prison guards in his back pocket; that is, he was buying alcohol, food, drugs, and pussy from the guard. (Women were regularly snuck into prison.) In a very real sense, this was a major crack in the façade of the prison. If a guard is willing to take several thousand dollars to look the other way for contraband, you can pretty much count on the fact that he would do anything for a hundred thousand dollars. No matter how you cut it, Amuso was a very wealthy man. He could have easily bestowed millions of dollars upon this crooked guard. Gaspipe immediately summoned other crew members and put a plan together to get Amuso out of Danbury. He rented a home within one mile of the prison to work out the details without being noticed. One of the first orders of business was to have McCarthy get the air frequency numbers off the guard's prison walkie-talkie so that they could actually hear—from outside the prison—exactly what the guards said the day they took Amuso out. Casso put a great deal of time and money into this audacious effort, this even after Amuso had accused him of being untrustworthy . . . of not being a "friend."

Through the crooked guard and with the help of McCarthy, a change of clothes was left for Amuso. He was to walk out of the prison with a group of visitors at 4:00 P.M. on May 17, 1992. Casso arranged for a car to be outside the prison to bring Amuso directly to him in New Jersey.

When the day arrived, the prison guard and McCarthy went to get Amuso to show him the way and give him the change of clothes. But Amuso refused to leave his cell.

"I changed my mind," he said.

"Are you fucking kiddin'?" McCarthy said.

"I ain't going," Amuso said.

People in the know suggest that Amuso felt he was walking into a trap, that Gaspipe was going to kill him. Amuso knew how truly dangerous Casso could be . . . not because of an out-of-control, raging psychosis, but because of a very rare, cold cunning.

No doubt that is what kept Amuso in his cell that day.

But Casso had no plan to kill Amuso. He just wanted Amuso out of jail.

CHAPTER 61

TIGHT-LIPPED VIC

In mid-January 1993, Vic Amuso was convicted of RICO charges and given a life sentence. With Al D'Arco, Fat Pete Chiodo, and Tumac Accetturo cooperating with prosecutors, it was a slam-dunk case for the government. Amuso never offered to testify or become a witness for the prosecution. He stayed loyal to his pledge of *omerta*; he did not name names, talk about crimes or murders, or discuss anything else. Vic Amuso was going to take his punishment like a man, go off and do his time. From the onset, Amuso knew that jail was part and parcel of the world he was in and he accepted that. Tight lipped and quiet when sentenced, his head bowed down, his ankles and wrists shackled, Amuso was led away by federal marshals without saying a word to anyone.

Over the next several days, as mafiosi around the country heard what he had done, they toasted him in respect.

Yet everyone knew, the government knew, that the brains behind the Lucchese family, the pistons that drove the engine—since Tony Ducks had been sent away—was Anthony Gaspipe Casso. U.S. Attorney Andrew Maloney declared at a press conference after Amuso's trial that Anthony Casso was "the most dangerous, cunning, ruthless Mafia leader left on the streets. He is number one on the hit parade of wanted criminals."

Greg O'Connell, one of the federal prosecutors, said, "We consider him the most dangerous organized criminal in our scope. He is the one responsible for countless murders and could do the most damage to the public."

The head of the Justice Department's New York branch, Jim Fox, added, "Casso is a psychopath whose name should be Mad Dog."

The federal prosecutors failed, it would be revealed, to fully understand the subtleties of Anthony Casso's hold on not only the Lucchese family but on the New York Mafia as a whole.

An interesting sidebar is how the federal government refused to acknowledge that Casso had FBI agents working on his behalf, that Casso had New York police detectives killing people for him. It seemed, for all intents and purposes, that the federal government believed that if they dubbed Casso a "psychopath," a "mad dog," and so on, they would diminish the far-reaching aspects of what Anthony Casso was about—that he had turned FBI agents the way the Justice Department had turned Mob guys.

It is obvious that the Justice Department did not want to acknowledge how manipulative and smart Gaspipe had been.

The government had shit in its underwear, but wouldn't acknowledge it. If no one mentioned it, they hoped, no one would notice the stink; it would not become public.

For the most part, the government had taken on the guise of cop, jury, judge, and executioner. The belief was that any tactic used against the Mafia was okay, that it was all right to fight dirty. Perhaps this is so. The Mafia was like a vampire drawing sustenance from the whole of society. Though this country's success is based on the rule of law and the rule of law must be applied to all equally, you can't fight clean if your opponent is fighting dirty; you have to get down to his level and take the fight to him.

Another interesting sidebar is how amazingly political the prosecution of Mob figures can be. Rudolph Giuliani used his prosecution of Mob figures to establish a brilliant political career. Giuliani was not the kind of prosecutor who worked behind the scenes, did his job quietly, and kept himself out of the limelight. It was common knowledge among people in the U.S. Justice Department during Giuliani's reign that there wasn't a camera he didn't like. He was constantly holding press conferences and constantly announcing the indictments, arrests, and convictions of Mob guys.

He was doing a good job of fighting criminals but a lot of people in the press began to believe that Giuliani was more concerned with his profile, his reputation—his own notoriety—than justice.

Clearly, Giuliani used his successful tenure in the U.S. Justice Department to run for mayor of New York City. Although he lost to David Dinkins in 1989, he challenged Dinkins again in 1993 and beat the incumbent. He won again in 1997. One of his mayoral platforms was that he was "tough on crime." He recently had his sights set on the Oval Office. Many political pundits say that that's what Giuliani was always after. He wanted to use his career as a crime-fighting prosecutor as the first rung on the ladder to high office. He always wanted to be the boss of bosses, to tell everyone what to do and how to do it.

Another prime example of crime fighting being political is Thomas E. Dewey. With an unprecedented tenacity, Dewey went after Mob figures such as Waxey Gordon, Dutch Schultz, and Lucky Luciano in the 1930s and used his successful stint as a prosecutor to become the governor of New York State. He, too, wanted to be president of the United States, but except for the *Chicago Daily Tribune* prematurely trumpeting his defeat of Harry Truman in 1948, it was not in the cards for him.

CHAPTER 62

KING GASPIPE

By Amuso refusing to leave his jail cell, he had effectively resigned his position as head of the Lucchese family. Anthony Casso, therefore, became the official head of the Luccheses.

The irony was that for years, Casso had been running away from positions of power. Casso was all about working the streets, making money, doing what he was comfortable with—he didn't want to be a boss. But here he was, the result of a series of Kafka-like turns and twists that put him in the driver's seat of the Lucchese family.

On a daily basis now, Casso would travel to Brooklyn and to two different town houses he had purchased in Rockaway, New Jersey. His trusted driver was George Zappola Jr. George's father, George Sr., was a dear friend of Casso's. They had been kids together in South Brooklyn. The senior Zappola was part of Casso's original bypass gang, and Casso thought the world of him.

But Chin Gigante ordered George Sr.'s murder in 1980 over the divvying up of a jewelry heist. His body had been cut up and dumped in the ocean off Long Island. His severed head had found its way to a lonely stretch of beach on Staten Island. When George Sr. was laid out, just his head was in the coffin. The Gigante people also wanted to kill George Jr., because they felt it was just a matter of time before he came looking for revenge. They knew George Jr. to be a stand-up tough guy and that he wouldn't lie down over his father's murder . . . not just his murder, but how he had been cut up like a side of beef. Casso was not about to let this happen. He had a meeting with Genovese underboss Benny Eggs and he asked Eggs to petition the Chin to release George Jr. to the Luccheses as a personal favor. The Chin agreed and Casso had George Jr. inducted into the Lucchese family.

The Genovese killers—the men who killed the senior Zappola—weren't pleased when they were told about this. But Casso had to take, in the public domain of La Cosa Nostra, full responsibility for George Jr.'s actions. Later, Casso, who was very fond of the junior Zappola, would make him a captain.

The key to Casso's staying free was fluid mobility—he was here, there, and everywhere all at once. Casso became more and more confident in his ability to stay off the FBI's radar. He even allowed his wife to visit him on weekends. Brazenly, they would shop for the kids at different malls in Rockaway, go to lunch, take in an afternoon movie, have a nice enjoyable dinner, and then make love—all while Gaspipe was America's most wanted fugitive and number one on the FBI's Ten Most Wanted list . . . a Mafia superstar.

Casso had come to view the FBI as a bunch of Keystone Cops. He thought they were incompetent, crooked, and not worthy adversaries.

Casso figured if he could stay free another twelve to seventeen months, the Windows Case would be over; he would be able to beat it and resume life as normal. Every hour that Casso was free, the government became more and more frustrated.

Mafia aficionados, John Q. Citizen, were rooting for Gaspipe in a big way. He had become the antiestablishment hero, a Mafia rock star. News accounts envisioned Casso moving around in esoteric disguises—as a hunchback, as a Hasidic rabbi, as a clown in full regalia.

Money. Everyone in the Justice Department knew that if they could find Casso's money, that would help flush him out. They knew his wealth to be enormous but still they went about the meticulous business of locating Casso's stashes. In their quest to locate the funds, they did find six bank accounts in various names totaling $684,558. They also located a safety deposit box in Lillian's name that contained $200,000 cash in a dog food container. However, the confiscation of these funds was a mere drop in the bucket. Casso would later say, "I had rooms filled with money."

———

Once again Burton Kaplan entered Casso's life. Casso still believed that Kaplan could be trusted, not out of friendship or loyalty, but more because Kaplan was afraid of him; Casso really felt Kaplan wouldn't do anything to undermine Casso or his interests.

On Friday, January 16, 1993, Kaplan drove Lillian Casso to meet Anthony at the Rockaway Mall. Kaplan did this with the understanding that he was to pick up Lillian on Sunday and bring her home. It was Kaplan's job, as he was bringing Lillian to the Jersey mall, to make sure neither the police nor the FBI followed him. When Kaplan came back to pick up Lillian, Anthony sat him down and told him that it was time to sign the deed back to Lillian for the Seventy-second Street house, and for Kaplan to put Lillian's name in a partnership agreement he and Casso had with Harold Lee's factories in the free trade zone in Arizona. Harold Lee was an astute Chinese businessman well connected to the Chinese government who had partnered up with Casso and Kaplan in a clock manufacturing business in the free trade zone. At that point, Casso knew that Kaplan was contemplating having his percentage transferred to his daughter's name to keep the government from finding out about this enterprise. Kaplan assured Casso he would follow his instructions, that he would have the deed to the home transferred back to Lillian's name and that Casso's interest in Harold Lee's factory would be put into Lillian's name as well. Anthony hugged and kissed Lillian good-bye that day. He walked away believing Kaplan would carry out his requests with speed and diligence.

Less than twenty-four hours later, a heavily armed FBI SWAT team descended upon Anthony's Mount Olive house.

CHAPTER 63

NO, YOU COME UP

January 19, 1993, was a major turning point in Anthony Casso's life. It was also a turning point in the world of La Cosa Nostra. It was a bitterly cold, very clear day. Frigid winds hurried off Budd Lake. Bare trees with long, arthritic fingers bent and swayed with each gust.

According to the FBI, it had managed to pinpoint Casso's location by using a tracking device that gave the locale of a newfangled apparatus called a cellular telephone. It was one of those early, clumsy versions that was the size of a walkie-talkie with a conspicuous antenna sticking out of it. According to people in the know, Burton Kaplan gave up Casso's locale. As more than a dozen FBI SWAT team members converged on Casso's hideaway, sporting Kevlar vests and carrying machine guns, shotguns, and tear gas guns, Casso was taking a hot shower. They banged on the front door, banged on the windows.

"FBI!" they shouted. "FBI! Come on out with your hands up!"

Upstairs, in the shower, Casso didn't even hear them. It was not unusual for him to take a shower for a full hour; he scrubbed with great diligence with imported brushes.

When he stepped from the shower that day, he was as squeaky clean as a newborn babe. It was now, for the first time, that he heard the *bang . . . bang . . . bang . . . bang.*

"FBI! Come on out with your hands up!"

For the FBI agents there that day, Anthony Casso was the worst of the worst. He was John Dillinger, Baby Face Nelson, Billy the Kid, and Clyde Barrow all rolled into one. Gaspipe's reputation as a senseless, remorseless killer was legendary among these law enforcement officials. Although rumors of Casso's killing prowess were completely disproportionate to reality, it is not an exaggeration to say that the agents there that day were on pins and needles, that their trigger fingers were itchy, that they were actually anxious to shoot holes in Casso. From upstairs Casso now listened to agents bang on the door with clenched, angry fists, demanding entrance.

Casso always knew this day would come. Now it was here. The thought of putting up some kind of struggle or pulling out a weapon was anathema to Casso. He still viewed himself as a businessman and what was happening that morning was nothing more than a business dispute.

Yes, Casso had been caught. But in his mind, this was just the beginning, the first bell in a fifteen-round championship fight. The agents downstairs were fed up with waiting. The door was kicked open by heavy, black combat boots. The agents rushed in, a stream of heavily armed humanity.

"Gaspipe! Give it up!" Agent John Sullivan shouted.

They stood still, pointing their guns every which way, very much like you'd see in a movie, but this was real.

"Anthony, give it up!"

"I'm upstairs," Casso shouted down.

"Come on downstairs," Agent Richard Rudolph shouted back.

"I'm getting dressed," he shouted down.

"Get dressed down here," he was told.

"I ain't coming down until I'm dressed," Casso said.

"We're coming up," he was told.

"Suit yourself," he said, as he sat on the bed and put on a pair of silk socks.

When the agents reached the bedroom, guns cocked and ready, Casso was nonchalantly putting on his pants.

"How you doing?" he asked. And he was soon dressed and whisked away.

Federal agents found $375,000 in the house that day. They also found the key to another safety deposit box containing $200,000, which was to help pay for Casso's daughter's upcoming wedding. In still another safety deposit box, they found another half-million dollars' worth of his wife's jewelry. Anthony did not know that Lillian had put her jewelry in that safety deposit box. Now it was gone.

Casso was whisked to Manhattan, where he appeared before a federal judge in the Eastern District; he was then housed in the Metropolitan Correction Center (MCC) without bail.

Lillian had heard over the news that Anthony had been arrested in the home of a childhood *girlfriend*. She was incensed, outraged, and felt betrayed—violated—used. She knew Rosemarie Billotti and had never liked her. For the life of her, she could not understand how Anthony could be so deceitful, duplicitous—such a two-faced pig. It would take, in fact, many months for Lillian's anger to abate and for her to agree to go visit her husband. Anthony sent her message after message imploring her to come.

In Casso's mind, his course of action was as clear as the ringing of a bell—he'd escape. Casso believed that with the cash he had available and with his contacts and resources, and his Machiavellian-type cunning, he'd surely be able to buy his way out of this predicament. For Casso, that's what this was—a mere predicament, a state of being that was forced upon him but was only temporary.

Casso's first strategy was to try to get moved to the Danbury Federal Prison. There, he knew, he'd surely be able to escape. But unfortunately for Casso, the prison had been turned into a women's facility; men were no longer housed there.

The storm clouds and lightning he'd seen from afar were now upon him. Lady Luck had turned her back on Anthony Casso.

———

The MCC was literally bursting at the seams with mafiosi. Every made man arrested in the Southern District was housed there. Casso was suddenly sitting with members of all the five families—soldiers, lieutenants, capos, and bosses. It was like some kind of camp for wayward mafiosi. Among this group, Gaspipe was a hero, a king, a man of respect. They all spoke the same language, they all walked the same walk, and they all came from the same culture. In a very real sense, they were not many, they were one.

At night, alone in his MCC cell, Casso paced. To an observer, he looked like a large jungle cat that had been suddenly taken from the jungle and put in a six-by-eight-foot cage. Back and forth, slowly, back and forth he moved.

Escape; escape; escape!

Casso obsessed on the word.

Casso obsessed on the deed.

Soon, Anthony put the wheels in motion for his escape. He was housed on the eleventh floor, in section Eleven North, with the Gambino brothers, Joe and John. Also there were Spero the Greek, who was with the Luccheses, Gregory Scarpa Sr., Anthony Bowat, and many others. Just across the hall, in Eleven South, Vic Orena, the acting boss of the Colombos, was housed. Orena was surrounded by dozens of mafiosi. Orena, Casso quickly learned, had an officer named Thomas Moore on the pad—he was taking money to look the other way. When Casso heard that, lights went off in his head. His eyes seemed to brighten. He immediately arranged to have Greg Scarpa moved to Eleven South; there were cells on this side.

Without preamble, Casso put Officer Moore on the payroll. He gave him five hundred dollars a week. For that, Moore would gladly go to an Italian restaurant on Mulberry Street every afternoon before going to work at the MCC and pick up hot cooked food that was waiting for him and bring it to Casso and Joey Gambino, along with a bottle of wine and a bottle of fine brandy. (This continued for over a year.)

Casso related for this book: "Later, when I knew Moore could be trusted, I had him bring in two pistols, a knife, and a cell phone. I had the keys made for the doors leading to the visitors' elevator. I made clay impressions from Moore's keys while on duty. I had the impressions smuggled out and new keys smuggled in. I had the officer smuggle in new clothes for my escape. The first plan was to wait 'til Moore was working in the control room located on the ground floor, where he would be watching all the prison monitors and controlling the elevators. And right before I would let myself out with the key, Moore would summon the street guard to check another part of the building that would allow me to walk outside unnoticed, and to freedom.

"While the escape plan was in motion, Officer Moore was working in the control room. At six o'clock on Saturday morning, the Eleven North floor officer came to my cell to inform me that I had a legal visit down on the third floor. I knew it was Moore calling, that there was no legal visit. Immediately I put street clothes on under my brown jumpsuit. The guards buzzed the doors open so I could get to the hall floor elevators. I entered the elevator, knowing that Moore was watching me on camera. Moore started bringing the elevator down to the ground-floor level. The doors opened and another officer was standing there, dumbfounded to see me alone, unescorted. And especially on the ground floor. Moore tells the officer I was called for a legal visit. The officer checks it out. No attorneys are present. I was returned to Eleven North escorted by two officers. Lucky for me that I hadn't taken off the brown jumpsuit. I was supposed to leave the jumpsuit inside the elevator and walk out through the garage and through the side door. That was the end of plan number one. It all happened so fast and unexpected, I had no time to get the pistols from Moore."

[Plan B]: "I was to go down the visitors' elevator and out the side door that was guarded only by one officer with a pistol. I was to call the bypass crew on a cell phone to unarm the outside guard and handcuff him inside so that I could walk out to a car. This plan never took place because days before it was about to happen the World Trade Center was bombed in the garage and the security around the MCC was tightened 24/7."

[Plan C]: "Was," Casso explained, "to overpower the U.S. marshals' van, when I was being taken back from Brooklyn Court to the MCC. This might have worked if not for Amuso ordering a Lucchese member *not* to show up and block off the street with a cement truck. This was needed to stop the traffic while the van was overpowered. The marshals always drove with their windows down, one guy and one woman.

"That's the end of escapes from the MCC. I didn't have the same opportunity to walk out of prison like Amuso had."

Casso and his incarcerated LCN cronies were facing sentences that would amount to dying in jail. The MCC was the last stop before being sent to hell—life in prison.

CHAPTER 64

EARTHQUAKE ROCKS MAFIADOM

On April 18, 1906, San Francisco was hit with an earthquake that just about destroyed the entire city: many were killed; thousands of buildings were flattened. When Sammy the Bull Gravano decided to become an informer, the net effect of that decision was like the Mafia being hit with a devastating quake.

Not only had Gravano agree to testify against John Gotti, but Gravano agreed to tell all he knew about the workings of the Mafia. This was a monumental occurrence because no mafioso who had the stature, the high position, of underboss had ever testified against La Cosa Nostra.

Over the years, there were Mafia informants who had actually been made, the first of whom was Joe Valachi at a Senate subcommittee meeting in 1952. At the time, and for years thereafter, he was the only made man to tell about the structure and inner workings of the American Mafia. But Valachi was a coarse thug—he carried out orders, he did not give them. He did not know the inner workings of the upper echelon of any of the families, including his own.

Still, back in 1952, what Joe Valachi had to say was shocking—that there was a concentrated group of men who were highly motivated and highly successful, whose purpose was successfully carrying out murder, racketeering, larceny, hijacking, bootlegging, and kidnapping . . . just about every crime but rape. Valachi likened the modern Mafia to ancient Roman legions because of the similarity in structure—that is, how orders were given and followed.

Now Sammy the Bull was telling all he knew in a Manhattan courtroom. The government managed to get Gravano to talk by playing surreptitiously taped conversations of John Gotti, recorded in a small apartment above the Ravenite Social Club in Little Italy. Gotti believed he could speak freely, believed he could say anything he wanted, when he wanted, how he wanted. The FBI had planted bugs in the Ravenite Social Club without problem. However, over a few months, all they heard was music, mostly Italian operas, being played. They finally figured out that Gotti had access to one of the apartments upstairs, number 10 on the third floor, and through clever machinations, they managed to get inside the apartment while its permanent tenant, seventy-two-year-old Nettie Cirelli, went shopping. The FBI hit pay dirt when Ms. Cirelli went to visit her family on Staten Island for a long weekend. Brash and overconfident, Gotti held meetings in Cirelli's apartment and thus the FBI managed to get excellent recordings of him talking about myriad crimes, including murder, extortions, robberies, and hijacks. This was a fatal flaw in Gotti's judgment because the FBI was gleefully recording every single word. Later, the FBI played the tapes for Gravano in which John Gotti castigated Gravano, called him names, and spoke in detail about murders that Gravano committed. Stunned and shocked, Gravano listened to Gotti belittle him and put him in the position of being charged with the murders Gotti talked about. After hearing this, Gravano agreed to become an informer, and what an informer he became. He was quickly put in the Witness Protection Program and from that secretive place, the government plotted and planned their strategy to take apart the Mafia piece by piece, bone by bone.

Federal prosecutors had what they always wanted: somebody who was part of the inner workings of the upper echelon of the Mafia willing to talk with authority, precision, and, more important, believability.

Gravano, dressed in a conservative, well-cut suit, wearing a white shirt and tie, was an impressive sight. He had an unassuming baby face, blue eyes, and dirty blond hair. On the witness stand, he seemed more like a beat-up Malibu surfer than a Mafia underboss.

The net effect of Gravano turning was profound for LCN, for Gravano knew, in colorful detail, about crimes all the families were involved with.

———

From his vantage point in the MCC, Casso followed what Gravano did via television and newspaper accounts with great interest—and with great disdain. Since he was five years old, Casso had hated informers—"rats."

Even in grade school, to be called a rat, a stool pigeon, was the worst possible insult, worse even than being called a motherfucker. Casso's father hated rats. All his uncles hated rats. His mother hated rats. Sitting on his bunk bed in the MCC, Casso could clearly remember his mother bad-mouthing rats.

The whole concept of *omerta* was swearing to silence, swearing on your life and on a holy saint. It was a literal blood oath, an oath that could not be broken, yet here was Gravano not only breaking the oath but happily naming names, crimes, dates, and places. Casso cringed at the thought of becoming a rat.

Anthony remembered as a young boy going for Sunday drives with his father to Sally Callinbrano's club. He remembered the respect Sally Callinbrano and the other men in LCN received. To those men, Anthony knew, a rat was the lowest form of life; a rat was little more than a rabid dog who could be shot and killed on sight. Casso remembered the case of the Blue Beetle. When he was in his midteens, the Blue Beetle, a South Brooklyn character who had been a noted jockey for a while, testified that he saw Alley Persico kill a man. It was an amazing sight to see the Blue Beetle take the stand and point at Persico and tell the court how he had seen him kill. The Blue Beetle came from this neighborhood. He knew the consequences of such an act. Persico was convicted and, upon his sentencing, the trial judge turned to Persico and said, "If anything happens to this witness, your sentence will be doubled. It's high time that you and your type stop scaring the citizenry, stop terrorizing brave people like the witness here."

Persico stared at the judge with dead eyes. He didn't acknowledge him, he didn't nod his head, he just stared.

Persico, Casso remembered, went away and did his time . . . ten years. During those years, the Blue Beetle was never seen in the neighborhood. He then, however, came back to the neighborhood because, supposedly, his mother was ill. Alley Persico at this point had been released from jail. Alley's brother Carmine heard that the Blue Beetle was at a card game in the neighborhood. He went and found him and shot him dead in front of five people. None of those five people saw or knew anything. Carmine Persico was never charged with the killing of the Blue Beetle.

This was, in Casso's mind, just and correct and the way things should be. Yet, here was Sammy Gravano, the underboss of the Gambino family, a rat, a stool pigeon, singing like a caged canary on a beautiful spring day.

Among the mafiosi at the MCC that year, the turning of Gravano was big news. That's all everyone talked about. They were like a bunch of old washerwomen talking over the fence, and all they talked about was what a scumbag Sammy Gravano was.

———

Soon word got out that Gaspipe was living the good life in Eleven North, and everyone he knew wanted to be moved over to the section he was in. There were Johnny and Joe Gambino, Alley Persico, and Virgil Alessi—a captain in the DeCavalcante family—also capo Bobby Carvert.

The authorities quickly learned that mafiosi were gathering around Casso like bees around honey and they shipped him out of the MCC and sent him to Otisville in upstate New York. Lucchese capo Sal Avellino was there as well as Baldy Mike Spinelli, who had tried to kill Fat Pete's sister, and Marat Balagula, arrested for gasoline tax fraud. Also, two guys from Casso's bypass crew were housed in Otisville.

Now absolutely intent upon escape, Casso immediately began looking to buy corrupt officials. With the kind of money he had to offer, and considering his reputation, it didn't take long for him to find an officer who was willing to help him escape on horseback. Since Otisville was located in the middle of a forest, the plan was for Casso to get on a waiting horse, ride through the trees to a waiting car, and drive away.

Again, Casso saw a bright light at the end of the tunnel—his escape. Freedom. Before he left, however, he was able to have a good talk with Lucchese capo Sal Avellino. Avellino had pled guilty to the murders of Robert Kubecka and Donald Barstow, the two men who had owned a private sanitation company in Long Island. As part of a conspiracy, Casso and Amuso had been indicted for these murders. Casso said to Sal,

"Where the fuck do you get off pleading guilty to murder charges that I'm indicted for without even talking to me, without trying to talk to me?"

Both Casso and Avellino knew that this was a cardinal sin—you do not undermine a boss's chance to beat a case by pleading guilty. Looking at Casso, Avellino knew he could very well be killed for what he'd done.

Telling the truth, Avellino said, "Anthony, I spoke with Amuso about this and he gave me permission to plead guilty. Otherwise I never would have. I swear. I swear on my mother's life!"

Casso took a long, exasperated breath. He knew this was just the kind of thing Amuso would do. Still, Casso thought of Avellino as a scumbag and he pretty much told him he was not in the family anymore—that he was persona non grata.

Back in his cell, Casso paced back and forth, thinking about escaping, dreaming about freedom, scheming about ways he would not get caught and sent back to jail. He would set up new identities for himself, go to South America, start businesses down there. After a while he'd send for Lillian and his kids—they'd have a good life. A happy ending.

Perhaps, he thought, he'd go to Italy. He'd buy a nice villa in the south somewhere, open some kind of import-export company, and not commit any crimes. He had enough money now to last many lifetimes.

What concerned him was freedom, having the ability to spend the money. Being in jail during these months taught Gaspipe several very important lessons—the least of which was to treat freedom with reverence and respect and never take it for granted. While at Otisville, Casso *made* Baldy Mike in an impromptu ceremony there in his cell. Casso looked forward to the following week because he'd be escaping from Otisville.

He saw himself jumping on a horse and riding quickly through the forest. Casso was an excellent horseman, as he'd been riding in Prospect Park and upstate New York since he was a kid, and he'd be shot dead before he allowed himself to be captured. Once he got on a horse, the next stop was *freedom*.

Before Casso's fateful, fanciful horseback ride, however, he was moved back to the MCC and housed on the seventh floor, not in Eleven North anymore. Here Casso ran into a dozen members of the Colombo family and Wild Bill Cutolo, a tough Colombo capo. Cutolo and Casso knew each other well from the street—Cutolo trusted Casso, and without reservation, Cutolo told Casso about a plot the Colombos had to kill a federal judge named Eugene Nickerson. This little tidbit of information would later come back and haunt Casso in a big way. Wild Bill said that Nickerson had to be taken off the case he and his codefendants were in together because he kept ruling against them and because he felt that they'd never get a fair shake in front of Nickerson. Wild Bill also told Casso that they knew where the judge lived and they knew his route to work every day. Casso wished him luck. As far as Casso was concerned, the incident was over—forgotten; it really had nothing to do with him.

Casso had been brought back to the MCC because he was to appear the following week in front of Judge Nickerson's court. Casso saw this as another opportunity for escape; he'd been waiting for just such an event, to be brought to a court in Brooklyn. Immediately, Casso contacted the bypass crew. He wanted them to take over the marshals' van he was in after leaving court and heading back to the MCC. The plan was to use an oversized cement truck to block a narrow city street, trapping the van, and then to overcome the two marshals with firepower. Everything quickly fell into place except for the cement truck and a driver that were needed to block off the street.

Casso quickly learned that Vic Amuso had ordered the driver not to help Casso escape and so he didn't show up at the prescribed time. Without interception or intervention, Casso was taken from the MCC in lower Manhattan to Brooklyn, appeared in front of Judge Nickerson, and returned to the MCC without event.

———

Slowly, Gaspipe's outlook was changing. He no longer held LCN in great esteem. He saw LCN as a broken shell of what it had been. Casso grew to hate Vic Amuso, and he hated Chin Gigante for not killing Peter Savino.

After all, Casso reasoned, *if Gigante had killed Savino like he was supposed to, none of us would have gotten arrested.* Casso had come to view them all as selfish, self-serving scumbags. Casso could not help but think of the deal Gravano had gotten, that he would be getting his freedom.

Alone, back and forth, back and forth, Casso walked, logging a good ten miles in that little cell every day. He thought about Fat Pete and

D'Arco. He wasn't stupid; he knew his chances of winning any kind of trial were nil.

Anthony wished his father were still alive. He wanted his consultation; he wanted his advice. At least he knew he could trust his father not to double-cross him. The more Casso thought about what had been done to him, the more angry he became. He believed in his heart of hearts that he'd always been fair and equitable and honest with all the people he'd ever dealt with in LCN, with all the people he'd ever dealt with on the street. And because Casso believed he'd been equitable through his entire career, he felt all the more slighted and outraged at how different members of LCN had acted—and how their actions had hurt him.

Back in the MCC, Casso was placed in Seven North. For a few weeks all he did was contemplate his next move. The government had offered Casso a twenty-two-year plea bargain. If Casso accepted such a plea, he'd be out of jail after doing two-thirds of the sentence . . . some fifteen years—in 2008.

Again and again, what Gravano did played through Casso's mind, but even the *idea* of cooperating with the government bothered Anthony deeply and profoundly—it caused him to feel a kind of inner earthquake that left him all broken up. Casso also knew that Philadelphia Mob underboss Phil Leonetti had pleaded guilty and been given a six-and-a-half-year sentence.

Casso's mind turned to his wife and children. They would play, ultimately, a huge role in what he ended up deciding. Casso knew that if he did take the twenty-two-year plea, by the time he got out of prison, his children would be grown up, married with children of their own, and moved away. If he knew he could get a six-and-a-half-year plea bargain, he'd be out in time to enjoy a good, full life with his wife, Lillian. They'd move to another state. They'd buy a home. They would enjoy the fall of their lives together. Casso owned a trucking company worth, at one point, $5 million, and he would try to keep that as part of his agreement—he'd sell it, he decided.

Like a slowly bending thick piece of steel under a great weight, little by little, Gaspipe's mind moved in the direction of his becoming an informant. He felt no allegiance anymore to Vic Amuso, Chin Gigante, or anybody else.

Lillian still hadn't come to visit Anthony. She was still very upset about his living with Rosemarie Billotti. But he felt confident that once she saw the new Anthony, understood that he had changed and how sorry he was, she'd come onboard and she'd go anywhere with him, including Siberia if need be. Anthony started thinking of his plan as "my new life."

It echoed in his head like the words to a favorite song. *My new life; my new life; my new life* it went.

———

In January 1994, as blustery winds pushed against the MCC, chilling the citizenry of New York City to the very bone, a request from the FBI came to Casso for handwriting samples. Casso refused. Judge Nickerson ordered that he pay a fine of $5,000 a day until he provided his handwriting.

Casso's Machiavellian mind began to churn. He called his attorney Mike Rosen from the pay phone at the MCC. He thought of Mike as a great guy and an eminently fine attorney. He told Rosen to arrange an appointment with a government agent for him to give handwriting samples. Casso was willing to use this as only a ruse that would allow him to get close to the people who would ultimately make the decision about a plea.

Gaspipe was moved from the MCC to the Brooklyn U.S. Attorney's Office. Upon his arrival, he was greeted by FBI agent Richard Rudolph. Rudolph had been one of the agents present when Casso was arrested in New Jersey. He was a large dour man who had obvious disdain for LCN and its members. In Rudolph's mind they were bloodsucking, murdering vampires—the scourge of society. Conversely, Casso felt equal disdain for Rudolph and the FBI. He thought of them as corrupt bullies with guns and badges, nothing more. But Casso would do business with anybody to get what he was after. Dealing with Rudolph, taking a plea was only a means to an end. He'd use the FBI like a carpenter a hammer, an electrician a piece of wire.

Mike Rosen didn't come to the U.S. Attorney's Office that day; rather, he sent a woman who worked for him named Jeannie Graziano. In the office there was Jeannie, Casso, and Agent Rudolph. Jeannie excused herself to go for coffee. Casso saw this as an opportunity to make a move. He turned to Agent Rudolph. Knowing Charlie Rose's office was just right down the hall, Casso said, "If you guys make me a good offer, I'll . . . I'll work with you."

Rudolph was stunned by this, and Casso could see the surprise on his face. Gaspipe was thought of as a stoic, old-world mafioso—the fact that he had just offered to become an informer was startling. For several seconds, Rudolph couldn't bring himself to believe that Anthony Casso just said what he'd said.

"Excuse me?" Rudolph said. Casso repeated it.

Agent Rudolph asked Casso to wait, said he had to go talk to Charlie Rose. Before he left the room, he said to Casso, who was shackled to the chair, "You're willing to cooperate?"—he wanted to get it clear in his head. Casso nodded yes.

The reason Casso did not consult with Mike Rosen was because he knew Rosen would not condone such a thing. But Casso was his own man, and he would do what his conscience told him to. He had become focused on his freedom. He would get it—no matter what. He had tried guile, he had tried escaping. That didn't work. Now he would play the last card left to him. Now, he thought, he'd go the route of Philadelphia underboss Phil Leonetti and Gambino underboss Sammy the Bull Gravano.

Anthony knew his father would roll over in his grave if he knew what his son was contemplating. Within minutes, Agent Rudolph returned and said he had spoken to Charlie Rose and that Charlie Rose agreed on the six-and-a-half-year plea. This pleased Casso, but always the quintessential poker player, he showed nothing on his face. At that moment, Charlie Rose walked past the office, locked eyes with Casso, smiled, and gave him the thumbs-up sign.

For Charlie Rose, this was truly a monumental occasion. Anthony Gaspipe Casso *turning* was a milestone in the annals of crime history. Casso was in a class of his own. He was responsible for a long list of crimes; he was responsible for dozens of murders; he was, Charlie Rose knew, the most well-informed, potentially best witness the government had ever gotten its hands on. If Charlie Rose could bring this to fruition, his name would become legendary in the U.S. Attorney's Office. He could, in years to come, no doubt, run for public office with such a large, colorful feather in his cap. He could be mayor. He could be governor.

Rose, who had been planning in the near future to go into private practice with his partner, Greg O'Connell, was so excited by the prospect of shepherding Casso into federal courtrooms and using him as a star witness that he and his partner immediately canceled their plans to retire from public service.

Charlie Rose bringing Casso to bay was like harpooning Moby-Dick. Gaspipe was a rare mafioso—at the very pinnacle of the food chain that is organized crime.

Now, Agent Rudolph and Casso shook hands on their deal. All this had occurred before the lawyer from Mike Rosen's office, Jeannie, returned with coffee. When she did return some moments later, neither Casso nor Rudolph said anything to her about Casso's cooperating. Casso proceeded to give the handwriting samples and was quickly taken back to Seven North of the MCC. He paced his cell. He waited. He informed Mike Rosen that he had decided to cooperate with the government. This shocked Rosen. Never in a million years would he have believed that hard-ass Anthony Casso, the notorious Gaspipe, would have become a government informer, yet he was hearing it from Casso himself. Rosen refused to cooperate with Casso or help facilitate his cooperation with the government. He worked with many mafiosi, and he did not want to get a reputation as an attorney who facilitated such cooperation. Rosen wanted his reputation to be pristine and unmarred by his cooperating with the Justice Department or the FBI. A week passed. The FBI came to the MCC and took Casso to the Brooklyn Federal Courthouse and introduced him to his new attorney, Matthew Brief. Knowing that Casso needed counsel, the Justice Department had arranged, without Casso's knowledge, for Brief to represent him. Not wanting to rock the boat, Casso accepted Brief as his attorney.

Matthew Brief had been a former federal prosecutor. He was an average-sized, balding man, an able attorney who knew the law as well as he knew the inside of his left hand; but the fact remained that he had been on the other team. When Casso learned about this, he had certain reservations about Brief representing him. Nevertheless, Casso accepted the goodwill of the government and of the counsel they were offering him . . . for free.

Casso was taken to the Brooklyn Federal Courthouse on February 28, 1994, and found himself in front of Judge Gold. Brief was to witness the rough pro-offer that Casso had agreed to. However, Brief, out of earshot of Casso, told Charlie Rose and Greg O'Connell that he wanted to withdraw from Casso's case because the rough pro-offer was only twenty minutes long and it did not "in any shape, manner, or form" guarantee the legal assurances Casso should have received.

Brief said, "Mr. Casso is a major crime figure. This pro-offer is woefully inadequate. I cannot in good conscience allow my client to take it. I wish to withdraw my representation, I feel so strongly about this inadequate pro-offer." He continued, "As far as I'm concerned, the government is showing that they have no true intention of honoring Casso's cooperation and agreement."

Federal prosecutor Gregory O'Connell threatened Brief with sanctions and told him to stay on as counsel until Casso pled guilty.

Shockingly, O'Connell ordered Brief not to tell his client, Anthony Casso, about him wanting to withdraw from the case because then Casso would know that something was wrong and would not want to plead guilty.

Brief, Casso recently explained, did exactly what the government told him to. He never mentioned to Casso that he thought the government was acting in bad faith from the start, and he remained Casso's lawyer and allowed Casso to plead guilty on March 1, 1994, to a seventy-two-count indictment while having a gut feeling that the government was going to renege on Casso's agreement. Casso further explained that Matthew kept this from him until 1997.

Four days after the rough twenty-minute pro-offer Casso had accepted, the government brought Casso into the chambers of Judge Eugene Nickerson. There, they asked Casso to plead guilty to all seventy-two counts in the indictment, which included thirty-eight murders—as well as racketeering, drug dealing, and so on.

Gaspipe pled guilty to all the charges. If, in reality, Casso had gone to trial, it was almost a certainty the government could never have convicted him on all seventy-two counts. Nevertheless, on March 1, 1994, Gaspipe pulled the plug on his La Cosa Nostra life. He was now in bed with the government. Soon, it would be known throughout Mafiadom that Anthony Casso was a *rat*.

One would think, considering that Casso had spent his life on the other side of the law, that he knew the game, that he knew the ropes, that he would have taken more precautions before agreeing to this plea deal. But that was not the case.

Casso left the courthouse that day and was rushed by FBI agent Richard Rudolph and several other agents to a private jet at LaGuardia Airport and flown to El Paso, Texas. There he was housed in La Tuna Prison, where, ironically, he was kept in the "Joe Valachi Suite."

Now it was time to put together the colossal amount of information Gaspipe had so it could be used effectively in the prosecution of just about everyone in the New York Mafia, for Casso knew everything about everyone. He was, in a very real sense, the Walter Winchell of organized crime.

CHAPTER 65

THE 302S

asso was brought to La Tuna for the sole purpose of the government fully understanding what exactly he knew and to verify that what he said was truthful and valid. From past experiences the government well knew that when mafiosi agreed to cooperate, they often provided no more than colorful variations of hot wind. Government prosecutors were particularly skeptical of Gaspipe because they never really believed he would turn.

The FBI agents who interviewed Casso were his case agents Richard Rudolph, James Brennan, and John Kapp.

One of the first things Casso began to talk about, as always using his hands when he spoke, his Brooklyn accent strong and tangible in the warm El Paso air, was his relationship with corrupt police and FBI agents he had dealt with over the years. As part of the debriefing process, the agents were taking notes to memorialize exactly what Casso said. It is mandated that notes are written down on what is referred to as a "302" form. The 302s would become viable legal documents that could be, and more than likely would be, used in a court of law.

The first crooked agent Gaspipe mentioned was New York FBI agent Doug McCane. McCane had for many years worked the Gambino division of the FBI and, according to Casso, had supplied the Lucchese family with vitally important information. Halfway through Casso's story about Agent McCane, Agent Rudolph "literally jumped up," according to Casso, from the table and shouted that he didn't want to hear anything more about McCane. He threw his pen down on the table and refused to take notes. Agent Rudolph leaned over, pointed his finger in Casso's face, and warned him not to mention McCane or any other corrupt agents to them or to any assistant U.S. attorneys, that is, Charlie Rose and Greg O'Connell. Both Rose and O'Connell were slated to arrive the next day to begin the task of making Casso a viable government witness. Writing up the 302s was the first step in that process and it wasn't going well at all.

Casso was shocked. He expected the agents to be happy; he expected them to be pleased that he was exposing crooked FBI agents. Just the opposite was true. When Agent Richard Rudolph was contacted for this book, he did not return phone calls.

Aghast, Casso sat there, looking at the agent and really not believing his eyes. Because Casso was an amazingly quick study and a good judge of character, he immediately knew what was in the wind, and he didn't like it. It was foul and it smelled. All his life, Casso had, for the most part, kept his word when he made a promise. To Casso, a handshake agreement was a bond you didn't break.

Yet, now, right in front of him, he was being told to keep his mouth shut about corruption. Rather than acquiesce to what Rudolph was ordering him to do, Casso questioned it. This was a mistake.

It didn't take long for Casso to understand why Rudolph was so upset because the agent outright told Casso that Agent Doug McCane and he had been friends for more than twenty years, that Agent McCane had integrity and honesty and was above reproach. Casso sarcastically suggested to Rudolph that maybe McCane had been getting the information that he gave Casso from Rudolph. With that, Rudolph's face twisted into a tight knot and the anger he felt was tangible.

Casso did not mention the crooked agent in front of Agent Rudolph again. He knew the wind was already blowing against him. Casso said, "Okay, if that's the way you want it—okay. I know of another crooked agent. Let's talk about him."

According to Casso, Rudolph abruptly stopped him again and said, "Don't you get it? I don't want to hear about any crooked agents here. We aren't here to talk about crooked agents. We're here to talk about what you know about the Mafia—got it?"

Casso suddenly felt like he was standing naked in a cold room, his skin reddened by the frigid air. As he looked at Agent Rudolph, he saw enmity, anger, foreboding in his face.

"I thought you wanted to know the truth about all the criminal things I was involved with," Casso said.

"Yes, I do," the agent said. "But I'm not interested in hearing your bullshit about crooked agents, Casso. If you're here to pull my chain, I'm going to end this right here, right now, and you can go fuck yourself. You got that?"

Silently, Casso stared at Agent Rudolph. He knew a bully when he saw one. All his life Casso had dealt with bullies. They didn't cow him. They didn't scare him.

"Okay," he said. "How about this—I had two NYPD detectives killing people for me, you interested in that?"

"Getting warm," Agent Rudolph said.

And Casso went on to describe all his interactions with Louis Eppolito and Stephen Caracappa—in great detail. He told the agents how the detectives supplied him with information and committed murder at his behest, how they murdered Gambino capo Eddie Lino and the others.

This both stunned and fascinated the federal agents. They had all been hearing for years about crooked cops under the control of the Mafia, and now suddenly, finally, the details were coming from Casso's mouth. It was obvious to all in the room that day that Gaspipe was telling the truth. What he said was so detailed and logical that it fit together seamlessly. He then detailed each of the murders Caracappa and Eppolito carried out for him. He told them about Burton Kaplan and how Kaplan had acted as the go-between for Caracappa and Eppolito and himself. The FBI knew about Kaplan, that he was a rogue Jewish gangster who'd do anything to turn a buck.

It appears odd that the first thing Casso talked about was his association with crooked cops and agents—saying nothing about the inner workings of the Mafia. Although Casso had made up his mind to be an informer, it was so anathema to him that he could barely talk. Words carrying the truth about the people who were once his colleagues and cohorts had a hard time coming out of his mouth.

For him, sitting there and telling about what he knew was absolutely surreal. Surely, this had to be a bad dream.

Still, he knew that for him to pull this off he had to deliver the goods, so little by little, Casso willingly told the agents what they wanted to hear.

———

The next day, Casso met federal prosecutors Charlie Rose and Greg O'Connell. Both O'Connell and Rose had dealt with many Mafia turncoats. They knew the walk. They knew the talk. They had an intimate understanding of the Mafia culture. They met with Casso in the Valachi Suite. It was like a room you would find in a Motel 6, with a table, chairs, a stereo, a television, and a hot plate for making tea and coffee. At night Casso slept in the adjoining room, which was a conventional six-by-eight-foot cell.

The agents were struck by Casso's fastidiousness, how obsessively clean he was. He served them coffee and tea and neatly cut pieces of cake. As they talked and ate, Casso was careful to wipe up crumbs and ring marks from the coffee cups lest the table become stained. Neither the federal prosecutors—none of the agents there—had ever come across such "a neat freak," Mafia or otherwise, as Anthony Casso. As he sat there, serving tea and coffee and cake, wiping up crumbs and stains, he gave them a litany of murders they knew nothing about. Shocked, the feds looked at one another, realizing, perhaps for the first time, who Anthony Casso really was, what he was about . . . the world of information in his head. What also struck them about Casso was the profound knowledge he had of why murders occurred. Time and time again they were shocked to learn that Gaspipe had ordered murders because agents and police officials had informed Casso that so-and-so had gotten themselves into trouble, and to get out of trouble, they'd agreed to become informers . . . moles . . . double agents.

Casso also now told them, in great detail—for the first time—about the murder of Frank DeCicco some seven years earlier. They also learned at La Tuna that the Genovese and Lucchese families were out to kill John Gotti, that his days had been numbered since he murdered Paul Castellano. Casso said, "What Gotti did was the beginning of the end of the Mafia the way we knew it. You don't do what he did. There's protocol, rules, regulations. Personally I liked John. He kept his word. But his killing Paul like that was a big mistake. He was thinking with his ego, not his head. In reality it was just a matter of time before we got him. Trouble was, everywhere he went there were either agents there or a news crew and all the time he was downtown it was impossible to get the job done because of traffic. There was no way to get away."

This the federal officers found both amusing and edifying. Casso now told his interrogators, there in the Valachi suite at La Tuna Federal Prison, that he had also taken out a contract to kill Charlie Rose. He said this somewhat apologetically. The reason, he said, "I was going to kill you was because I believed you were the one that put in the *Post* that I killed the architect Anthony Fava because he had an affair with my wife. But later I found out that it wasn't you that said that. Sorry."

Bemused, Rose told Casso that he forgave him, and they continued.

Anthony Casso was very much like the cartoon snowball that rolled down the hill, getting bigger and bigger and bigger as it went. The more he talked, the more the agents realized he was truly going to divulge all—that what he was doing was not going through the motions of telling the truth or just giving them little tidbits here and there that they could use as sound bites. What he was doing was describing the world he came from, the world he knew, the world he controlled, in three-dimensional living color.

Casso had always been a great raconteur. He knew when to pause, when to draw out scenes. He now willingly told the feds about his drug dealing—about the shrimp trawlers they had converted into a means to get tons of marijuana, heroin, and Quaaludes from South America to the eastern seaboard.

Again, as always, he was detailed, and his candor struck all in the room. When he mentioned that Sammy the Bull Gravano was one of his best customers, however, Agent Brennan stopped him—said they didn't want to hear about that now. That struck Casso as odd, but he continued to talk. He described killing the son of the captain of *Terry's Dream* after the trawler had been busted as they unloaded several tons of marijuana from it. Casso believed the son would become an informer. He invited him to a meeting in Florida. Before the young man arrived, Casso explained to the feds, he had an associate dig a grave. The man arrived. Casso shot him. They put him in the grave. As the victim was being buried, he stood up and tried to get out of the grave. Casso cracked him in the face with a shovel, knocked him back down, and they proceeded to bury the young man alive.

"Did doing that bother you?" Charlie Rose asked Casso.

Without hesitation, Casso said, "No. It had to be done. It was done."

To a degree, even these hardened, seasoned feds were somewhat appalled by Casso's response. It wasn't so much the crime he had described but the way he described it—without any feelings or any kind of emotions. He could have been talking about a meal he liked; he could have been talking about a good wine.

The feds there that day, like most of society, did not realize that to a mafioso, murder is something that has to be done as a part of that business. You don't feel remorse. You don't feel anything. It's no accident that to be inducted into any borgata, the inductee must kill somebody; he has to show that he can kill without second thought, without remorse.

Everyone listening to Gaspipe talking about murder like he was talking about the weather thought he was a psychopath, thought he was evil, thought he was a monster. Casso very well might be a psychopath, but in the world he had come from, he was none of the above. What he was, was good at what he did . . . a dedicated general—LCN's George Patton.

At one point during these debriefings, assistant U.S. attorneys Rose and O'Connell argued with Agents Rudolph and Brennan. The basis of the argument was the fact that Casso had told Rudolph and Brennan about the contract he had taken out on Rose's life, and they had opted not to tell the prosecutors.

O'Connell, according to Casso, said, "Fuck them [the FBI agents]. Tell [us] what you have to say. Tell them nothing. You can't trust them."

O'Connell said this not knowing that, in truth, Agents Rudolph and Brennan had told Casso not to say anything about corrupt federal agents. Casso sat in the middle of these two camps now, not sure what to do—not sure whom to sidle up to.

Interestingly, when Charlie Rose and Greg O'Connell left El Paso and returned to New York, all they did regarding Caracappa and Eppolito was leak the story about the detectives to the media, showing no interest in investigating further what Casso had said. Shockingly so, the story would not break in a large way for another ten years.

Pacing the Valachi suite at La Tuna, Casso waited impatiently. He

began to get a bad feeling in his gut about what was to happen. He realized that the feds would never truly let him change his stripes. To them,
he would always be a predatory creature, an out-of-control, bloodthirsty,
murdering psychopath. But Gaspipe didn't give a flying fuck about who
thought what of him. He was who he was, and he was proud of his life in
the Mafia. Casso knew that Sammy Gravano, Pete Chiodo, and Al D'Arco
had all told the feds—memorialized in their 302s—that Anthony Casso
had FBI agents working for him. How, he wondered, could they not be
interested in that?

Casso still didn't seem to grasp the fact that the FBI was a political
entity that functioned in the most self-serving ways possible. How would
it look if it became public knowledge that there were FBI agents working with the Mafia when Congress was allocating the FBI's budget that
year? In a sense, Agents Brennan and Rudolph would be undermining
their own jobs by allowing Casso to detail in the 302s what FBI agents
had done for him.

Casso waited to hear from Charlie Rose and Greg O'Connell. He was
concerned. Why, he wondered, weren't they bringing him to New York
and putting him before a judge so he could tell what he knew? He wanted
to get on with his life. He wanted what Sammy the Bull Gravano had
received. He was still estranged from Lillian, from his children.

Now when Casso looked into the future, he didn't see freedom and
a new life . . . he saw more storm clouds, darkening skies; he heard lightning and thunder.

Finally, FBI agent Chris Favo came to interview Gaspipe. He was from
the Colombo squad.

Agent Rudolph made sure he sat between Casso and Agent Favo
and he constantly gave Casso the hairy eyeball, making sure that Casso
said nothing about crooked agents. When Agent Favo left, Rudolph told
Casso that no one would listen to Favo and that Favo would be put out
to pasture, which very nearly became true. Yet, still, as Casso told about
what he knew regarding government corruption within the FBI, he was
summarily shut down by Agents Rudolph and Brennan.

On another day at La Tuna, Agents Rudolph and Brennan received
a phone call from the Brooklyn D.A. informing them that Drug Enforcement Agency (DEA) agents would arrive very early the next morning to
interview Gaspipe. Rudolph got very panicky, according to Casso, and

ordered him not to speak to the DEA people under any circumstances unless Rudolph was present. Rudolph seemed dismayed by the mere thought of the DEA interviewing Gaspipe. Casso welcomed an opportunity to talk to the DEA agents for he saw it as a chance to air the truth—that Sammy the Bull Gravano was a drug dealer, that Gravano was a cunning liar.

Even back then, the government was hell-bent on protecting Gravano's interest at all costs. But the public at large was not served well. When Gravano was ultimately given his freedom by the federal court system, he went on to sell Ecstasy to children in Arizona. This not only would bolster what Casso had tried repeatedly to tell the government but also would be a major embarrassment for the U.S. Attorney's Office because their star witness in over twelve Mafia trials turned out to be a low-life drug dealer.

Nevertheless, back at La Tuna in 1994, when Casso tried to get the truth out, he was stonewalled and told to shut up—and he was threatened with solitary confinement.

As hard as it for the average citizen to feel any kind of sympathy for Anthony Casso, the rule of law is still the *rule of law*. For everyone.

CHAPTER 66

THE TEFLON DON

John Gotti, like Anthony Casso, was born and raised in the Mafia culture. Unlike Gaspipe he did not come from South Brooklyn, but from another area thick with mafiosi—he was born in the Pleasant Avenue section of northeast Manhattan, now known as Spanish Harlem. For many years, this area had as many Italian immigrants as Little Italy did.

Early on in life, John Gotti, like Casso, learned to strike first and strike fast and to make the blow lethal. He was a physically tough man, an adept street fighter, and he had a very quick mind. Gotti had a high IQ and was very good at memorizing numbers. He seemed to have an ability to see beyond the obvious and take advantage of what he saw. He was glib, quick-witted—and very dangerous.

Gotti was a Neapolitan. Many old-timers in the Mafia believed that Neapolitans should not have the right to become mafiosi. They were thought of as loud and boisterous, and they drew attention to themselves. The Sicilians were all about blending in with the woodwork. The Neapolitans, however, were just the opposite. They seemed to thrive on the limelight, on ostentatious clothing, fancy cars, fancy women, fancy restaurants. Gotti loved all of the preceding.

Gotti was brash; he was outspoken; he seemed to think that he was above the law—even the Mafia's law. As John Gotti rose in the ranks of the Mafia, he ended up becoming head of the Gambino family by murdering Paul Castellano. It was this outrageous public act that initially drew the ire of the federal government.

The federal government in the form of the U.S. Justice Department declared all-out war on John Gotti. Agents and prosecutors in the Justice Department hated the way he defied them. They hated the way he disrespected them. They hated seeing his colorful, larger-than-life persona on news reports and TV specials about the Mafia, and they hated reading about him in numerous books.

As mentioned, the FBI managed to get recording devices into Nettie Cirelli's apartment and Gotti on tape talking about myriad crimes—including murders. This was not, however, before he beat the FBI in two highly publicized trials, earning himself the sobriquet "the Teflon Don."

John Gotti made everybody's skin crawl at the U.S. Justice Department. He not only was a public embarrassment to them, he also made them seem like incompetent buffoons. Gotti also had a second sobriquet—"the Dapper Don"—so dubbed by the New York media because he dressed well and was seen in the best New York restaurants every night. He flaunted not only who he was but what he was about. He defied the government to put him in jail; he defied the government to enforce the law.

Ultimately, on April 2, 1992, John Gotti was convicted with the help of Gravano. As explained earlier, the government had managed to turn Gravano into an informer by playing tapes of John Gotti bad-mouthing him endlessly. Whatever bond that existed between Gravano and Gotti, it was over and done with when Gravano heard those tapes. On them, Gotti talked about multiple murders that Gravano did, a no-no in the world of the Mafia. Because there is no statute of limitations on murder, no one in the Mafia ever discussed it. Once a successful murder has been completed, it is over and done and must never be referred to, for if it was picked up through government surveillance, a murder that is ten, fifteen, or even twenty years old can come back and haunt the killer. In a very real sense, it would be as if the murder happened the day before. Yet here was John Gotti in this little apartment above the Ravenite Social Club talking about numerous murders and crimes that Gravano and he had been involved with, that Gravano and Gotti had done together, as though he was talking about sports.

Ultimately, John Gotti was given a life sentence and sent away to a prison where he would die a long, slow death from cancer. Gravano went on to be hailed as a hero by the U.S. Department of Justice. In the course of Gravano helping the government, he not only testified at the Gotti trial but at twelve other trials. Gravano was responsible for putting away forty-one high-ranking mafiosi.

In his plea bargain and deal with the government, Gravano was promised that he would never have to testify against any of the men in his immediate crew and that he would be able to keep all the money he had earned in his life of crime—about $11 million. It was an amazing, unprecedented, sweetheart deal that would, ultimately, end up haunting the government in a very real way.

When Anthony Casso, in the course of being debriefed by federal agents, talked about dealing drugs with Gravano, talked about murders by Gravano other than the ones Gravano said he committed, the agents didn't want to hear it. No one in the federal government was interested.

CHAPTER 67

ANATHEMA

Anathema: 1: an ecclesiastical ban, curse, or excommunication
2: one that is detested
—Webster's II New Riverside Dictionary

As Gaspipe tried to cooperate with the federal government, word quickly spread throughout Mafiadom that he had become a rat. This was a shocking, stunning revelation not only to mafiosi around the world, but also to their wives and children, to all the associates who worked with the Mafia, to the lawyers who represented them, to the secretaries who worked for those lawyers, and to all the different union people.

Like jungle drums warning of war, warning of strife, word of Anthony Gaspipe Casso becoming a rat resonated in his old Brooklyn neighborhood.

What had the world become? became the collective question asked by all those involved in La Cosa Nostra. If a person like Anthony Casso could become an informer, if a person of Gaspipe's stature in that world could turn on them, what was left of the honored society they had once believed in? The bells were tolling for LCN.

———

From the Valachi suite at the La Tuna Federal Prison, Casso could actually feel the hatred he had brought upon himself. He had nightmares about what he'd done. When he looked in the mirror, he hated what he saw.

Anthony thought about his father, the man he respected most in life. Oh, how ashamed his father would have been of what he had done! He dreamed about his father coming to him and asking him *Why? Why, son, why?*

Anthony could envision the hurt that would have spread across his father's face. Anthony had always thought of his father as his best friend, his mentor, the person who loved him the most in life. Sitting alone in the Valachi suite, Anthony remembered his childhood, how made men were treated—the respect that they were given, the deference they received, how people from all walks of life had come to his godfather, Sally Callinbrano, asking for help with this or that problem, and how Sally Callinbrano did all he could to help those who came to him. Like his father, Sally Callinbrano would hold Casso in great disdain for what he was doing now.

Anthony thought, too, about Lillian and his children, how shocked and stunned they had to have been when they heard what he was doing. Like Anthony, Lillian had come from a world in which people who cooperated with the police were anathema. Anthony had written Lillian many times since his arrest and had never gotten a response. This added further fuel to the pain and suffering he was feeling there alone at La Tuna.

Little by little, Casso slipped into depression, became morose, quiet, and withdrawn, just staring at the wall or at the television set. He wrote Lillian more letters, to which he got no response. Casso knew if he now walked along Fifth Avenue in South Brooklyn, which was rapidly gentrifying into Park Slope, he would be booed, scorned, ridiculed, and spat at. Hated. If he could find any old-time Italians there at all.

Casso felt he now was alone and adrift in a turbulent, shark-infested sea. He had no friends anymore; no family; no country.

But all his life, Casso was all about being tough, meeting all challenges and dangers head-on. He was not about to let the present circumstances do him in. He would fight. He would turn things around. He would convince the world that he was a direct product of his environment, that he was not evil, that he was not a psychopath, that he merely did his job the way it should be done in the world into which he was born.

If I have to go down, he thought, *I'll go down fighting. I'll go down a man.*

Still, Anthony worried about his children—especially his son. He knew his son had to be suffering ridicule and embarrassment because of what Anthony had done. He wanted to sit down with his boy and explain the reality of life the way he saw it, but that was not in the cards. This was just another painful reality Casso had to endure—the estrangement from his son, the hatred that his son, Anthony believed, was surely feeling for him.

There, alone in the Valachi suite at La Tuna, Gaspipe took long, thorough showers, did push-ups and sit-ups, and plotted and planned how to get himself out of prison; how to get a new life; how to win back the affections of his family . . . his beloved Lillian.

CHAPTER 68

A NEW REGIME

In the summer of 1994, Charlie Rose and Greg O'Connell, crime-fighting superstars for many years now, decided to quit the U.S. Department of Justice and open a private law practice together. Between the two of them, they had put away several busloads of mafiosi, drug dealers, gang bangers, and Russian and Latin mobsters (including MS13), the worst any society could provide. Each of them had a world of information about criminals, their motivations, and the inner working of crime in America. Rose and O'Connell were supremely suited to protect society at large from the scourge that is the criminal element.

Yet, now, they were effectively joining the other side, for when they went into private practice, they would be representing and protecting the very criminals they'd been so steadfastly going after during their stellar tenures at the Justice Department.

When Casso first heard that Rose and O'Connell were going into private practice, he was surprised, but he had no idea of the far-reaching, dire implications this would have upon him and his life. The deal Gaspipe had made with the government had been made directly through Rose and O'Connell, and with them suddenly out of the picture, Casso would have to deal with strangers who had neither a liking nor any kind of affinity for him. When Casso shook Charlie Rose's hand and agreed to become an informer, the bond that Casso felt with Rose was strong and tangible and real. Casso resigned himself now to getting along with whoever the new prosecutors were.

———

Toward the end of June 1994, Gaspipe was moved into the Witness Protection Unit of Fairton Federal Prison in New Jersey. He learned that the U.S. Attorney's Office's Valerie Caproni and George Stamboulidis had taken over his case.

When Casso arrived at Fairton, he was greeted by Colombo consigliere Carmine Sessa and a captain in Nicky Scarpo's family, Larry "Yogi" Mellano. Both men, like Casso, had agreed to become government witnesses. Yogi Mellano, in fact, had never testified at any trials but would still be given his freedom after eight years at Fairton. Also housed at Fairton was Phil Leonetti, who had been given a six-and-a-half-year sentence for cooperation, the deal that Charlie Rose and Richard Rudolph had promised Casso.

This was the sentence Casso felt he should have gotten. He'd bide his time—and be as patient as possible.

———

Valerie Caproni, an attractive, tall, high-cheekboned brunette and a no-holds-barred U.S. attorney, and Casso's attorney, Matthew Brief, along with FBI agents Richard Rudolph and Jim Brennan, drove out to Fairton to meet Casso for the very first time. For the most part the meeting was stiff, formal, and unfriendly—Casso sensed trouble in the wind.

On their return trip to New York, Casso would later learn, Caproni was seated in the front seat, Brief in the backseat. Caproni turned to Agent Rudolph, who was driving the car, and said, "We can never use Casso as a witness." Brief heard this as plain as the nose on his face, and according to Casso, he never repeated this comment to him.

The crux of the problem with Gaspipe as a witness was Sammy the Bull. All the attorneys at the Justice Department knew that if Casso were put on the stand in a court of law and told about how he dealt drugs with Gravano, told that there were more murders than the nineteen Gravano had admitted to, Gravano's credibility as a witness would go out the window. Not only that but Gravano would have clearly committed perjury because he had said in open court—while under oath—that he never sold drugs.

Perjury not only in the John Gotti trial but in twelve other cases. This would immediately create fertile ground for all the defense attorneys representing the people Gravano had put away to file appeals.

If the defense attorneys could prove that Gravano had perjured himself, there would surely be a wave of appeals and an influx of complaints, creating a nightmare for the Justice Department and an embarrassment of monumental proportions. The Justice Department also felt that Casso could never be a credible witness because of the voluminous amount of crimes that he had been involved in, not only as a participant but as a boss, and not only calling the shots . . . but as the mastermind behind the crimes.

Emphatically, Casso said that had he known, when at Fairton, that the Justice Department planned not to use him as a witness, he would not have said anything to anyone about any crimes he was ever involved in. "Why in God's name would I continue to cooperate with them if I knew they weren't going to cooperate with me? The only reason I told them all I knew, the only reason I cooperated, the only reason I was helpful, was because I thought they would honor the deal they made with me. I stupidly believed that these were people who would honor their agreement. On the street, the place where I came from, you shook somebody's hand and you kept your word. I realize now that all they were doing was playing me, using me."

Gregory O'Connell would say of Gaspipe as a witness, "It was impossible to overcome his history and make him sound credible. Using Casso as a witness would have been like putting Adolf Hitler on the witness stand."

Perhaps, but no one in the Justice Department told Casso they felt that way, no one in the Justice Department told Casso that he would *not* be used as a witness, and the government would continue to get information from him. Prosecutor George Stamboulidis would later relate for a book on organized crime that "Casso had more horrendous baggage than virtually any cooperating witness the government had ever signed up."

CHAPTER 69

CONTRABAND

The Witness Protection Unit at Fairton Federal Prison in New Jersey was filled with men whose lives, whose very existences, revolved around crime. They came from the street. They had all been cunning, clever criminals on the outside; now most of them schemed, day and night, to figure out new ways to commit new crimes. If the world was a sea, the men housed in Fairton's Witness Protection Unit were the sharks and barracudas.

These men had one foot in prison and one foot out the door. Technically, theoretically, they were to be given their freedom after cooperating with the federal government. They thought of themselves as elite. They thought of themselves as better than the other prisoners—a criminal aristocracy, as it were, smarter. It was not unusual, indeed it was the conventional norm, for these men to be allowed—under the table—conjugal visits, special foods, even alcohol and drugs.

When Casso looked around and saw what was going on, he, naturally, wanted the benefit of being in the Witness Protection Unit and would, of course, jump at anything that could make his time in this place better. To a large degree, Casso still felt he was on the side of the government, that he would be cooperating with the government to put away some of

America's most notorious criminals. He felt he should receive whatever privileged treatment was available in the unit.

Casso quickly discerned that two of the counselors in charge of the unit, a man and a woman, were bought and paid for. Carmine Sessa had the woman under his wing, and the male counselor was on the pad of Spanish drug lord Alfonso Perez. Casso managed to strike up a friendship with Alfonso. They had similar backgrounds. Both had been the heads of large criminal enterprises that involved the importation of huge amounts of drugs into the United States. Both had been involved with murder when necessary.

Within several months, Casso was allowed to have boxes weighing up to seventy pounds of contraband brought to his cell. Sessa and Perez were smuggling in everything under the sun. Once a month, like clockwork, the boxes of contraband were picked up at the local post office by the counselors and brought back to the prisoners' mailroom. Sometimes Sessa had his wife mail his box right at the Fairton post office on a Saturday to make sure that the box was there when the counselor went to pick it up Monday morning.

Sessa was going to testify at many organized crime trials. According to Casso, the government prosecutors Valerie Caproni, George Stamboulidis, and Andrew Weissman all catered to Sessa's every need. When they came out to Fairton to debrief Sessa, he would literally start crying to get what he wanted. Over a period of time, Casso grew to know Sessa for what he was—a "punk crybaby," as Casso put it. Casso personally saw an inmate push Sessa into a slop sink in the mop room and Sessa start to cry and hold his hands over his head. The inmate told Sessa to stop crying—that he was not going to hit him. Some tough guy.

This was the world that Gaspipe now found himself in. He didn't like being there. Although he disdained the place, he kept looking down the road and seeing light at the end of a dark tunnel, and he resigned himself to being patient and waiting for the government to use him as a witness. Anthony had resigned himself to being a good witness. He planned to don a sharp suit, get on the witness stand, swear on a Bible, and tell the truth as he knew it. At this point, at this late juncture, Casso was not about trying to deceive the government about anything. For real and straight-up, he had effectively become a "rat," as he was referred to now by everyone in the outside world. As hard a moniker as that was for Casso to accept, accept it he did. He had come to view La Cosa Nostra as a failing, hypocritical organization; there was no honor; there was no loyalty. Casso recently said, "The Mafia is dying."

Perhaps Casso's buying into being a witness for the government to such a large degree had to do with the fact that he was surrounded 24/7 by men who planned to take the stand and testify against their brethren.

For the most part he wasn't thinking anymore about what he was doing—he didn't think about what his father would feel; he didn't think about what his wife thought; he didn't think about what his children thought. He certainly did not think about his Mafia contemporaries on the outside world. At this point in Fairton, Anthony Casso had grown to disdain all those who had once been his partners in crime.

Like this, slowly, weeks turned into months and months turned into years. Sometimes for Casso, time went by very quickly, but most of the time it moved slowly—indeed, torturously slow. He felt like a piece of flotsam drifting on an endless sea.

CHAPTER 70

A NEW NEW LEASE

In June of 1995, FBI agents James Brennan and John Kapp came to Fairton to debrief Casso. To jazz up his profile as a cooperating witness, Casso decided to inform the agents of the smuggling of contraband into the Witness Protection Unit at Fairton, run by Sessa and Perez and two prison counselors. Casso also told Agents Brennan and Kapp that if they wished to send him a package with an operational gun, he not only would receive the gun but he also would bring it out to them on their next visit, which was held in a restricted area, he pointed out. This was not that shocking to Brennan and Kapp. They knew about the contraband that was brought in to the Witness Protection Unit. They knew that many looked the other way to keep these people happy. Yet as Casso spoke they carefully wrote down everything he said and listened with attention. When this session ended, the agents assured Casso that they would go back to Brooklyn and report what he had told them to his case agent, Richard Rudolph, and to federal prosecutors Valerie Caproni and George Stamboulidis.

"We'll get back to you," he was told.

Within a week, Agent Rudolph came out to visit Casso at Fairton and told him that he had spoken to Caproni and Stamboulidis about the report of Agents Brennan and Kapp. According to Casso, Rudolph said, "My advice to you, if I were you, I would forget what you reported."

Casso was trying to expose the corrupt system that had been set up to accommodate the needs of a government witness, so when Agent Rudolph told him that he should forget what he saw, Anthony couldn't believe what he was hearing. But it was not the first time Agent Rudolph had ordered Casso not to report corruption concerning the government.

The following week, on July 16, 1995, Valerie Caproni and George Stamboulidis had Gaspipe moved out of Fairton and sent him to Otisville Prison in upstate New York near Port Jervis. It was a Sunday. At 8:00 that morning Casso was having a cup of coffee with Tommy Ricciardi inside Fairton's Witness Protection Unit. Ricciardi was from the Lucchese faction in Newark, New Jersey. His captain had been Anthony Tumac Accetturo, who had flipped and become a government witness. Casso would later learn from the FBI that Accetturo had been an informant for law enforcement since the 1960s, for almost thirty years.

While Ricciardi and Casso were drinking their morning coffee, Tommy spotted two law enforcement vehicles coming through the prison gates. Wearing a pair of shorts and a T-shirt, Casso sat and watched the marshals drive onto the prison grounds.

The next thing Casso knew, within five minutes, he was roughly handcuffed, abruptly removed from prison, and driven to Otisville, New York. Without explanation, he was thrown into another cell, and the cell door was locked with a resounding *bang.* He was moved, Casso says, to protect Carmine Sessa's criminal activities at Fairton. According to Cass, he was caught in a catch-22 between the prosecutors—Caproni, Stamboulidis, and Weissman—and Carmine Sessa. The following morning, Casso called U.S. Attorney Stamboulidis and Agent Rudolph and "scumbagged" them to no end for transferring him in order to cover up Carmine Sessa's crimes at Fairton.

Agent Rudolph told Casso that Valerie Caproni said she would let him, Casso, know in thirty days what she had decided to do with Casso's report, which he said she had received two weeks earlier about the corruption at Fairton.

Casso said he'd be happy to sit down at a table with them so he could take a polygraph. "You people," Casso said to Agent Brennan, "are far more threatening and dangerous to the citizens of New York than the five organized crime families."

In prison, in the community of incarceration, Casso was a superstar. Everyone knew Gaspipe or knew of him. People gravitated toward him; people were in awe of him; people respected him.

Within two weeks of Gaspipe arriving at Otisville, he learned that the corruption there was exactly the same as it was at Fairton. A young tough kid named Bobby Mellino from Canarsie, waiting to testify at the drug trial of Gaspipe's old partner, Burton Kaplan, confided in Casso that he had two guards on his pad. And a black guy named Judd in Building #2 had the secretary on his pad. Over several months, Casso readily admits he paid to have food and drinks brought into him at Otisville. This included the finest vodka and scotch, cakes, all kinds of sausages, a variety of gourmet cheese, fresh baked bread, even caviar.

During Gaspipe's stay at Otisville, the trial of Chin Gigante was to begin, on June 23, 1997. Casso had told, in great detail, about all his dealings with Chin Gigante. Casso would have been the ideal witness to testify against Gigante; he had personally had meetings and sit-downs with the Chin, and he knew more about Chin's operations than anyone the government could put on the witness stand. The government, however, still did not want to put Gaspipe on the stand because they knew that once defense attorneys questioned him, they'd ask for Casso's 302s; and in Casso's 302s, he had said that Gravano was a drug dealer, that Gravano had committed more than nineteen murders. Come hell or high water, the government was intent upon protecting Gravano. The government seemed irrationally obsessed with protecting Gravano.

Rather than use Gaspipe in the trial against the Chin, the FBI agents wanted Casso to falsely implicate NYPD detective John McNally—to say that he was working hand in glove with Detectives Caracappa and Eppolito in a murder-for-hire scheme. The reason the government was intent on besmirching John McNally was because of what McNally discovered while working for numerous defense attorneys who had hired him to find the truth about Gravano's criminal dealings. In his quest to separate the truth from the lies, McNally found out that there were, in fact, more murders than the nineteen Gravano said he had committed. He found out, too, that Gravano was not only a drug dealer, but that this was known throughout Mafiadom. McNally learned that Gravano had sold tons of marijuana, and huge amounts of both cocaine and heroin. McNally also found out that Gravano himself was a heavy cocaine user. In addition, he heard rumors that Gravano was bisexual—that he had affairs with men while attending beautician school in Manhattan (this obviously before Gravano decided on a life of crime).

Thus, the government wanted to be able to undermine McNally by having him be a part of the Caracappa-Eppolito murder-for-hire scheme. Initially, the government was going to use Al D'Arco in the trial against the Chin. But D'Arco had become known as a chronic liar and had never been to any meetings at which the Chin was present. According to Casso, the prosecutors George Stamboulidis and Andrew Weissman, present at the meeting along with Gaspipe's government handlers, Agents Rudolph and Brennan, gave him this choice—if he wanted to testify at the upcoming Gigante trial, he had to implicate McNally in a few murders. Casso recently explained that he told the government to go fuck themselves.

"No way would I do that," he said.

———

Now *60 Minutes* contacted Casso and asked him if he would agree to do an interview. They wanted to focus on the Mafia Cop Case. Casso agreed, and a film crew headed by Ed Bradley came out to the prison. An older, heavier Gaspipe was put on camera. He wore large, thick aviator glasses. He still had a full head of hair, though somewhat gray. Speaking in a heavy Brooklyn accent, he told in detail about how he hired Caracappa and Eppolito, how he had specifically ordered different murders, how he had ordered the killing of Gambino capo Eddie Lino. He spoke about the amounts of money that he paid them and just what they did for that money—how they brought victims to him to be killed, how they went out and outright murdered at his behest. Fused with Casso's interviews were interviews with family members of the victims. When CBS executives saw and heard what Casso had to say, they decided to hold off airing the piece until law enforcement decided to take some action, one way or the other. For the time being, the Gaspipe interview and exposé of the Mafia cops were shelved by CBS. The interview wouldn't be aired for ten years.

———

Prosecutor Stamboulidis and his partner, Andrew Weissman, flew out to Arizona and convinced Sammy the Bull to testify against Chin Gigante in place of Casso, according to Casso.

It appears that Casso's descriptions of events were accurate and true. Sammy Gravano had far fewer dealings with Chin Gigante than Casso had, yet the government used Gravano. In the world of the Mafia, Casso had a far greater stature than Gravano ever had. Nevertheless, the government put Gravano on the stand rather than Gaspipe, and it appeared the government really wanted nothing to do with Casso anymore.

Interestingly, the week after federal agents flew down to Arizona to see Gravano about testifying against the Chin, FBI agent Brennan came back alone to ask Casso to change his original story from 1994 that Gravano had always been a drug dealer and that Gravano had dealt drugs on the street. At this point, Casso was so disgusted with the government, its lies and cover-ups, he says, that he did what Agent Brennan asked of him. The government's intention was, of course, to protect Gravano's reputation. It was very difficult for the federal government to offer sweetheart deals to mafiosi who were drug dealers. When mafiosi sold drugs they did so on a huge scale. Since drugs are a major scourge on society, with an extremely high social cost, it is incredibly bad PR for the government to allow such a criminal to walk.

Murder, strangely enough, however, didn't seem to have the stigma that drug dealing had. A man who admits to murder could, according to government standards, be given a sweetheart deal. Gravano had already admitted, after swearing on a stack of Bibles and raising his hand, that he had murdered nineteen people, personally. Some victims were businessmen that got in his way, some were LCN. Yet here was the U.S. government all ready, willing, and able to allow Gravano to get a pass; that is, to allow Gravano to get his freedom if he cooperated. If he said what they wanted the way they wanted—if he did what he was told.

But the government wanted John Gotti so bad they were willing to do *anything*, and in this case, this meant making a deal with a major drug dealer—Sammy the Bull Gravano.

In February 2000, Sammy Gravano would be arrested for selling large amounts of Ecstasy to junior high school children, causing the government major embarrassment. Suddenly its poster boy, the man it held up as the epitome of a criminal who had turned a new leaf, turned out to be a low-life, scumbag drug dealer. Now the press knew it. And now the public knew it. All along, government officials had been acting like ostriches with their heads in the ground.

It would have been an easy thing for Gravano to go on and lead a productive life with his freedom. He had $11 million. He was allowed the solace and comfort of his family while in the Witness Protection Program. Yet what Gravano did was turn back to a life of crime.

CHAPTER 71

GASPIPE MEETS THE UNITED STATES SENATE

n May of 1996, a U.S. Senate subcommittee held hearings on Russian organized crime in Washington, D.C. The subcommittee contacted Anthony Casso to ask if he would testify. Casso saw this as a golden opportunity to prove to the Justice Department that he was a viable, coherent witness. At this point, he had no allegiance toward most any of the people he had dealt with in the outside world, least of all the Russians.

When Valerie Caproni and George Stamboulidis heard that Casso had been invited to testify at the Senate subcommittee and that he had agreed, Caproni tried everything she could to stop it. Casso refused to acquiesce to Caproni's demand not to appear. He was brought to Washington by U.S. marshals.

On May 15, Casso, dressed in a blue silk suit, white shirt, and dark tie, closely shaved, well barbered—the picture-perfect image of a Mafia don—sat before the full Senate subcommittee on Russian organized crime. His demeanor, his physical presence, reminded those who saw him that day of Al Pacino in *The Godfather*. They were the same height, had the same coloring. Present were Senators William Roth, William Cohen, Sam Nunn, Joe Lieberman, and Byron Dorgan. To everyone's surprise, Casso was articulate and forthright, sincere and honest.

Casso said:

"Good afternoon, Mr. Chairman and members of the subcommittee. My name is Anthony Casso. Early on in my life, I was given the nickname Gaspipe.

"I have been in jail since 1993, when I was arrested after being a fugitive for almost three years. At that time, I was the underboss of the Lucchese organized crime family. Ultimately, I decided to cooperate rather than go to trial. As part of my deal with the Government, I pleaded guilty to a 72 count indictment, including murder, racketeering and extortion. I have not yet been sentenced, and no promises have been made to me for my testimony here today.

"As part of my cooperation agreement, I told the government about my life of crime. I gave a deposition for use in an Israeli trial, but I have not yet testified at a trial in the United States. I will testify, if requested by the government, at upcoming organized crime trials.

"I have been involved with organized crime for more than 35 years, since I was a kid working on the docks in Brooklyn, New York. When I was 21, I became associated with a guy named Chris Furnari of the Lucchese organized crime family. Everybody knows him as 'Christie Tick.'

"Before I was arrested this time, I had only been in jail once. That was in 1962 for five days when I was convicted of running a bookmaking operation on the docks and fined $50. After that, I was arrested several times for different federal and state charges, including assault with a gun, selling stolen property, dealing heroin, burglarizing a bank, and bribing state parole officers. In every case, I was either acquitted or the charges were dropped.

"In the early 1970s, I met Vic Amuso. Then, in 1974, I became a 'made' member of the Lucchese family. Vic was made in around 1977. At that time, 'Tony Ducks' Corallo was the boss of our family. But, in 1986, Tony Ducks went to jail so he had to name a new boss. I became a 'capo' in 1986. After discussions within the family, Tony Ducks made Vic Amuso the boss at the end of 1986. At the end of 1987, Vic told me I was the new consiglieri. Then, in 1989, Vic named me the underboss of the family. After Vic was arrested in July 1991, I ran the Lucchese family as underboss while I was a fugitive.

"In my position as a member of the Lucchese family, I came to know individuals associated with Russian organized crime, which is the subject I have been asked to testify [about] today.

"In the mid–1980s, our family got involved with Russian organized crime in the gasoline business in Brooklyn. Italian and Russian organized crime made large amounts of money by working scams to avoid paying taxes on gasoline. The Russians owned hundreds of gas stations and controlled the supply and distribution of gasoline. We provided them with protection they needed to maintain a cartel. We also helped them set up corporations to work the scam.

"The main Russian guy working with our family was Marat Balagula. Marat was one of the early leaders of Russian organized crime in Brooklyn. He made millions off gas tax business and our family made a lot of money with him.

"In around late 1986, another Russian named Vladimir, whose last name I did not know at the time, came up to Marat in a Russian restaurant in Brighton Beach. Vladimir had recently arrived in Brighton Beach from Russia. According to the Russians, the word on the street was that he was a tough guy with his own crew. Marat told me Vladimir pulled a gun, put it next to Marat's head, told Marat that he was his new partner, and demanded Marat pay him $600,000 or Marat would be dead.

"Marat reached out to us and told us what happened. We agreed to meet the next day. When we went to Marat's house, we found out that he was so scared that he had a heart attack but did not want to go to the hospital. I remember seeing Marat in bed hooked up to all kinds of machines, refusing his doctor's orders to go to the hospital. Marat's guy wanted us to kill Vladimir.

"Since Marat was with our family and especially since he was such a money-maker for us, this was not just a threat against Marat. This was a threat against the Lucchese family as well. We knew what we had to do. Vic and I agreed that Vladimir had to be killed. We took this situation to Christie Tick, who agreed we could have Vladimir killed. Vic gave the hit to Joey Testa.

"We asked Marat and one of his guys to get us some information to identify Vladimir. One of Marat's guys got us his picture and license plate number. We had Marat call Vladimir and arrange to have lunch with him in the same Russian restaurant in Brighton Beach where Marat was threatened. After leaving the restaurant, Vladimir was shot and killed.

"I heard about the murder on the radio. Marat was very thankful that we had gotten rid of his problem. We couldn't let somebody try to put the squeeze on one of our family's big money-makers. After that, Marat did not have any more problems from any other Russians.

"I found the Russian organized crime groups to be very clever. We knew the Russians were involved in heroin trafficking, as well as complicated scams involving forgery, and tax evasion in the oil and gas business. The Russians were also willing to use violence to achieve their goals.

"I will be happy to answer any questions you have about my knowledge of Russian organized crime."

For nearly two hours, each of the senators, in turn, questioned him. He was forthright and precise in his answers. He impressed all of the senators there that day as being a man who was telling the truth, as being a man who had turned over a new leaf, as being a man who had been in a unique position of power and had taken another turn in life; and no one who heard Gaspipe testify that day would ever forget him . . . the cold, austere way he described murder. All the senators in turn thanked Casso profusely for his appearance, smiling as they did so. Casso did not go to Washington that day to con or fool anybody. He went there to tell the truth as he knew it, and no one knew the truth better than Anthony Casso.

Graciously, Casso stood up, thanked them for their time, and thanked them for listening; and the quintessential gentleman was led away by four large U.S. marshals sporting crew cuts and heavily armed.

CHAPTER 72

NO COMMENT

The prosecutors Valerie Caproni, George Stamboulidis, and Andrew Weissman were contacted by the author. They refused to comment on the Anthony Casso case.

BOOK V

THE LIVING DEAD

CHAPTER 73

HELLHOLE

The government honored its agreement with "Big Sal" Miciotta. In December 1998, Big Sal admitted he had bribed prison guards at the Arizona Witness Protection Unit and assaulted another witness. Yet assistant U.S. attorneys had nine years cut off his sentence.

Vincent Gigante was tried and convicted the same summer Gaspipe was given thirteen life sentences plus 455 years. The Chin was ultimately convicted because of testimony of the government's superstar witnesses, Sammy the Bull Gravano and Al D'Arco. According to Casso, and according to defense attorneys and people in the know on the street, D'Arco—nicknamed the Professor by Casso—had lied through his teeth while on the stand. He bolstered his position in the Lucchese family by saying he had been the boss—not true; that he had attended sit-downs at which the Chin was present—not true. Gravano testified about things that Casso had initially told the government. The government had masterfully morphed the Bull into Casso—Gravano was parroting what Casso had initially said. Still, the Chin was ultimately convicted and sent to jail where he died of a heart attack on December 19, 2005.

CHAPTER 74

IMPARTIAL OBSERVATION

In 1999, Casso retained a new counsel to perfect and argue an appeal on his behalf. He was a young, sharp, particularly bright attorney out of New York City by the name of Joshua Dratel. Dratel was highly motivated, clearly, saw the duplicity of the government's position regarding Casso, and argued vehemently on Casso's behalf. Unfortunately, his argument was rejected by federal courts. But Josh Dratel was also an accomplished author. On November 22, 1999, an article he wrote regarding the government's use of informers was published in *Criminal Justice Weekly*. It was a succinct, accurate assessment of the particulars not only of Casso's case but also of a second case that clearly delineated how the government was managing to manipulate the rule of law at will. The article is entitled "Government Witnesses: Getting More—or Less—Than They Bargained For?" To read the article in its entirety, see the appendix.

CHAPTER 75

CHINESE TORTURE

Back at ADX Florence, the U.S. supermax federal prison in Florence, Colorado, Anthony Casso waited for justice. For him, seconds were like weeks, minutes were like months, hours were like years. A less resilient man than Casso might very well have cracked under the strain of having cooperated, yet not reaping any of the benefits. He felt fooled, duped—used.

Yet, regardless of how Gaspipe had been used, very few people were interested in his fate. He was an admitted Mafia boss, an admitted killer, a ruthless mercenary for organized crime.

As time passed, Casso grew more and more bitter. He recently explained, "Going over to the government's side in 1994 was like a terrible cancer throughout my body and mind. I lost my family; I lost my friends; I lost my dignity . . . I lost all respect not only from others but from my own self. I believed Charlie Rose when he promised me six and a half years for my cooperation. I was all ready to start a new life. Funny . . . I liked Charlie Rose. He wanted to be a gangster in real life. He told me one time, laughing as he said it, that he was the underboss of the U.S. Attorney's Office. My biggest problem, I know now, was Judge Block. He was made prejudiced against me by the prosecutors telling him that I was going to kill his colleague Judge Nickerson, which was a bold-faced lie. I never had any dealings with Nickerson's court. There was no reason for me to have anything to do with a plot to kill Nickerson. It was the Colombo crew that told me they wanted to do in Nickerson and I told the feds about that."

As far as Casso was concerned, his battle with the government was, in reality, just beginning. He likened it to a heavyweight championship fight. There were still many rounds left, and he was intent upon winning. He felt his honesty and integrity in dealing with the government would ultimately be rewarded. Perhaps, in this, he was being somewhat naive. He didn't seem to fully comprehend how truly hateful the federal prosecutors felt toward him. He didn't seem to understand that all those in the U.S. Department of Justice and the FBI would move in lockstep. They had built around them an impenetrable moat filled with piranhas.

Time in prison is a very subjective thing. It can be realistically likened to dreams. One does not know if a dream is an hour or a lifetime. Being locked up in a small cell is a very unnatural state for our species. Some experts contend that keeping men locked up as they are at ADX Florence causes a certain kind of mental illness—people become violent, sedentary, disoriented, paranoid. They, too, hallucinate and imagine things. The fine line between reality and illusion, under those circumstances, is often hair thin. Some days Casso feels calm, somewhat at peace with his surroundings, but those days are, for the most part, rare. Most days he feels like a prisoner of war—being held captive by a hostile foreign entity that has no place in a civilized society. He likens himself to a political prisoner in the faraway, northern reaches of Siberia. He has come to think of the federal government as an untrustworthy, unsavory, totalitarian monster.

Strangely, a bizarre turn of events forced the government to acknowledge what Casso had been contending all along—that Sammy Gravano was a committed drug dealer. It came in the form of a shocking revelation.

CHAPTER 76

DUMB FUCK

In February of 2000, in the wide open expanse of the state of Arizona, with its perfect weather and low crime rate—the place where the federal government decided Sammy the Bull Gravano would lead a new life—Gravano was busted for dealing drugs. Not only was he arrested, but his wife, son, and daughter were also busted.

Apparently, Gravano felt that no law enforcement agency could touch him, that he was unlike anyone else. Gravano used his freedom not only to return to a life of crime, but also to create the largest Ecstasy ring in the United States. Using two Israeli men who were making the drug in Israel, Gravano set up a large distribution network in Arizona that was connected directly to children in junior high and high school. There, Gravano knew, was the largest market for the drug—and he exploited it. Through a series of wiretaps and police surveillance, the Arizona State Police put together an airtight case against Gravano and arrested him and his family.

This was a major embarrassment for the federal government. Its poster boy was caught with his hand in the cookie jar. When the federal prosecutors heard about the arrest, they all suddenly got migraine headaches. The media was all over this story like white on rice. From one end of the country to the other, the story of how Sammy the Bull Gravano had turned against the people who had protected him was the lead story.

When Casso heard about Gravano's arrest, and the reason why he was arrested, he wanted to do a jig. He knew that now, no matter what the government said, what he had said would be seen as true. Finally, the truth would be known, he thought. He viewed this as a major vindication of everything he'd said.

Overjoyed, he paced his cell back and forth, waiting for something to happen . . . waiting for a change, waiting to be taken back to New York where he would go in front of a federal judge and be given an opportunity to tell all he knew—to tell the truth.

Time kept passing and nothing kept happening. Casso wrote letters to different federal judges—to which he got no response. He wrote prosecutors, reminding them of his help, reminding them that what he said had been vindicated by way of Gravano's arrest for selling drugs; he reminded them that the conviction of Chin Gigante was based on inside information he had provided. He got no response from them, either.

———

He paced his cell, he waited. Time inexorably passed. Gaspipe continued writing letters to the powers that be. The powers that be were no longer interested in him.

Then, in February of 2004, Casso was called upon by the defense attorney of Frank Federico, who was going to be tried for the murders of the two Long Island carters, Robert Kubecka and Donald Barstow. The trial was to be held in front of Judge Frederic Block. As Casso was being transferred from one prison to another, heading east, which is the way the federal government moves prisoners, he had to stay overnight at Atlantic Federal Prison. At 2:00 A.M. the following morning, guards came to get him. He was ready to leave to catch a Con-Air plane back to New York. While walking from one cell to another, Vic Amuso and Casso came face-to-face for the first time in ten years. They had both aged considerably in those ten years. Hard time is not good for a youthful appearance.

Vic, according to Casso, looked older and very tired. Unbeknownst to either one of them, they had both been called by the defense in the Federico case. They also ran into one Kid George Conti from Benson-hurst, a Colombo soldier. They were all on the same Con-Air plane. When they landed in New York, the same bus took the three of them to the

Metropolitan Detention Center (MDC) in Brooklyn. Amuso and Casso were housed on the ninth floor. At this point, Amuso had not, like Casso, become an informer. As the two men were led to different cells that day, Amuso said to Casso, "I can see in your face you are sorry for going with the government."

How right he was, Casso mused that day. Casso quickly told him how the FBI and federal prosecutors in Brooklyn were more corrupt than the Mafia ever was.

"On the street, if you shook somebody's hand," Casso said, "you could take it to the bank. With these people, you shake their hand one minute and the next minute they act as though they've never heard your name, I swear."

Amuso had steadfastly refused to cooperate with the government, had steadfastly kept his mouth shut. He did not have the dilemma that Casso had; he did not have the sobriquet—rat.

Gaspipe was kept in the MDC in Brooklyn for four months. Lillian finally came to visit him for the first time since he'd been arrested. Casso explained how Rosemarie Billotti meant nothing to him, that she was just a friend, that he used her to run errands and the like. Lillian wasn't buying it. As much as she wanted to believe Anthony, she was still very hurt. She'd been publicly embarrassed by what he had done. Everyone in their world knew what he had done, knew that he had cheated on her. It was hard now for Lillian to walk with her head high knowing that Anthony had betrayed her so. When Anthony looked at her now, her face was stoic and rigid . . . there was no mirth, there was no laughter. In reality, Casso had no feelings for Rosemarie Billotti. He didn't have the emotional bond with her that he had with Lillian. He didn't have the trust that he had with Lillian. Though Casso had known Rosemarie just as long as he had known Lillian, he never thought of her as more than a warm body on a cold night. When he wanted to, Anthony could be very convincing, and now, at MDC, he poured his heart out. He cried in front of Lillian. He begged for her forgiveness. Lillian would never truly forgive him for what he had done, but suddenly she was back at his side.

The Brooklyn District Attorney's Office contacted Casso's lawyer, John Lewis, and told Lewis that Anthony Casso's information was extremely accurate and truthful, right on the money, concerning corrupt cops Eppolito and Caracappa. They further told Lewis that they wanted

Casso to be a witness at the upcoming trial of the Mob cops in Brooklyn. If Casso agreed, the Brooklyn District Attorney's Office would have him out of the MDC within hours and on his way to a Brooklyn court. With Casso's permission, Attorney Lewis told the District Attorney's Office that Casso would testify provided that he got immunity from the U.S. Attorney's Office in Brooklyn. Later that same day, the assistant U.S. attorney Mark Feldman refused the Brooklyn D.A.'s request to give Gaspipe immunity. They were still concerned about Casso being put on the stand and a defense lawyer demanding his 302s. It was, as it always was, all about Casso's 302s, about Gravano being a drug dealer, about Gravano killing more than nineteen people.

———

The second incident that hugely bolstered Casso's credibility, that he had told the truth all along, was the 2005 arrest of crooked NYPD detectives Stephen Caracappa and Louis Eppolito, who were charged with the eight murders Gaspipe had ordered.

CHAPTER 77

RECONCILIATION

Every day Anthony was in prison, he loved Lillian more. He wrote her frequently. She was the only reason he cried. He could deal with whatever else came his way—even the monsters he was housed with and the strict regiment of ADX Florence, known as Alcatraz in the Rockies. He could deal with bitter and sadistic guards. The only vulnerability Anthony had was Lillian. In his mind's eye, he could clearly see the first day he had seen her. He remembered the time in Prospect Park in the pouring rain when Lillian demanded that he stop the car so she could save a German shepherd on the road there. She was the only person he ever trusted in life. She had never let him down. It was he who had let her down; it was he who had betrayed her. Yet she had accepted what he'd done, which only bolstered his love for her. As bad as Anthony's circumstances were, especially and particularly from his point of view, they would soon get worse . . . far worse.

———

In the world of the Mafia, Anthony Casso was not only persona non grata, he was thought of as a rat's rat. Everyone in La Cosa Nostra knew that he had told the government about the contraband at Otisville and Fairton, that he had told the government about all the workings of the Lucchese family, and that he had told the government everything he knew about all the other families, such as the Colombo family's intention to kill Judge Nickerson. Wild Bill Cutolo and five of his cohorts were arrested and charged with plotting to kill a judge because of what Casso had told the government.

Thus, Casso had become fair game for all manner of retribution. Because he had been thrown out of the Witness Protection Unit (for allegedly fighting and being involved in contraband), he was vulnerable, and so was his family. Lillian and Anthony's children were not afforded the safety of the government's Witness Protection Program. The government had no use for Anthony Casso or his wife and children.

Lillian Casso had opened a boutique called Lillian's that sold women's undergarments . . . a kind of local version of Victoria's Secret on Avenue N and Flatbush Avenue. Lillian went to work every day. She was intent upon keeping herself busy. Anthony had given her enough money to live as comfortably as she wanted, but what Lillian wanted was her own business, her own source of income.

While Anthony was free, while he was a rising star in LCN, Lillian had been by his side through thick and thin. An attractive woman with a sharp, acerbic wit, Lillian was not only easy to like, but she gave people a feeling of confidence—that they could tell her anything, and she'd keep her mouth shut. Lillian was a good friend to have; in the sorority of "Mafia wives," Lillian was well known and liked. In that all Mob wives and girlfriends have ridiculous, inordinate amounts of money to spend on shopping, Lillian's business prospered. She sold expensive panties and underwear sets from La Perla and Natori and these women would spend three hundred dollars on a simple bra and panty set. Lillian's business did very well.

On a regular basis, she went out to dinner with the wives, sisters, and mothers of mafiosi; she lunched with them. Because Lillian had nothing to do with Anthony turning into a rat, she was still very much embraced by the society that is LCN. However, she felt the stares, she saw the finger-pointing when she walked into a room, and she knew what was being said. "That's that fucking rat Gaspipe's wife!"

Lillian could very well have divorced Anthony, publicly condemning him by that act, but she didn't.

No matter what, the fervent, intense love that Anthony felt for Lillian,

Lillian in turn felt for Anthony. She thought of him constantly. She remembered fun times they had as kids, she remembered hard times they had as adults. For her, Anthony was a walking dichotomy—he could be the most fun-loving man one moment, then the next moment as cold as ice.

Lillian had rarely seen the cold Anthony, but she understood what her husband was capable of. Yet Anthony had never raised his voice to Lillian, never laid a finger on her or their children. When he was home and he was angry, he kept his anger to himself.

Anthony had high hopes that circumstances would change for him, that he would get a second chance at freedom, that because of the Gravano drug arrest and the arrest of Caracappa and Eppolito there would soon be a change. He felt certain that soon FBI agents would come knocking on his cell door. Anthony passed his optimism on to Lillian . . . and she believed him. How could she not? She knew Gravano for what he was. She knew all about his arrest and his turning, about all the trials he testified at. It could very well be in the cards that her husband would also be treated the same way.

Lillian went to work at her shop every day, socialized with her friends, and hoped for the best. She was concerned, however, about her and Anthony's children. She knew her son, particularly, had been stigmatized because of what Anthony had done. He was called names at school. Friends of his put him down for what his father had done—becoming a rat. All Lillian could do was hope for a better day—a new future somewhere.

In the fall of 2004, Frankie "the Bug" Sciortino, a vicious, dour, stoic Colombo soldier, came knocking. Casso knew the Bug well. As he puts it, "This guy was crazy. He would do anything. They didn't call him the Bug for nothing. One time I remember he wanted to kill Teddy Persico, the youngest son of Carmine Persico, and I had to stop him. I mean, he was that nuts."

The Bug was a scary-looking man. He had hard eyes, a hard jawline, a hard face. His shoulders were wide; he was stocky and walked like a gorilla. In fact, he was very simian in his appearance. He was, in the world of LCN, a feared man, a killer. A man like Paul Castellano was never really feared. He wasn't a physically tough man. He was a businessman who chose organized crime as his business. But the Bug came from the same mold that Greg Scarpa, Eddie Lino, and Roy DeMeo had come from. Of course, when he walked into Lillian's store that day, she knew who he was. She knew he was with the Colombos. This was a day that Lillian had been dreading. She well knew that she had no insulation, that she had no one to turn to, that no one in LCN would come to her rescue.

The Bug told Lillian exactly what he wanted. He pulled no punches. He was not in the least bit delicate. He said, "This is the last time I'm going to come here and talk to you nicely. What I'm saying to you is that I want money. I want a lot of money. Your husband created a lot of problems for a good friend of mine. It's funny how your husband seemed to think he could get away with anything . . . that he was above all of us. Well, that ain't true. And just the fact that I'm standing in front of you proves it."

"I had nothing to do with anything my husband said," Lillian said.

"You don't understand. I ain't interested in anything like that. I'm interested in one thing—money."

He stared at her long and hard. In his stare, Lillian saw the truth. This man would, without question, commit the kind of violence that she had seen in the movies but had never experienced herself; this man represented all the worst of what we, as a species, are about. He'd kill a child; he'd kill a woman; of this there was no doubt. It was written in his eyes as clear as day. He said, "As far as we are concerned, all bets are off. I'm coming back next week, and I want money—a lot of it. Do you understand, Lillian?"

She nodded that she understood. He ambled apelike toward the door.

Thus began the slow bleeding of Lillian Casso . . .

———

Lillian was wary of telling Anthony about Frankie the Bug. She knew from the position he was in he could do nothing. She knew, in a very real sense, he was as helpless as a newborn babe in this. As is natural, she thought about who she could turn to for help, and she kept coming up with the same answer: no one. She was in this alone.

Lillian, like Anthony, was suddenly adrift, alone in a turbulent, shark-infested sea. Unlike Anthony, Lillian had done nothing to deserve to be in this position. Yes, she had married a fledgling mafioso and had reaped the benefits of millions of ill-gotten gain, but she had committed no crimes.

Now, all that was quite literally turned upside down. The world she had once known was no more. It was a thing of the past. Yet here it came, from the past, to destroy whatever she had left.

More out of desperation than because of a cohesive plan, Lillian decided to give the Bug $100,000 and tell him to go away, that Anthony had no more money, that she had no more money. Maybe, she hoped, reasoned, he'd leave her alone.

Lillian did not seem to grasp the fact that the Bug's goal was to not only torment her, but also to torment Anthony. He knew that the only vulnerabilities Anthony had were his wife and children.

The following week Lillian gave the Bug $100,000 cash. He said he'd be back for more. The following week he came around looking for more. She gave him more. He bled her little by little. After this had gone on for several months, she said no to him . . . she said, "There is no more money."

"Find money, or you'll find your children dead."

Lillian, in a fleeting way, thought about telling the police, the FBI, about her being shaken down. But she couldn't do such a thing without Anthony knowing. She finally decided that Anthony had to know what was happening, so she told him.

This was the thing, of all the things in the world, that Anthony dreaded the most. His wife being threatened, his children being threatened . . . it was his worst dream come true. He punched walls, he screamed, he looked in the mirror and hated what he saw. It was bad enough that he had become an informer, bad enough that the whole world he knew had turned on him, bad enough that his own father would've disowned him for what he did. But now it got worse . . . unspeakably worse.

Gaspipe well knew that the animal circling his wife would tear his family apart limb by limb, without reservation or hesitation. He thought the anger and turmoil that he felt, like the pressure in a pressure cooker, would grow and grow and grow until he exploded. After the explosion, bits and pieces of Anthony would be strewn about the cell. But no such explosion occurred, no such solace.

Out of sheer desperation, Casso turned to the federal government. He wrote letters, he petitioned federal judges, again he petitioned federal prosecutors. At one point, he did get word from U.S. Justice Department personnel that they would "look into it."

But they never looked into it. They didn't care. Anthony Casso, they collectively felt, was getting what he deserved. When you played both ends against the middle, as they say he had done, you get what you deserve.

He felt as though he had been run over by a eighteen-wheel truck and left on the side of the road. Roadkill.

———

Now that Caracappa and Eppolito had been arrested for working with Anthony Casso, *60 Minutes* finally had the backbone to air the piece they began some ten years earlier. From a journalistic point of view, it was an insightful, cohesive, well-put-together piece. It was also a very disturbing piece that caused an uproar across the country. Americans from every state wondered how such things could happen, wondered what this country was coming to.

CHAPTER 78

NO MORE PAIN

Lillian was a strong woman, but dealing with what was happening now, the threat against her children, was taking a heavy toll on her. In a matter of weeks, she seemed to age ten years. Dark circles formed under her eyes. She grew thin. Her daughter asked after her, worried about her. When she asked her mother what was wrong, of course Lillian said nothing. No one in the government, as Anthony feared would happen, came to help Lillian deal with the Bug.

In February 2005, Lillian came home from the store. She was particularly fatigued. She was standing at the kitchen counter when she began to feel woozy, weak . . . disoriented. She passed out and hit the ground with terrific force. The delicate bones in her face were broken. Lillian had had a massive stroke.

She lay there, unmoving, as still as any of the kitchen appliances, the only sound that of the ticking clock, the hum of the refrigerator. It's hard to say exactly what goes through the mind of someone as he or she is struck down by a massive stroke. Was Lillian conscious? Was she aware of the world around her? Was she, in that state of being, aware of Anthony and the problems he had brought to the Casso home? Whatever was transpiring in Lillian's brain, it was apparently very stressful because as the prostrate, unmoving Lillian Casso lay there, she had a massive heart attack. She was on the kitchen floor that August day for four full hours before she was discovered. Anthony Junior kept calling—there was no answer. Finally he drove to the house and found her unmoving, unresponsive. At this point, she was a sickly pale blue color, her tongue protruding from her mouth, the whites of her eyes showing. In a panic, he dialed 911. An ambulance arrived quickly. The ambulance attendees tried to stabilize Lillian as best as possible. They hurried her off to Kings Highway Hospital. In reality, that was the best place she could've gone because Kings Highway had a very good trauma unit. They were ready for life-and-death circumstances. When Lillian was brought in, she was unconscious.

She was quickly examined and tested, and X-rays were taken. The stroke and heart attack were correctly diagnosed. Anthony Junior and Jolene were shocked and traumatized by their mother's being struck down as she had been, so severely, a heart attack and a stroke at the same time . . . *my God.* A team of doctors and nurses worked triple time to save Lillian. They managed to stabilize her, and she was put in intensive care. By now it was the wee hours of the morning. When she came to the next day, she could not talk at all. She wrote a note asking if Anthony knew. Jolene had called him. Over the next few days, Lillian had another heart attack, a second stroke. Late one night, in a drug-induced delirium fused with the effects of the stroke, Lillian pulled out all the tubes and lines. At that point they were giving her life. Just like that, in the intensive ward at Kings Highway Hospital, Lillian Casso died. All the pain was over. Anthony's childhood sweetheart from Union Street, South Brooklyn, was no more.

CHAPTER 79

THE WORLD SUDDENLY TURNED UPSIDE DOWN

A t Alcatraz in the Rockies, there is no such thing as rehabilitation. The function of the facility is to keep under lock and key America's most dreaded criminals. There is no work for the prisoners. There is scant recreation. The cells are six by eight feet, containing a stainless steel sink, a stainless steel toilet, and a cement-type bunk bed that the prisoners can cover with a three-inch mattress. It's like sleeping on a slab of concrete. Prisoners are allowed a thirteen-inch black-and-white television and a radio. Prisoners are also allowed reading material, provided it's approved by the prison. Casso hated this facility. It wasn't so much the fact that the place was so austere, foreboding, unforgiving—so hard. It was because, he felt, it was against all things American. It seemed more like a place you would find in Communist China, or Soviet Russia, certainly not the greatest democracy in the world. In this, all the people housed at ADX Florence felt the same way. Here, the thought of escape was a joke.

There were few other mafiosi at ADX Florence. One mafioso prisoner of note was Greg Scarpa Jr. He, like Casso, had agreed to become an informer. The problem with him was that he had committed such heinous crimes, was such a despicable character, that the government was hesitant to put him on the stand. He was hated by the other prisoners and constantly exposed himself to the female guards. He was a bad apple among the worst apples.

Anthony read magazines, he watched television, he listened to radio. He liked the oldies. They reminded him of the days of his youth, the great times he had had with Lillian.

Lillian . . . he constantly thought of her, envisioning her as a safe harbor, a stabilizing anchor.

Anthony was first made aware of Lillian's death the day following her passing. His daughter, Jolene, very distraught about the loss of her mother, called the prison to make Anthony aware of what happened. A guard came to Casso's cell and gave him the news. For Anthony, this felt like being shot in the head. In reality Anthony had been shot numerous times, but nothing, none of that pain, matched the pain he felt now. He banged the walls with his fist. He banged his head against the walls. He cried uncontrollably for hours on end. His safe harbor was gone. His beloved Lillian was dead.

CHAPTER 80

PHOENIX

Ten months after Lillian's death, in March 2005, during a blisteringly cold winter, U.S. Attorney Mark Feldman's office indicted and arrested Mob cops Stephen Caracappa and Louis Eppolito on information that Gaspipe had initially provided to the FBI and federal prosecutors some ten years earlier. The government failed to launch an investigation. The government, in fact, failed to do anything. When they were finally ready to act, they tied the murders Caracappa and Eppolito committed to an "ongoing criminal enterprise" by claiming that Eppolito had sold an ounce of amphetamine to an undercover operative in Las Vegas. In reality, Caracappa and Eppolito should have been tried in a New York State court, but the feds wanted the bells and whistles—the press—that prosecuting killer cops would inevitably generate. However, Judge Jack Weinstein threw out the convictions in the 2006 trial because he said too much time had passed between the murders and the purchase of the one ounce of amphetamine to claim an ongoing criminal enterprise. This, inadvertently, proved that the federal prosecution of Caracappa and Eppolito was ill conceived at the very least. As of this writing, the Brooklyn District Attorney's Office is planning on trying Caracappa and Eppolito for the eight murders Casso said they committed at his behest. This trial should take place in the spring of 2008.

The first trial, with all its gory details about abduction and murder, was the lead story on every news show during its twenty-six-day length. CNN, Fox News, and MSNBC had a virtual field day with the trial of the Mob cops. They did endless stories, a daily summary of the trial, and interviews with the main participants. Not even Paris Hilton or Lindsay Lohan could upstage the Mafia cops. One would think, logically speaking, that the government would surely have invited Casso to testify at the trial of Eppolito and Caracappa. After all, it was Casso who had hired them; it was Casso who first told the feds about them; it was Casso who was constantly referred to in the media and in the courtroom as the man responsible for paying Caracappa and Eppolito to do his bidding.

That, however, did not take place. Instead, the government used Burton Kaplan in place of Gaspipe. By now Kaplan was a completely bald old man with huge oversized glasses. Up on the witness stand he appeared like a beat-up vulture who at any moment would fall over and drop dead.

Kaplan had been serving federal time for the selling of tons of marijuana. Over the years, he had opportunities to spill the beans on what he knew, to become an informer, but he had steadfastly kept quiet. However, when the U.S. Attorney's Office prosecutors Valerie Caproni and George Stamboulidis approached him in early 2005 and asked if he'd be a witness in the Caracappa-Eppolito trial, he said he would—if he could get consideration, if he could get out of jail. They promised that if he cooperated with them, they would in fact petition the courts to get him out of prison.

As Kaplan testified, it became obvious that he was taking the place of Gaspipe, that he was talking about things that he really had nothing to do with. He was taking on not only the guise of Anthony Casso, but the literal role of Casso. At this point in time, all Burton Kaplan was interested in was getting out of jail and spending whatever days he had left with his wife, children, and grandchildren. He even made reference to his grandson and family while on the stand. Even though, as Casso contends, Burton Kaplan was perjuring himself right and left about his interactions with Caracappa and Eppolito, defense attorneys who observed him would comment that he seemed believable and forthright, like someone's grandfather whom you would be happy to leave your children with. The jury warmed to Kaplan and liked his demeanor.

When famous Mafia lawyer defense attorney Bruce Cutler—a powerful man with the physical appearance of a linebacker—cross-examined Burton Kaplan, he tried to undermine him by casting him as a liar; he tried to show him as a man looking to get out of jail whose testimony was "self-serving." Cutler had a booming, powerful voice, yet his courtroom acumen was apparently lost on the jury because they ultimately convicted the two cops.

Gaspipe, back in ADX Florence, was angry beyond words. It was obvious to him exactly what the government was doing, he says. At one point during the trial, seeking revenge, Casso wrote letters and contacted both the defense attorneys, Bruce Cutler and Ed Hayes, and he told them that their clients, Caracappa and Eppolito, had nothing to do with the killings the government was charging them with. Casso even sent a letter to the presiding judge, Jack Weinstein, that stated that the government had it all wrong, that the two cops were "innocent."

This could not be overlooked by either the defense counsel or the prosecuting attorneys. Casso said he'd be willing to testify, even via the phone. There was in fact a phone conference between Casso and all the interested parties—the two cops, their attorneys, and their attorneys' assistants, and federal prosecutors Valerie Caproni and George Stamboulidis. With a stenographer present, Gaspipe, on the phone from ADX, gave a detailed account of what he said was the truth. The sum of what he said that day was that the two cops were innocent, that Burton Kaplan was lying, that the federal government had it all wrong, that what he had previously said about the two cops was "all bullshit."

At the end of what Casso had to say, rogue cop Louis Eppolito said, "Anthony, thank you. Thank you very much."

After the phone call, the defense attorneys sat down for a meeting. They decided that putting Casso on the stand would be a liability, that he wouldn't come across as a believable, viable witness.

Louis Eppolito adamantly disagreed with his lawyers. He thought Casso should take the stand, that the jury should hear Casso say that they were innocent. Casso had been referred to during the trial literally hundreds of times. Eppolito asked why they wouldn't let the jury hear what Casso had to say. Could he be less believable than Kaplan?

However, the two defense attorneys refused to put Casso on the stand, and the two detectives ultimately acquiesced to their lawyers' advice. The case was given to the jury and they were both convicted, though the convictions were quickly thrown out because, said Judge Weinstein, the federal government had overextended itself in trying to connect a one-ounce sale of amphetamine by Louis Eppolito in Las Vegas to the eight murders via "an ongoing conspiracy."

Federal prosecutors Valerie Caproni and George Stamboulidis had egg on their faces.

Back in Alcatraz in the Rockies, Casso was overjoyed. He knew that the government had not only screwed themselves, but had been publicly made a laughingstock.

Still, the government proved that Detective Eppolito had sold an ounce of amphetamine to an undercover agent. In reality, Caracappa and Eppolito were guilty of the murders. There's no doubt that they were guilty. Even Judge Jack Weinstein said they were guilty. Yet the Justice Department contrivance of a drug/murder conspiracy did not hold water.

Anthony had again been vindicated. But what good would it do? Would anybody listen to him now?

CHAPTER 81

THE DEATH OF LA COSA NOSTRA

In the words of Anthony Casso, "La Cosa Nostra is dying. It's not what it once was. There are no rules, there are no regulations. Everybody's a cowboy out for their own good. La Cosa Nostra is not an honored society of men anymore. It is a society of self-serving scumbags that would give up their mother to turn a buck. To this day, I hate myself for coming over to the government's side. But I still don't think of myself as a rat. I saw a chance at a new life, I saw a chance to get away from the cancer that LCN had become, and I took it. Back then, I had no idea the government would take everything I gave them, use it for their benefit, use it to get a lot of convictions, and not give me so much as a thank-you. I should have known better, maybe. But where I came from, when you shook somebody's hand, you kept your word. I really believe the government is more treacherous, more untrustworthy than any of the Mob people I ever dealt with.

"I truly feel sorry for the younger generation who wants to belong to that life. It's sad for them. There is absolutely no honor and respect today. Little do the newcomers know that there are many made members in the Mafia that wish not to be there and would like nothing better than to walk away from it. So they do the second best thing: stay low key if possible. The young newcomers will never see the kind of big money that was once made. That's long gone. They don't realize what it means to be free, and have peace of mind until it's taken away from them.

"I'm here—I'm here until the day I die. I've accepted that. No matter what the government does to me, I will never allow them to beat me. They've done everything in their power to destroy my body, to destroy my mind, but my mind is good. My body's still strong. And they have not, I repeat this, they have not beaten me. When I die, when I take my last breath, I can do so knowing that the government never beat me. Far as I'm concerned, I'm the last man standing."

———

A typical day for Casso at ADX Florence: he must wake up at 5:00 every morning. He washes and cleans his cell meticulously. Without question he is the cleanest person who was ever inducted into the Mafia. His cell is always impeccably clean. At 6:00 A.M., guards bring him breakfast. At 8:00 A.M. every other day, Casso can go to the inside rec area or the outside rec area for several hours per day. There he is able to see and have some contact with the other prisoners—the terrorists, notorious Aryans, mirthless serial killers. When in the outside rec area, Casso works out on the high bar, and briskly walks at least five miles a day.

Ironically, interestingly, as of this writing, Sammy the Bull Gravano also is being kept at ADX Florence. On several occasions Casso has seen him. According to Casso, Gravano is a little more than a hundred pounds, completely bald, and most of his teeth are missing; he looks as though he was just released from a Nazi concentration camp. He has, Casso says, some kind of disease—it might be cancer—but Casso does not definitively know. At 11:00 A.M., he must go back to his cell, where lunch is served. After lunch he showers in his cell and then tries passing the day by writing and reading. For the most part, Casso keeps his fellow prisoners at arm's length, though in the fraternity of convicts at ADX Florence, Casso is well known. Every single one of them knows that he was the head of a Mafia family, and a certain amount of cachet comes along with that position. After all, no matter how you cut it, the Mafia was the most successful criminal enterprise that's ever existed, everyone at ADX knows.

At 4:00 P.M. every day, the prison holds a stand-up count. The guards go from cell to cell counting each prisoner, making certain they are all present. At 5:00 P.M. dinner is served. Casso is allowed to shave on

Wednesdays, Fridays, and Sundays only. Once a month a Catholic priest comes to his cell with the holy sacrament and Casso receives Holy Communion. Casso is allowed one haircut a month. After dinner is served, whatever mail he has received is brought to his cell. At 9:00 P.M. sharp, it's lights out and back to bed, back to the terrible monotony of Alcatraz in the Rockies.

He is still hopeful that a fair-minded federal judge will allow him a hearing, so he can get the deal he was promised—release after six and a half years for telling all he knew, which is exactly what he did. As of this book's publication, Casso will have been behind bars for fifteen years.

Meanwhile, Anthony Gaspipe Casso paces his immaculate cell and waits for his freedom.

POSTSCRIPT

- U.S. Assistant District Attorney Charlie Rose died of a brain tumor at age fifty-one.
- U.S. Assistant District Attorney Greg O'Connell is in private practice in New York representing white-collar criminals.
- Attorney Matthew Brief is in private practice, specializing in criminal law, in New York City.
- Assistant U.S. District Attorneys Valerie Caproni and George Stamboulidis are currently working for the U.S. Justice Department.
- Gambino boss John Gotti died of cancer on June 10, 2002, while in prison, after being convicted on Gravano's testimony.
- Chin Gigante died on December 19, 2005, of a heart attack while serving his time as a result of the Windows Case.
- Tony Ducks Corallo died on August 23, 2000, in prison.
- Vic Amuso is alive and well and doing his time in federal prison.
- Dante and Nina Carlo sold their home in Bensonhurst, Brooklyn, and moved to Long Island in 2002.
- Lucchese capo Fat Pete Chiodo is in the Witness Protection Program.

- Al D'Arco is also in the Witness Protection Program.
- Sammy the Bull Gravano is also being housed at federal prison ADX. He never comes out of his cell. He has lost a considerable amount of weight and is down to a hundred pounds. He has no teeth and is bald. The author has recently learned that Gravano in fact has Graves' Disease, a disease that causes overactivity of the thyroid gland and hyperthyroidism. Symptoms include trouble sleeping, irritability, rapid weight loss, severe muscular weakness, radical altering in the appearance of the eyes, rapid heartbeat, and severe hand tremors.
- As a result of his testimony at the Mafia cops trial, Burton Kaplan did receive his freedom. Upon his release from jail, he sued to evict Anthony's son, Anthony Jr., from the home on Seventy-second Street. This further enraged Anthony Senior. Today Burton Kaplan is enjoying his freedom, spending time with his family and grandson. An out-of-court settlement between Anthony Casso Jr. and Burton Kaplan was reached in October of 2007, in which Mr. Casso Jr. was to pay Burton Kaplan $600,000 for the home.
- The so-called Mafia cops are languishing in federal prison trying to get the conviction for the one-ounce sale of amphetamines overturned. Both Caracappa and Eppolito are scheduled to be tried in Brooklyn State Court for the eight murders they committed at Anthony Casso's orders. Anthony Casso is scheduled to be the star witness against them.
- Anthony Casso's club the 19th Hole today is an optometry center.
- As a result of Gravano, Casso, the Windows Case, and the Commission Case, the Mafia has been severely diminished. However, the five families are still intact. La Cosa Nostra still has its tentacles in all the businesses that they always controlled. But LCN now has heated competition from other ethnic gangs—the Jamaicans, the Chinese, the Dominicans, the Colombians, the Mexicans, the Hondurans, and particularly the Russians have all developed lean, mean gangs, hungry for the riches America can provide.
- Today, South Brooklyn—Park Slope—has turned into a yuppie mecca, filled with upscale restaurants and clothing stores. Most

all of the mafiosi who once lived here have moved away and taken up residency along Brooklyn's Shore Road, in Mill Basin, all over Long Island, and on Staten Island's Todt Hill, although Bensonhurst is still home to a large LCN community. Park Slope is still a good place to bring up children.

- Rudy Giuliani failed miserably in his attempt to run for president of the United States. His platform had been that he was the crime-fighting superhero of 9/11. He regularly said on his campaign tour, "I can keep you safer than anyone else."

- If you wish to contact Philip Carlo, you may do so at www.philipcarlo.com.

GASPIPE REVELATIONS

In Casso's own words:

Who killed Hoffa and why?

"New York's Genovese crime family boss 'Benny Squint' Lombardo had contacted the Chicago crime family that controlled the Teamsters Union and Hoffa. The Genovese family had claimed that Hoffa's continuous public hatred for the Kennedys was bringing much unwanted attention to La Cosa Nostra nationwide. The Chicago family tried talking to Hoffa to ease up on the Kennedys, but Hoffa was headstrong with leadership and refused to listen, the same way Joe Colombo had refused to listen with his leadership of the Italian American movement. Hoffa was making heat for everyone. He, too, was headstrong with power until assassinated in Columbus Circle. Later, he did the same thing—was threatening people, telling everybody that he wasn't scared of us; he was making noise and had to be silenced. The Genovese family arranged for Hoffa to meet with Tony Pro (Provenzano) from New Jersey. Hoffa's killers were from the Genovese Jersey crew. I don't know their names."

Why was Paul Castellano killed?

"Paul Castellano was killed because he ordered that John Gotti and his best friend, Fat Angelo Ruggiero, turn over the FBI tapes from the bug planted in Ruggiero's Long Island home that led to a drug arrest. Gotti kept on stalling Paul with the tapes, but once Castellano's underboss died, Aniello Dellacroce was no longer around to protect Gotti and Ruggiero. Therefore, they would be killed by Castellano and Gotti knew this, so Gotti acted first and took the risk of killing Castellano.

"If Castellano were a true gangster, he would be alive today."

Why was the Mafia so successful?

"A lot had to do with the ruling body of the Commission. Everyone played by the rules. There were no exceptions. At one time there was honor and respect amongst the Mafia. The businessmen wanted to be involved with the Mafia. They became richer and fascinated with the Mafia's abilities to deal with any kind of a project, movie stars, law enforcement. People, state and government officials, are all [so] fascinated with the Mafia that they risk going to prison for supplying information to the Mafia. The Mafia gave the American people what they wanted with no questions asked. The people will always turn to the local Mafia for any kind of help before going to the police. The Mafia protects their neighborhood."

Who was the smartest boss?

"Thomas Lucchese was business smart. He controlled the New York airport unions, the garment district, and many, many more unions throughout New York for many years.

"Carlo Gambino, who got his start in the unions through Tommy Lucchese.

"Joseph Profaci.

"Vito Genovese.

"Joseph Bonanno.

"I would say that these five were all smart."

John F. Kennedy assassination plot?

"Talk in the Mafia was that the government killed him."

J. Edgar Hoover?

"He had always denied the existence of the Mafia for so many years because criminal attorney Roy Cohn had arranged a party with young boys at a hotel for him, Roy, and his buddy Hoover, who were both gay men. The Genovese crime family had gotten hold of a compromising photo of Hoover but turned it over to Roy Cohn in good faith. Hoover was thankful to the Mafia, in his own way.

———

A Letter from Anthony Casso to Philip Carlo dated September 22, 2006:

Personal Statement

I am truly regretful for my decision to cooperate with the govern-ment. It was against all my beliefs and upbringing. I know for certain, had my father been alive, I would have never done so. I have disgraced my family heritage, lost the respect of my children and close friends, and most probably added to the sudden death of my wife and confidant for more than 35 years.

I wish the clock could be turned back only to bring her back. I have never in my life informed on anyone. I have always hated rats and as strange as it may sound I still do. I surely hate myself, day after day.

It would have definitely been different had the government had honest witnesses from inception. I would have had a second chance to start a new life, and my wife Lillian would still be alive.

It seems that the only people the government rewards free-dom to are the ones who give prejudiced testimony to win convic-tions. "The Truth Will Set You Free" means nothing in the Federal courts.

Even at this point in my life I still consider myself to be a better man than most people of the people on the streets these days.

A Casso

APPENDIX

GOVERNMENT WITNESSES: GETTING MORE— OR LESS—THAN THEY BARGAINED FOR?

BY JOSHUA L. DRATEL

I n my more cynical moments, contemplating the future of the federal criminal justice system, I foresee ten years from now a division of criminal defendants into only two categories: those who cooperate, and those who try but fail. The advent of the Sentencing Guidelines in 1987 left cooperation as the only certain path to leniency—the Section 5K1.1 letter as the "Holy Grail" of the sentencing process.

Yet, like the mythical Grail, many are doomed by their pursuit of it. An ever-increasing number of defendants find themselves cast aside by the government even after providing undisputed "substantial assistance" and saddled with harsh sentences—often life imprisonment. The reason from their ejection from "Team America" is a "violation" of the terms of the cooperation agreement: a purely subjective determination by the prosecutor that the defendant has either lied in the course of cooperation or committed some post-agreement act that nullifies the government's obligation to file a Section 5K1.1 letter.

WHO'S THE LIAR?

For example, Anthony Casso was underboss of the Lucchese Family of organized crime in New York City before he was apprehended and began cooperation. He gave the government abundant information about the Mob's influence in a variety of legitimate and illegitimate businesses, including the identity of two New York City police officers who served as hit men for John Gotti. Yet Casso made the mistake of accusing Sammy "The Bull" Gravano and Alphonse D'Arco of lying in their testimony at the trial of Vincent "The Chin" Gigante, the reputed boss of the Genovese Family. The government deemed Casso the liar without any investigation, revoked Casso's agreement, expelled him from the Witness Security Program, and watched with smug self-righteousness as he was sentenced to 15 concurrent life terms.

Similarly, Blue (whose name has been changed because he resides in general population at a federal correctional facility, where he fears any word of cooperation will endanger his life) was the leader of [a] murderous drug-dealing gang in Harlem. Based on his cooperation, the government returned an indictment that prosecutors claimed was responsible for an astounding 54-percent drop in the precinct's murder rate. Yet Blue informed on one confederate too many; one such target, Green, disputed Blue's version of certain events, and since it was Green's testimony that was needed at trial, Blue was jettisoned by the government. He, too, now serves a life sentence.

The problem for Casso and Blue is that the appellate courts, with the current exception of the U.S. Court of Appeals for the Eighth Circuit, afford the government unfettered discretion in deciding whether it is "honestly dissatisfied" with a cooperator's performance. The result of this deference is that cooperators are stuck with the government's decision whether to rescind the cooperation agreement. As a consequence, at oral arguments of Casso's appeal, the assistant U.S. attorney could tell the court with impunity that if the government decided in "good faith" that "spitting on the subway" warranted termination of the cooperation agreement, that decision was unreviewable. For Blue it meant that the sentencing judge could deem "irrelevant" the objective accuracy of the government's decision as to whether Blue or his accuser was telling the truth, since all that mattered was the government's "good faith" belief in its position.

COURTS FEEL HANDS ARE TIED

Of course, the government's decision in either case was influenced far more by other factors than merely the instances of misconduct upon which the government ultimately relied in rescinding the cooperation agreements. Indeed, I have represented cooperators who have (a) violently assaulted and injured other inmates while cooperating; (b) violated bail conditions by leaving the jurisdiction for months without permission; or (c) lied to law enforcement agents and prosecutors to the extent of having to plead guilty to a false statement charge.

Yet each of them received their Section 5K1.1 letters, while Casso and Blue were denied theirs on the basis of far less serious misconduct. It is that disparity in the treatment of cooperators—manifesting the arbitrariness of the government's decision-making—that requires the type of judicial monitoring that the courts are unwilling to perform.

For Casso and Blue, their fate was sealed by their differences with other cooperators who were considered more valuable because their testimony was required, while Casso and Blue's testimony was unnecessary. Thus, the credibility contest between Casso and Gravano, and Casso and D'Arco was resolved by the government not on the basis of evidence but on the basis of need. Since Gravano's and D'Arco's testimony was responsible for the conviction of, among others, two bosses of New York organized crime families, by necessity they were deemed truthful. Otherwise, the veracity of their trial testimony, and the convictions secured thereby, would be thrown into grave doubt in the ensuing flood of habeas corpus petitions. The same was true for Blue's conflict with a testifying cooperator, since the subjects of Blue's cooperation had all already pleaded guilty.

The government's repudiation of its agreements with Casso and Blue constitutes an ironic twist that defies logic: while in the past, cooperators whose assistance prompted guilty pleas from co-defendants received maximum benefit due to the conservation of government resources, those cooperators are now in the most jeopardy of losing their agreements due to some genuine or contrived misconduct. Now, cooperators who are required to testify enjoy the only leverage over the government, which must stand by them in order to preserve convictions.

NO SAINTS IN THE STREETS

The failure of the courts to enforce agreements that the government disavows leaves cooperators helpless. It also provides a perfect opportunity for cooperators to settle scores with each other, since accusations of lying endanger the accused's agreement. That is what happened to Blue. One of his confederates against whom he had provided information turned the tables, and alleged that Blue had withheld information about his involvement in two homicides. While that might constitute poetic justice, it is not criminal justice.

The government's unbridled discretion also allows it to procure the cooperation of notorious criminals, suck them bone-dry of information, and then, because of a distaste for affording such grand evildoers any leniency, later seize upon some violation to terminate the agreement. For Casso, since he had admitted tangential involvement in inchoate assassination plots against both the assistant U.S. attorney prosecuting his case, as well as the presiding judge, the government's reluctance from the outset to afford him any benefit for his prodigious cooperation likely motivated its decision not to use him as a witness at trial, since testimony would have effectively protected his agreement from revocation.

Nor is finding misbehavior upon which to premise revocation of a cooperation agreement an arduous task for the government. Almost all cooperators shade the truth, at least at first; many initially minimize their own culpability. They most often arrive at cooperation fresh from a culture of secrecy and deviousness, and they do not make an immediate conversion to complete and truthful disclosure.

And since the population of cooperators is not composed of seminary candidates, the likelihood of some post-agreement misbehavior is high. The government takes full advantage of that imperfection, as it provides a storehouse of potential rationales for the ultimate denial of a Section 5K1.1 letter. For Casso, it was his assault on another cooperating witness—who previously had assaulted Casso in prison (as well as committed offenses on bail while cooperating, including carrying a weapon, fraud, and assault) but did not lose his agreement—and his "lies" about Gravano and D'Arco. Yet D'Arco himself was judged "untrustworthy" in another case when he attacked Gravano's credibility. Nevertheless, the need for D'Arco's testimony against Gigante insulated him from sanction. For Blue it was his alleged minimization of his role in two homicides, even though his accuser told the government four different versions of the events in question.

That double standard creates a situation unprecedented in the context of contract law that the courts ostensibly apply to cooperation agreements: one party (the cooperator) fully performs, the other party (the government) receives the full benefit of the other party's performance (the "substantial assistance"), yet the fully performing party is deprived of any benefit of his bargain. That is called having your cake, and eating it, too.

Indeed, Casso and Blue, like other cooperators whose agreements are not honored by the government, found themselves in a demonstrably worse position than if they had stonewalled from the outset. Since the result of their cooperation was that the accusatory instruments were redrawn to include all of their confessed crimes, their sentences were harsher than if they had proceeded to trial on the initial indictments, which alleged far fewer, and far less serious, offenses.

The solution is the Eighth Circuit's approach, which it devised in the *United States v. Anzalone*, 149 F.3d 940 (8th Cir. 1998), en banc hearing order vacated, and panel opinion reinstated, 161 F.3d 1125 (8th Cir. 1998). Restoring sentencing authority to the court, the Anzalone opinion prohibits the government from denying a Section 5K1.1 letter on any basis other than the simple failure to provide "substantial assistance" in the first place. Any other subsequent misconduct is a matter for the sentencing court, and not the government, to weigh. That, in fact, is all Blue asked for at sentencing—just to have the sentencing court balance his cooperation against his alleged violations of his agreement. Yet even that modest request was denied.

As more and more federal criminal defendants opt for cooperation in the face of onerous sentencing prospects, the prosecutor, already in control of most of the sentencing process, will arrogate even more sentencing power unless more courts apply a brake to this prosecutorial caprice. While some criminal defense attorneys and their clients will crow that the cooperators will have gotten their just desserts, we all know from bitter and repeated experience that what starts as an abuse of the rights of the least attractive elements of the system spreads inexorably to the rights of all.

ACKNOWLEDGMENTS

Many thanks to my agent, Matt Bialer, for his constant enthusiasm and support and all the wonderful people at Sanford Greenburger, a literary agency where they still treat writers like sensitive artists. Also, a thank-you to Jerry Kalajian for always quickly returning phone calls, for helping me deal with the sharks that swim so adeptly in the waters of Hollywood. Many thanks to my always conscientious, always precise, always with good cheer, always on time assistant Kelsey Osgood.

Special thanks to my mother and father, Dante and Nina Carlo, for all their help and support . . . their friendship with Anthony and Lillian Casso. It was my parents' unique friendship with Anthony and his wife, Lillian, that enabled me to gain Anthony's trust and confidence.

I want to thank Karen Garofalo-Scala for holding pages in the wind so I could read one of the many drafts of this book.

Doug Grad, my editor at HarperCollins, has been an invaluable asset to this book on all levels. He's a hell of an astute editor—patient and accommodating—and a hell of a nice man. I'd be remiss if I didn't thank Sarah Durand for picking up the ball and running with it . . . for her good advice and good cheer. Thanks also to all the terrific people at HarperCollins who helped with the birth of this book. Many thanks to Stephen Byer, for all his help and for his sincere, enduring friendship.

My sincere gratitude to all my friends at the Savoy Hotel in South Beach, where I wrote most of this book, for their gracious hospitality— Brian Mendez, Raf Pasquet, Sergio Corniglio, Alex Hernandez, Luis Liranzo, Michael and Perry Boucher, and Carlos Mendez.

Many thanks to Dr. Ray Onders, Dr. Daniel Alpert, Dr. Richard Ash, and Dr. Mark Sivak at Mount Sinai for all their help and friendship.